Mrs Ferguson's Tea-set, Japan, and the Second World War

THE GLOBAL CONSEQUENCES FOLLOWING GERMANY'S SINKING OF THE SS *AUTOMEDON* IN 1940

Eiji Seki

GLOBAL
ORIENTAL

MRS FERGUSON'S TEA-SET, JAPAN, AND THE SECOND WORLD WAR

THE GLOBAL CONSEQUENCES FOLLOWING GERMANY'S SINKING OF THE SS *AUTOMEDON* IN 1940

By Eiji Seki

First published in 2007 by
GLOBAL ORIENTAL LTD
PO Box 219
Folkestone
Kent CT20 2WP
UK

www.globaloriental.co.uk

ISBN 978-1-905246-28-1

British Library Cataloguing in Publication Data
A CIP catalogue entry for this book is available from the British Library

Set in Bembo 11 on 12pt by Servis Filmsetting Ltd, Manchester
Printed and bound in England by Antony Rowe Ltd, Chippenham, Wilts

Contents

Acknowledgements

DURING THE INTERVIEWS and research I carried out both at home and abroad I received the help and support of many people and made many new friends. In particular, the late Samuel Harper and Frank Walker and their families. They not only willingly agreed to be interviewed but also supplied me with much valuable material in the form of written records and photographs. I am grateful to Alex Parsons for the interview and replies to my numerous queries as well as Heather Stewart who kindly made available precious material related to her grandfather Captain Donald Stewart. I am also greatly indebted to the following people for taking part in my interviews and providing me with written resources and photographs: Mrs Ferguson's younger sister, Madge Christmas, whom I finally traced at the start of October 2003 after a long search, and Mr Ferguson's niece, Ann Nelis.

Mrs Ferguson, one of the protagonists of this story, died in April 2003 at the age of ninety-six. I did not manage to meet her and regretted that my research had taken so long. Mrs Christmas repeatedly told me that it was a pity that her sister was no longer alive as she would have gladly told me all about her story. Sadly, Samuel Harper also died in October 2003, one year after our interview.

I should like to express my sincere gratitude to the following people for the information they supplied and their support: Kanji Kanazawa, Director of the Nippon Yūsen Kaisha (NYK) Maritime Museum, for his guidance on maritime matters; Kazuo Hata and Itō of the Association to Honour Seafarers Who Died on Duty for the statistics on the Merchant Seamen at War; Kazuyuki Uetani, formerly with the Shōsen Mitsui Kaisha for the material on the Kashiimaru; my good friends Mr and Mrs Edgar Harrell, who found time in their busy schedules as academics to assist with my information-gathering in the United States; Professor K.G. Tregonning, former Raffles Professor of History at the University of Singapore; Gabe Thomas of the MILAG Prisoner of War Association, James Waggott and Ken Dunn; everybody connected to the Blue Funnel Line, especially Ray Wurtzburg, Harold Smyth, Graham MaCallum, Stuart Walker, Hugh Ferguson and Dave Molyneux; Andrea Biberger and Andreas Tabeling of Stiftung Liebenau; Dr Dieter Schmidt of the Wissenschaftliches Institut für Schiffahrts und Marinegeschichte; and Heinrich Siemers, historian on the German Navy. I am also grateful to Anne Hemingway, Richard Thomson and the many other people who helped me with carrying out interviews, researching the people in this story and giving me introductions. In particular, it would have been impossible to find Mrs Christmas without Richard Thomson's journalistic network.

As to the sources of material, I must say first of all that I have been very fortunate to have had available Professor John Chapman's outstanding work, *The Price of Admiralty*, without which many of the essential elements would have been missing from the book. I am also most grateful to him for his valuable comments and advice after reading the typescript. I owe much to the National Archives: the Public Record Office; the Imperial War Museum; the Merseyside Maritime Museum; the SOAS Library; the University of London Library; the British Museum Library; the National Library and the National Archives of Australia; the Militärgeschichtliches Forschungsamt; the Military Archives and the U-Boot Archiv. My gratitude also goes to the Ministry of Foreign Affairs Library and Diplomatic Record Office; the Military Archives of the National Institute for Defence Studies; the National Diet Library of Japan; the Hydrographic and Oceanographic Department of the Coast Guard; the Geographical Survey Institute; the Transportation Museum Archive; the Meteorological Agency and the Kobe Maritime

Meteorological Observatory; the Metropolitan Central Library and the Shinagawa Municipal Library.

Once again I should like to express my appreciation to all those who lent me their support, as well as to my family who assisted me along the way. Last but not least, I must mention with many thanks the excellent professional and painstaking work of Maya Nakamura who produced the translation from the Japanese text.

List of Plates *(facing page 84)*

Introduction

ON 11 NOVEMBER 1940, approximately one year before the outbreak of the Pacific War, in the Indian Ocean to the west of Sumatra, a British merchant ship heading for Penang, the SS *Automedon*, was captured and sunk by a German commerce raider, the *Atlantis*, commanded by Captain Bernhard Rogge.

With the first salvo fired, the captain of the *Automedon* and five of his officers were killed, while the First Officer sustained severe injuries and lost consciousness. Consequently, an important mailbag was not disposed of and was instead discovered by the German boarding party buried in the debris of the *Automedon's* bridge. When this was found to contain top-secret British Cabinet papers, even Captain Rogge, who was used to seizing quantities of confidential material from the British ships he attacked, could not hide his astonishment at their significance. That was not all. Through his kindness, Rogge had his men search the *Automedon* for the luggage of one of her passengers, Mrs Violet Ferguson. As a result, despite the determined efforts of the Second Mate Donald Stewart to keep the Germans off track, they discovered the ship's strong room and obtained a large quantity of other classified documents and information. The *Atlantis* had truly struck gold.

The British Cabinet papers were nothing other than a Joint Chiefs of Staff Committee report entitled: 'The Situation in the Far East in the Event of Japanese Intervention Against Us'. It revealed details of the British forces' preparations in the Far East and Britain's strategies in the event of a war with Japan. This valuable information, which was sent to Berlin via Kōbe, caught the eye of Hitler, who had been inciting Japan to attack Singapore, and he personally ordered it to be shared with the Japanese Navy without delay. Based on this information, Admiral Isoroku Yamamoto, Commander-in-Chief of the Japanese Combined Fleet, became convinced that the British forces were not yet ready and there was no danger of the British Far Eastern Fleet attacking Japan from the rear while she was occupied with a campaign in the eastern Pacific, and so pressed on with planning the final details of the surprise attack on Pearl Harbor. Thus, Japan was now firmly on a path to war and her march gathered pace.

The *Atlantis* criss-crossed the Atlantic and Indian oceans and achieved a high tally of successful operations, capturing or sinking twenty-two Allied ships in a period of 655 days, from the spring of 1940 to the autumn of 1941. As a result, a considerable number of merchant seamen and civilian passengers from Allied and neutral countries lost their lives, and the many who were taken prisoner were subjected to hardship on German prison ships, like the *Storstad*, and then in internment camps in Germany. Among those taken prisoner from the *Automedon* were Third Engineer Samuel Harper and a young Deck Boy, Frank Walker.

For operational reasons stipulated by the German Navy, the prison ship *Storstad*, carrying the crew and passengers of the *Automedon*, was required to wander backwards and forwards in the Indian and Atlantic oceans for two months. Finally, she arrived at Bordeaux on 5 February 1941. For Mr and Mrs Ferguson, Former passengers of the *Automedon*, this was their lucky port, from where they had made a narrow escape from the German army, and successfully returned to England about eight months earlier. When the couple had originally left England from Liverpool aboard the *Automedon* on 24 September 1940, they could not have imagined that they would be brought back to Bordeaux in this manner four months later.

Harper could not bear the thought of losing his freedom and so jumped off a prison train in France with some of his colleagues. He crossed France, hiding from the Germans, and made an arduous journey over the Pyrenees, finally succeeding in his great escape. However, in Franco's Spain he was incarcerated on a charge of illegal entry. He was later freed with the help of the British Naval Attaché and returned to Britain, via Gibraltar, for the first time in 229 days. Sad news awaited him at home: his younger brother Frank had been killed by a U-boat in the Atlantic a month before his own capture by the *Atlantis*. His mother Jessie, who believed she had lost her elder son, whom she had been informed was missing, as well as her beloved younger son, had become mentally unstable and had been hospitalized. At around this time, Walker was in a German prison camp being forced to dig peat.

Captain Rogge was a true warrior and a highly capable man. He kept his distance from the Nazi authorities and did not appoint any crewmembers who held extreme National Socialist views or racial prejudices for fear of them upsetting the harmony on board his ship. He was not concerned by the fact that his attitude brought him into disfavour with the Nazi leadership and his career progression was hampered. His English was excellent, and in battle he had his men adhere strictly to international law. He always treated his prisoners with fairness and kindness and gave them as much freedom as possible. As a result, he was respected and well-liked by allies and enemies alike.

However, finally on 22 November 1941, the *Atlantis* was cornered by the British heavy cruiser HMS *Devonshire* and so she scuttled herself in the South Atlantic. Rogge endured all manner of challenges on a 6,000-mile voyage back to Europe, all the while maintaining the morale of his men who were being transported in several lifeboats and submarines, and finally reached St Nazaire in France on Christmas Day. Six hundred and fifty-five days had passed since the *Atlantis* had first set sail from Kiel.

Rogge subsequently became involved in the German Navy's training programmes, and then entered fleet combat service in 1945. He hoisted the flag on the heavy cruiser *Prinz Eugen*, the nucleus of the remaining German fleet, as Commander of the Third Battle Group in the Baltic. He lent all his strength to the campaign, bombarding the Soviet forces that were driving towards Berlin. The Merchant Navy POW camp, where Walker and the other crewmen of the *Automedon* were held, was liberated by British forces in late April 1945. It was then Rogge's turn to be imprisoned by the Allies, but he was soon released. The Allies trusted him and he went on to dedicate all his efforts to the challenging task of building a new navy for the Federal Republic of Germany.

Violet Ferguson had been repatriated ahead of her husband in March 1943, and she was reunited with him in February 1945 when he, too, was sent home early. In the December of that year the couple returned to Singapore where they had lived before the war. There, Violet's trunks and other pieces of luggage 'unwanted on voyage', which had been retrieved by Rogge from the *Automedon* just before the ship was sunk, were returned to her intact. Among them was her favourite tea-set which she had used at the German internment camp. When she was repatriated the German Navy had stored all the belongings she had left behind, including this tea-set, in a warehouse in Hamburg. Given that the war was raging all around, this was simply miraculous. She had long since given up on her belongings in a Germany devastated by war.

I became interested in the possibility that the secret British documents seized from the *Automedon* served to facilitate Japan's entry into the Second World War by lessening Admiral Yamamoto's worries regarding the presence of the British fleet in the Far East as he planned the attack on Pearl Harbor. As I traced the *Automedon*'s path I learnt that, behind the scenes of the fierce naval contest between Germany, which aimed to disrupt Allied shipping, and Britain which strove to defend it, and on which the survival of each nation was at stake, so many human dramas were unfolding. I was gripped by the desire to portray these as faithfully as possible. I hoped that, by doing so, I could illustrate that there are no limits to the futility and cruelty of war and the human agony it engenders. Also, I hoped to make a contribution, however small, to any debate about the direction Japan should take in the future. The book was never intended to be any sort of treatise on the naval, military or political history of the Second World War. The author himself is more than aware that this is far beyond his own academic competence.

This book was first written with the Japanese reader in mind. Accordingly, it contains descriptions that may appear superfluous to others. The Chapter on the Battle of Britain, the additional explanatory notes on the Cabinet War Rooms and the history of the Straits Steamship Company and Singapore are such examples. It was in response to the rather unexpected but strong interest expressed by many people abroad, especially my friends and those who kindly helped me, and the encouragement I received from many of them that I decided to publish it in English first. As a matter of fact, the *Automedon* story is essentially more British rather than Japanese, especially with regard to the human interest element in the narrative.

1

A Fateful Decision

'Proceed on Course'

AT DAWN ON 11 November 1940, the British merchant ship SS *Automedon* (7,528 tonnes) was steaming 250 miles southwest of Achin Head, the northwestern tip of Sumatra. She was just one-and-a-half days away from Penang, her next port of call. It was the twenty-second anniversary of Armistice Day, when Kaiser Wilhelm II of Germany abdicated and a ceasefire agreement was signed to end the First World War. The sea was calm like a sheet of glass and visibility was excellent. The *Automedon* was making good progress.

With Penang so close, a rather more relaxed atmosphere began to prevail on board, and conversation became more cheerful. Forty-eight days had passed since the *Automedon* had set sail from Liverpool. The voyage had been particularly testing since she had left Durban and entered the Indian Ocean: it had been two weeks of nothing but sea and sky, day and night. All but the most seasoned seafarers were bound to begin doubting whether they would ever reach their destination and to yearn for dry land. This would also be the mood on board the SS *Asakamaru* (7,399 tonnes), owned by the Japanese Nippon Yūsen Kaisha (NYK) and chartered by the Japanese Navy, the following April.[1]

Homeward bound for Japan, which was preparing for war at a frenetic pace, the *Asakamaru* was carrying a full cargo of munitions and supplies from Germany and Switzerland, including 20mm Oerlikon cannons for Zero Fighters, machine tools and mercury. Setting sail from Bilbao, she had rounded the Cape of Good Hope and steered a course similar to that of the *Automedon*. She was crossing the Indian Ocean non-stop, heading northeast to the Lombok Strait. Her crew did not sight land for days at a time and were on guard for British Navy visitations, blacking out all lights at night. Even the naval officers on board became unnerved by the endless days at sea, and repeatedly sought reassurance from Captain Kingo Toriumi of NYK that they would reach Japan safely.

On the bridge of the *Automedon* that November morning in 1940 Able Seaman Stanley Hugill was at the wheel, while Second Officer Donald Stewart, struggling to stay awake, was the Officer of the Watch. As the clock on the bridge struck 7.00 the end of his shift approached, and he looked forward to his breakfast. It was then that he spotted another boat, which was a mere speck in the distance. The *Automedon* was steering north-north-east and this vessel was at 34 degrees off the port bow. She was hull down, and even through the telescope Stewart could barely make out the tip of her mast. He could not discern her shape, let alone what type of vessel she was or her nationality or name. Nevertheless, he made the precautionary decision to inform the Captain, W.B. Ewan. Since leaving Durban the crew had been particularly vigilant, and it was required that any sighting of a ship was reported to the Captain. Having checked through the telescope once more Stewart ran down from the bridge to wake Ewan who was still asleep in his cabin.

Dismissing his momentary misgivings, the Captain dressed hurriedly and proceeded to the bridge. He stood next to Stewart, who asked whether they should alter their course slightly, and stared through his binoculars without reply. The unidentified vessel appeared to be following the shipping lane from Madras to the Sunda Strait. The ship that eventually emerged more clearly in the circular field of the telescope closely resembled the Dutch ships often encountered in these seas, *en route* to the Dutch East Indies. Moreover, the Royal Navy had only warned of ambushes by German raiders and U-boats in the waters north of Madagascar; to avoid this area as much as possible the *Automedon* had been steering an easterly course since leaving Durban.

At around 7.30, Hugill heard the Captain, who had been pacing up and down the bridge deep in thought, say to Stewart that he believed the unidentified ship to be Dutch. Ewan was inclined to think that the *Automedon* had come far enough to be out of danger. She had previously picked up distress calls from a couple of other ships in the area, one of which was the *Ole Jacob*, but apparently they had both turned out to be false. One concern weighed on Ewan's mind: in order to enter the Strait of Malacca, it was going to be necessary to make a major course alteration eastwards in the dark that night, relying on the direction finder. Any accomplished seaman knew of the strong and complex currents in those waters; so the previous morning the crew had even used the sextant to carefully calculate the point of course alteration. To be excessively fearful of phantom German cruisers and to make changes to good plans seemed inept. As it would soon become clear, the alarm raised by the *Ole Jacob* was in fact real. By a trick of fate, Ewan, unaware of this, would shortly invite disaster.

The Captain finally decided to maintain his course until the turning point that had been set. Having instructed Stewart, who was anxiously standing by his side, binoculars in hand, not to alter their course, Ewan returned to his cabin. He completed his preparations for the day and quickly ate some breakfast before returning to the bridge, for what would be his last time. Stewart wrote in the logbook that the course was to be maintained, also conveying this to his relief. Stewart had served under the command of Ewan for two years, and trusted and respected the Captain implicitly.

Captain Ewan was of medium-build, in his early fifties, with a full head of silver hair. Though taciturn, he was a man of distinction. Alex Parsons, who was Assistant Steward, recalls that Captain Ewan had vast experience after so many years at sea and that he exuded dignity and confidence.[2] There was a somewhat unapproachable air about him and he was strict in disciplining his men, yet he possessed a charisma that inspired their deference and devotion. He had worked for the Blue Funnel Line for many years and he was a figure held in high regard even among the other captains. Through his long years of sailing he had come to know all there was to know about the nature of the sea, and there should have been nothing that he feared.[3] However, in the seas of human conflict he eventually made an error of judgement. He had acquired all the arts of navigation and was intimately acquainted with the sea, but now he needed something else, not least good luck.

When Stewart suggested a change of course, had the *Automedon* turned her bow slightly to the east, steamed at a speed of fourteen knots or more and approached even a little closer to the Strait of Malacca, she might have been able to elude her pursuer. The *Atlantis* (7,862 tonnes) would have soon given up the chase as it was extremely dangerous for her to venture into busy shipping lanes. Indeed, Bernhard Rogge, the Captain of the *Atlantis*, later uttered something to this effect, probably to Stewart. This is recorded in a written statement by Samuel Harper, Third Engineer of the *Automedon*, which was received by the American consulate general in Marseilles, as we shall see.[4] Ewan's decision not to alter the *Automedon*'s course sealed her fate. A little over an hour after he was woken by Stewart, Ewan was dead. Further, the lives of the many crew and the passengers took an unimaginable turn, and the top-secret British Cabinet papers the *Automedon* was transporting were seized by the enemy. This in turn would serve to step up Japan's march to war.

It is said that the *Automedon* had been picked up by the Italian secret service's surveillance network while she docked at Durban on 29 October, and that the information had immediately been conveyed to the German Navy. At that time, in the Mediterranean and off the coast of Africa, the German and Italian secret services were intercepting and decoding Allied shipping communications and actively exchanging information with considerable success. The *Automedon*'s radio communications had been intercepted by the Italians and her movements closely followed. One theory was that an Italian submarine had tracked the *Automedon* and relayed information to Rogge at every stage, but this has not been verified.[5]

A Voyage Never To Be Completed

Around midnight on 8 November, masquerading as the British auxiliary cruiser *Antenor*, the *Atlantis* had captured, undamaged, the Norwegian oil tanker the *Teddy* (6,748 tonnes) in the seas to the east of Ceylon (Sri Lanka). The *Teddy* had been transporting 10,000 tonnes of crude oil from Abadan to Singapore. Twenty of the *Teddy*'s crew, including Captain Thor Lütken, had been transferred to the *Atlantis*. Under the command of the German prize crew, the remainder had been forced to steer the *Teddy* to a meeting point the German Navy referred to as 'Mangrove' just south of the equator, where she was to await further instructions.

On the 10th, taking advantage of the calm seas, the *Atlantis* had launched its spotter. The pilot had caught sight of another oil tanker, steaming west in the waters a little to the north of the spot where the *Teddy* had been seized two days earlier. Once again passing herself off as the *Antenor*, and under the cover of darkness, the *Atlantis* had approached this vessel. She had then deployed a somewhat hackneyed tactic which had been wholly successful: she had dispatched a small boat, carrying Adjutant Ulrich Mohr (wearing the Royal Navy uniform), an officer, and ten fully-armed marines concealed under a tarpaulin; they had flanked the tanker's broadside and launched a surprise attack, proceeding to take the ship with little resistance. She was the *Ole Jacob* (8,306 tonnes) that had set sail for Suez from Singapore on 7 November loaded with 9,000 tonnes of aviation fuel. She belonged to the Johannes Hansen Tanker Shipping Company based in Arendal in Norway, and she was a new vessel built by the Swedish Gotaverken Company and launched in April 1939.

The *Ole Jacob* had managed to raise the alarm, 'QQQ – *Ole Jacob* – latitude 6.3 degrees north, longitude 90.13 degrees east'. This had been picked up by the nearby *Automedon*. However, Mohr had been one step ahead, swiftly interrupting this transmission using the *Ole Jacob*'s own communication equipment. Captain Ewan had fallen for this clever trick and believed the message to be a false alarm.

The Royal Navy had standardized the emergency signals to be used by British ships or neutral ships under British charter. In the event of being attacked by an enemy raider, or of spotting or being pursued by a suspicious vessel, this procedure was to enable fast and accurate communication to the nearest British warship or shore-based communication centre. The ship under threat was only to wire her name and position preceded by 'RRR' in the case of an actual attack and 'QQQ' in the case of a potential attack.

While transmitting the 'QQQ' alert the *Ole Jacob* had been captured, and placed under the guard of a prize crew led by First Lieutenant Paul Kamenz. The Captain of the *Ole Jacob*, Leif Krogh, and twenty-three others had been ordered to board the *Atlantis* with enough clothes for three or four days. The rest of the company had been held on the *Ole Jacob*. She had then been transferred to a location named 'Ratan', at latitude 3.3 degrees south, longitude 93.15 degrees east, where she was to wait. It was close to Mangrove, the spot 300 miles south of the equator where the *Teddy* was also on standby awaiting orders from the *Atlantis*.

The moment of encounter between the *Atlantis* and the *Automedon* was now approaching.

According to Captain Rogge's memoirs[6] and the *Atlantis*'s war diary,[7] at 7.04 on the morning of 11 November, Able Seaman Jena, who was stationed at the crow's nest on the *Atlantis*'s foremast, had spotted a small and faint cloud of smoke. It was at 222 degrees – southwest of the *Atlantis* – over eighteen miles away on the horizon. This means that the *Atlantis* and the *Automedon* had caught sight of one another at around the same time.

Visibility was extremely good that day and the sea was calm and as smooth as a sheet of glass. At 7.11 Rogge had ordered his ship to stop briefly, so that an accurate calculation of his prey's course and speed could be made. He had then ordered the crew to be on the alert, steered onto a collision course with the target vessel, and proceeded at a speed of eleven knots. When he was about ten miles away, seeing her graceful silhouette, he had become fully convinced that the target was the Blue Funnel Line steamship *Automedon*. The distance between the two vessels had progressively closed and at 7.58 it was just 4,600 metres.

At 8.03 the *Atlantis* revealed her identity by displaying the flag signals 'Do not raise the alarm' and 'Stop' one after the other on her mast. A minute later, from the cannon on her bow and from a distance of 600 metres, she put a shot across the bow of the *Automedon*. The tragedy of the *Automedon* was now about to unfold. It was impossible for her to prevent the ensuing assault, because her crew, staggered by the sudden confrontation, were unable to decode the flag signals quickly enough. As a result, in the wireless room the First Wireless Operator John Rawcliffe and the Second Wireless Operator Phillip Buck, following the Captain's orders, began tapping out the 'RRR' alert.

On the bridge, Captain Ewan shouted, 'Hard on the wheel!' to Hugill at the top of his voice. His aim was to turn the bow to starboard, to the maximum limit of 35 degrees, so that the stern faced the *Atlantis* and they were better positioned to evade the bombardment. 'Hard on the wheel!' Hugill repeated, and he turned with every ounce of strength in his body; he would not have cared if the wheel had shattered. 'Hard on the wheel, Sir,' he then replied once more. He heard the Captain call out with vigour and resolve, 'Come on everyone, let's do it – we're going to fight!' In Hugill's eyes, Captain Ewan, like Admiral Horatio Nelson, was the personification of valour.[8]

At the aft end of the midship housing on the port side, Deck Boy Frank Walker, who was only sixteen years old, and the ship's carpenter W.G. Diggle, had watched, astonished, as a mysterious ship had headed straight towards the *Automedon*. Diggle had hurriedly fetched his binoculars from his cabin, and leaning against the handrail, the two men had taken turns to look through them at the oncoming vessel. According to Walker's recollection this was around 8.30, and he remembers how the sea was flat like a sheet of glass and the visibility was exceptionally good. Diggle had said he thought the boat was an intermediate P&O steamship, not in the least suspecting its true identity. The men had watched the distance between the two ships close more and more, as neither made an attempt to alter its course.

Walker recalls how, when this ship was just forward of the *Automedon*'s beam, she emitted four sparks and four puffs of white smoke from the side of her hull. The next moment there was a tremendous bang and a crashing sound. This was the first salvo, which promptly followed the warning shot, striking the bridge. Three further salvos were fired in quick succession. They were targeted at the centrecastle where the officers' accommodation and the canteen were located. With each strike the *Automedon* seemed to scream and shudder in agony.

On the same port-side deck not far from Walker and Diggle, Parsons was watching full of curiosity and apprehension as the *Atlantis* approached his ship. Immediately after the first salvo, he began running for cover to the starboard side. But the moment he was passing No.3 hatch, a shell from the second salvo scored a direct hit and demolished it. He was showered with shrapnel from his waist upwards. His legs were uninjured only because of the protection from the hatch. He staggered on but collapsed into a lavatory on the way. He lay there unconscious until the German boarding party came and found him. Then he was zipped up to the neck in a body bag they had brought with them and lowered by rope into the boat to be transferred to the *Atlantis*. He was kept on the floor of the surgery on the *Atlantis* while the two German surgeons operated on someone who may have been Chief Steward Moseley. They did an excellent job on Parsons though even today some of the shrapnel remains buried in his chest and waist.

Walker had left home when he was fourteen years old to flee his strict father. First, he had worked as a bellboy for a coastal shipping company. Then, from May 1939 to the end of August 1940, he had continued to work on Canadian Pacific Railways ships, including the ocean liner the *Duchess of Richmond*. In those days approximately 23% of sailors were between the ages of fifteen and twenty-one, so a young mariner like Walker was not in the least bit unusual. He had turned sixteen just one month before the *Automedon* had set sail on her final doomed voyage in September 1940. He had applied to join her crew as soon as he heard that she was recruiting, and had boarded the ship for the first time just one day prior to her departure. He had enjoyed all his former voyages: the food had always been good, and he had experienced exotic foreign cultures. However, from the beginning, things had been different aboard the *Automedon*. Day after day, he spent a miserable time being shouted at by a particularly spiteful senior colleague, who was nicknamed the 'Terror of the China Sea' and was universally disliked. Things went from bad to worse, of course, when the *Automedon* was captured and sunk; Walker was subsequently to endure four long years of captivity and hardship.

Alex Parsons was fond of everything about the sea because he had been brought up near the sea in New Brighton, Merseyside. His interest increased because his uncle was in the Royal Navy but was killed in the First World War. Three times he tried to enlist in the Royal Navy but was refused because he was too small. So he decided to make a career of the Merchant Navy and started working on Cunard liners in 1939 at the age of seventeen.

The Ferocious Onslaught

At long last, Second Officer Stewart had been relieved from watch duty at 8.00. He had returned to his cabin which was adjacent to the Captain's accommodation on the boat deck. According to his recollections[9] written twenty-one years later, at around 8.20, as he was shaving in his underwear, he heard the sound of gunfire. Astonished, he looked out of the porthole to see that the ship that he had been convinced was Dutch was flying the Swastika and steaming parallel to the *Automedon* at close proximity. Immediately after firing the warning shot, the *Atlantis*, which had been on a collision course with the *Automedon*, had turned sharply to port and more or less aligned herself with her prey.

Recognizing the gravity of the situation Stewart dropped everything and rushed to the cabin next door, where T.G. Wilson, the extra Second Officer, was still asleep, and shook him awake. Then Stewart and Peter Evans, the First Officer, scrambled up the ladder to the bridge, almost tripping over one another as they went. Stewart noticed that the distress signal, 'RRR Automedon, latitude 4.18 degrees north', was being tapped out repeatedly. At that moment, an enormous blast accompanied by a thunderous bang tossed him into the air like a leaf, threw him against the floor and knocked him out. Hugill, who had been holding tight onto the wheel nearby, was instantly buried by the debris. When he managed to crawl his way out he was bleeding from the nose and his back was wounded. Miraculously, his life had been spared, and he would later marvel at his survival of the event.

Twelve shells in succession were pumped into the bridge and the boat deck. The extent of the devastation would even surprise the German boarding party. It is recorded in the *Atlantis*'s war diary that 'the *Automedon* presented a picture of devastation'. The passenger cabins were located two decks below in the after-centrecastle, so Mr and Mrs Ferguson and the other passengers were fortunately all unscathed. That morning the *Atlantis*, which was equipped with a sophisticated fire-control system, executed her attack with her usual precision. The *Automedon*'s wireless room which she targeted was in fact not in the vicinity of the bridge, but was situated at the aft end of the boat deck. Rogge recorded in the war diary that he only discovered this after the event. In the diary he also admitted to his irritation when the *Automedon* ignored his warnings. Though it may seem inhumane, for the aggressor not to allow any opportunity for his victim to raise the alarm was the rule of thumb on which his own survival depended.

For Walker, too, the blast was a very sudden shock. He held his body rigid, and though stunned, he managed to remain standing. The awning above his head was ripped to shreds, and the spars and the ship's structure around him were blown away. It was nothing less than a miracle that he was uninjured. When he looked around, Diggle, who he thought had been next to him, was nowhere to be seen.

One of the crew went to the poop deck and attempted to lower a raft onto the water. By then the *Atlantis* was positioned very close to the *Automedon* on her port quarter. Another man – possibly the gunner – ran towards the *Automedon*'s gun on the after deck. An officer of the *Atlantis*, who was keeping watch from her bridge, immediately spotted him and shouted in English over a loud hailer: 'Do not go near the gun. Or we will blow you out of the water!' Walker still clearly recalls hearing this.

This episode is recorded in the *Atlantis*'s war diary thus: she resumed the bombardment because, although the transmission of the emergency alarm had ceased, a figure was seen approaching the gun on the afterdeck of the *Automedon*, which had turned her stern towards her; she concentrated three salvos on the poop deck and the bow, which were all on target.

It seems that, because the *Automedon* had veered sharply to starboard and showed her stern immediately after the warning shot, and a crew member had rushed towards the gun, Captain Rogge judged the *Automedon* to be intent on fighting back. For raiders like the *Atlantis*, which spent long periods far offshore, replenishing supplies and making repairs were extremely difficult. This meant that even the slightest damage to the vessel could have serious consequences, so not even the smallest risk was taken.

Even so, why did the *Atlantis*, which was extremely close to the *Automedon*, not employ small-calibre weapons like machine-guns or rifles, but instead cause particularly extensive damage with her cannons? This is a question that still remains for Walker.

The *Automedon* was designated a DEMS (Defensively Equipped Merchant Ship) by the Royal Navy, and was armed with a 75mm gun. Usually a DEMS had an appointed gunner on board, a retired artilleryman or a marine, or just one of the crew. The all-important gun was often a relic from the First World War. It was impossible for a DEMS equipped with such a weapon, as the *Automedon* was, to compete with the *Atlantis*'s advanced fire-control system and sophisticated guns with barrels twice as wide. It was a foregone conclusion that it was useless to retaliate. On this occasion Captain Ewan's heroism undeniably backfired, and exacerbated the damage to his ship.

Walker heard loud groaning from the top deck. He drummed up enough courage and went there to find the Chief Steward, P.J. Moseley, lying very badly injured: his internal organs were exposed and he was bleeding heavily. Walker fetched him a blanket from a cabin nearby and gave him some water. He held him in his arms, comforting and encouraging him, as he groaned in agony. Through his strained gasps, Moseley asked him to give an envelope which was in his cabin to the Second Steward. Thinking that he was at least capable of doing this, Walker rushed to Moseley's cabin. He had to dodge the manifold objects scattered all over the floor as well as the sharp fragments of timber that hung here and there above his head. When he reached Moseley's cabin, he picked up the envelope to take it to the Second Steward. It contained petty cash for the crew.[10] For the young Walker, to nurse a man on the brink of death was extremely distressing. Moseley was later transferred to the *Atlantis* and he underwent surgery, but this was to no avail and he eventually died. On the starboard side of the same deck A. Parsons, the Assistant Steward, also lay showered with shrapnel from his waist upwards. Able Seaman J.J. Watts was dead.

The din of bombardment had ceased and the ship was shrouded in the eerie stillness of death. About an hour later Diggle's body was discovered. Half of his head and shoulder had been ripped off by a shell. He had been killed outright; there would have been nothing that anyone could have done. He was lying to the left of the windlass, so he had probably been running to his station in the forecastle when he was killed. The twenty-nine-years-old Diggle was never to see his wife and two beloved children, who were counting the days until his return to London, again; the war-ravaged seas were merciless.

On the bridge of the *Atlantis*, before the bombardment had begun, Adjutant Ulrich Mohr had stood next to Captain Rogge, who was firing off one order after another. Mohr had gripped the railing and leant far forward, staring fixedly at the bridge of the *Automedon*. He had felt an overwhelming urge to cry out: 'Sending a distress signal, in this hopeless situation, is the most ridiculous act of suicide. For pity's sake, don't force us to create unnecessary casualties!' However, within just seconds of the warning shot the *Atlantis* had picked up the *Automedon*'s 'RRR' alert being tapped out. As long as she was transmitting the message, she had to be silenced as quickly as possible. Although her two Wireless Operators were undeniably courageous, as Mohr feared, they brought about a catastrophe for the *Automedon*.

Harper later spoke of Captain Rogge's fair and sympathetic personality. However he also pointed to another, harsh aspect of his character, demonstrated by the ferocious attack to which he subjected the *Automedon*.[11] In the brutal battlefield of life or death, Rogge too did not shy away from taking ruthless measures in order to survive.

The German Navy's preferred strategy, instilled into those operating the commerce raiders, was to seize enemy ships undamaged and complete with their cargo, in order to serve Germany's war economy as well as to keep casualties to a minimum. To this end, target ships were to be stopped with a warning shot and ordered not to raise the alarm. In response, the Royal Navy instructed British ships to transmit distress calls to help establish the positions of the German vessels and help capture them. The two approaches conflicted, of course, and the number of British casualties rose continuously as many British ships, faithful to the Royal Navy's directive, emitted the 'RRR' signal in full knowledge of the consequences. Captain Rogge frequently had no choice but to fire on his prey to force it to halt and cease its transmission. After the war he revealed that, time and again, it pained him to think of the victims.

The *Automedon* was wrecked by a total of twenty-eight shells; she was now afloat having completely lost her functions. Her emergency dynamo house had been destroyed, and her aerial severed, leaving no possibility of communication. Absolutely no hope remained of her ever reaching Penang. At 9.09 Mohr was ordered to lead the boarding party, and he came on board the *Automedon* at 9.25.

Through her intensive operations the *Atlantis* achieved astonishing results in the short period between 8 and 11 November, taking three ships in succession. This shows that she was making efficient and detailed plans based on highly reliable information on the movements of Allied shipping. This is also indicated by the way she used her spotter plane. The fact that the crew of the *Ole Jacob* were ordered to take only enough clothes for three or four days when they transferred to the *Atlantis* is perhaps evidence that Rogge had anticipated the approach of the *Automedon* and had calculated that only one or two days were needed to deal with her. In any case, the activities of the *Atlantis* during this period were certainly well planned and highly coherent.

2

The Battle of Britain

BEFORE PROCEEDING WITH the story of the *Automedon* let us now take a look at its wider context, the European theatre of war. Though it was fought far away from the Far East, the Battle of Britain turned out to be critically important to the destiny of Japan when her leaders failed to recognize the fact that the tide of war had changed in favour of Britain as early as the middle of September 1940. Then Hitler gave up his plan to invade Britain and directed his attention towards the Soviet Union thereby sealing his own fate forever. The Japanese leaders' colossal failure led to another that committed Japan to her alliance with Germany and Italy on the 27th of the same month. Thereafter, naval cooperation between Japan and Germany was noticeably accelerated. It is regrettable that unbiased reports by the Japanese military attachés in London and other posts were accorded little attention in Tokyo. Thus, Japan placed herself on the final course to national disaster. Indeed, the Battle of Britain, which was the most crucial event in the history of the Second World War, continues to provide the main background to the story of the *Automedon*.

France's Defeat and the Allied Retreat from Dunkirk

Early in the morning of 1 September 1939, over a year before the *Automedon* incident, Germany invaded Poland with a coordinated air and land attack involving 1,300 aircraft and a large force of sixty-two divisions, triggering the Second World War. Britain and France declared war on Germany two days later. Yet Britain and France made no attempt to attack Germany from the rear while she progressed eastwards, and they appeared to abandon Poland.

In fact, the German defences on her western front were extremely weak. This was because Hitler, disregarding the protests of his General Staff and military leaders, had deployed almost all of his best-armed and mechanized divisions in the invasion of Poland. On the western front, thirty-three divisions, the majority of which were second-rate in terms of armaments and training, were stationed without aircraft or tanks. If Britain and France had seized this opportunity and invaded Germany in earnest the course of the war would have been very different.

Lacking in military strength and external support, the Poles capitulated to Hitler's invasion in spite of their ardent determination to defend their homeland. Their desperate fight was in vain and they were vanquished in less than a month. Through the collusion of Hitler and Stalin, Poland was promptly carved up between Germany and the Soviet Union, and was erased from the map.

The Polish secret service is said to have been the most advanced in breaking German codes during the 1930s. At the start of the decade it had already discovered the inner workings of the Enigma machine with the help of German collaborators and had succeeded in its replication.[1] Between 1932 and 1938, the Polish secret service had been intercepting and decoding German Enigma communications. Prior to the invasion it had supplied its British and French counterparts with all the documents, equipment and other materials it had accumulated. When France surrendered, the Polish decoding experts moved to England, where they assisted the code-breaking work of the Government Code and Cipher School at Bletchley Park in Buckinghamshire, and contributed to its successes.[2]

Soon the Royal Navy was in full command of the Enigma machine and was able to decode the German submarine fleet's communications. This helped considerably to suppress U-boat activity in the Atlantic, where they had been wreaking havoc. The

Royal Navy undermined the security not only of the U-boats but also of their supply ships that were required to communicate with them, and even raiders like the *Atlantis*.[3] In this way the Allies safeguarded their supply routes, which in turn helped pave their way to victory.

Although it was not one of her original duties, the *Atlantis* was enlisted to supply U-boats in her latter days in order to compensate for the lack of supply ships. Captain Rogge was very concerned that the U-boat codes had been broken.[4] Finally, his nightmare became a reality on 22 November 1941 when the *Atlantis* was caught by the British cruiser *Devonshire* in the South Atlantic. Even if her radio communication system was separate from that of the submarine fleet, if the latter's codes had been cracked it was impossible for a supply vessel to conceal her position.

After Poland was divided and annexed by Germany and the Soviet Union, the war in Europe reached stalemate. There was so little development that American journalists coined the term 'the phoney war'. However, the situation changed completely the following year, when Germany first attacked Norway and Denmark on 9 April, and then France and the Benelux countries on 10 May.

In the battle for France, 228,000 British troops and 110,000 French troops were pushed back by the German army and narrowly escaped by being evacuated from Dunkirk across the Strait of Dover between 27 May and 4 June. The Royal Navy initially estimated that only around 100,000 troops could be withdrawn but, owing to poor weather conditions which impeded German Luftwaffe operations, the evacuation was much more successful than expected. However, the British were forced to abandon a huge quantity of munitions in their retreat, including 120,000 vehicles, 7,000 tonnes of explosives, and 90,000 rifles. On 24 June, a truce was signed between Germany and France, and Britain would continue fighting alone. Now Britain was threatened with the prospect of being ravaged by an invading German army.

Franklin Roosevelt, President of the United States, had until then been indecisive over the matter of providing military assistance to Britain and France. This was partly because a presidential election loomed, and he was very conscious of domestic popular opinion, which staunchly favoured isolationism and non-interventionism. However, he now became very concerned that, with the weakening of Britain and France, a grave situation was developing in Europe which might affect American interests in the future. Even if it was too late to support France, he took rapid and drastic action in a bid to aid Britain.

First, Roosevelt gathered military aircraft and attempted to ship them to the French front on a French aircraft carrier from Halifax on the east coast of Canada. This was an urgent operation that was not completed in time. However, he did supply to Britain without delay considerable quantities of bombs and gunpowder as well as 900 field guns, 80,000 machine-guns, one million shells, over 500,000 rifles and 130 million bullets. Roosevelt was already becoming convinced that Hitler's Germany should not be permitted to take over Europe and that an Allied victory was vital to American security.

The Battle of Britain

After the Allied retreat from Dunkirk, the arena of combat switched to the skies of Britain. Although the German army was overwhelmingly the superior force on the battlefields of continental Europe, it was still essential that Hitler established aerial supremacy in order to succeed in his invasion of Britain over the English Channel where the Royal Navy and the Royal Air Force were consolidating their defences.

To this end the Marshal of the Luftwaffe, Hermann Goering, summoned all the strength of his fleets based in Germany, France and Belgium, and while sustaining considerable losses, bombarded British targets day and night. As well as London, Liverpool and other major cities, they included many of Britain's airbases, munitions factories and railway junctions. However, with the very survival of the nation at stake, the British fought back with every determination. From mid-July through to the end of October a vigorous and critical battle, the so-called Battle of Britain, was played out all over the country, although principally over southern England. The contest was unprecedented in the history of warfare in that the direction of the whole war hinged on the two countries' air forces alone, and their foiling of one another's tactics.

In terms of the numbers of fighter aircraft there was little difference between the two forces but the British possessed clear advantages: the conflict took place over their home territory and their fighting spirit was keener as they strove to defend it. The British pilots fervently resolved to protect, with their lives, the beautiful green country they saw below. There was even a pilot who, while returning to base having run out of ammunition, caught sight of a German bomber heading for London and brought it down by flying into it.

As soon as they took off from their home bases the British fighters climbed to the optimum operational altitude and, with the guidance of ground control, adeptly positioned themselves in wait for the enemy. There were numerous bases and runways where they could land in an emergency, and so there was little need to worry about running out of fuel or losing time in refuelling. While the German pilots who were brought down were taken prisoner, many of their British counterparts, provided they ejected successfully, could then return to the front, which many did.

The Luftwaffe faced additional challenges: its pilots were required to use unfamiliar bases in recently-occupied Belgium and northern France, in addition to those in Germany; and just when they began to tire, having flown considerable distances, they faced dogfights. Even if they ejected, if they were unlucky they were taken prisoner or drowned in the English Channel.

In addition, Goering, who had made his name as a pilot in the First World War, frequently changed targets on a whim. There were occasions when the British commanders, who had been concerned that they could not withstand a sustained attack on a given target, were actually relieved by this.

The Royal Air Force, on the other hand, was blessed with two very distinguished leaders, Sir Hugh Dowding, the Air Chief Marshal, and Sir Keith Park, the Air Vice-Marshal. Having learnt a hard lesson when they lost 300 precious pilots by misreading a situation in France, they were undeterred by criticism that they were too cautious, and they succeeded in maintaining a high degree of fighting capacity and morale throughout the force. They achieved this through the method of awaiting and attacking the enemy with efficiency, while attempting to conserve pilots and insisting on squadrons alternating combat with rest. Even Prime Minister Winston Churchill placed all his trust in these two men and did not attempt to interfere in their operations.

The RAF had been developing radar technology from the beginning of the 1930s and had succeeded in its practical implementation. Using frequently-updated information gathered by a radar network covering the whole country and a 50,000-strong anti-aircraft surveillance team, RAF fighters could position themselves very effectively in anticipation of the German planes. The

British subsequently developed a compact radar, which proved to be a highly effective part of their fighter planes' equipment. They were ahead of the Germans in terms of radar technology and they were able to jam the Luftwaffe's primitive radio communications.

The contribution of the ground staff, who worked without sleep or rest in an attempt to mobilize even just one plane, was also significant. Their devotion to their work was such that they were frustrated by having to stop and take shelter every time there was a German bombardment or machine-gun rake.

To counter the Luftwaffe's 800 Messerschmitt 109E fighters, the RAF was able to dispatch 600 high-capability Hurricanes and Spitfires every day throughout the duration of the battle. The aircraft factories, though subjected to bombings, continued to maintain a monthly production rate of 500 of these two principal fighters. Replacing lost aircraft posed no difficulty and repairs to damaged fighters were also completed quickly. Rather, it was the delay in training new pilots, on whom success depended, that was the major unresolved problem. The death of the 300 pilots in France remained a heavy loss from which the RAF could not really recover, primarily due to the stalling of the pilot training programme because of bad weather during the winter of 1939–40, as well as the need to put the training instructors at the frontline because of the urgency of the situation.

After 12 August, the emphasis of the German attacks shifted from British vessels in the Strait of Dover and the port cities along the coast to large-scale waves of daylight bombing of airbases and radar installations inland, and the Battle of Britain began in earnest. On the 15th, the weather improved from around midday and there was a clear blue sky. The RAF, which, before noon, had registered incoming German aircraft over the Strait of Dover on radar, swiftly took up position.

The first wave of German fighters and bombers attacked northeast England in the morning, and from midday to dusk the second and third waves attacked the southeast and the southwest. The large formations totalling 1,750 aircraft concentrated their raids on airbases and airplane factories and caused considerable damage. The RAF confronted them boldly by repeatedly despatching more than 600 fighters. While the British people looked on with bated breath, a valiant aerial mortal combat of unremitting dogfights unfolded. This was to be a crucial stage of the Battle of Britain.

That day, the front spanned 500 miles, and there were five major engagements excluding smaller clashes. Against the seventy-six Luftwaffe aircraft destroyed, RAF losses were limited to thirty-four fighters and eighteen pilots. Churchill, who had been informed of every new development, could not contain his excitement at this result, and on an impulse rushed from his residence to the RAF base at Stanmore on the northwestern outskirts of London.[5] This was quite understandable as he had been following, closely and prayerfully, the course of the battle on which the fate of the nation rested. Fighter Command was located at Stanmore and from here there were repeated sorties of two squadrons of young pilots, fuelled with a resolve to protect their homeland. Churchill expressed gratitude and encouragement to these men, who were willing to sacrifice their lives in their desperate fight to defend the country.

When London was submitted to intense German air raids, Churchill installed himself in the Cabinet War Rooms, a citadel-like fortified underground shelter,[6] and spearheaded the defence of the country by undertaking the command of the forces. He rose to the occasion spectacularly, like a great actor on stage delivering the performance of his life. He presided over War Cabinet meetings on a daily basis. He seated the Chiefs of Staff of the army, navy and air force in a row in front of him, relentlessly fired one incisive question after another regarding any situation reports or explanations of strategies and tactics that he did not understand, and sometimes raised his voice in directing or admonishing them.

There was a stark difference between Churchill and the Japanese Prime Minister, who was totally isolated from the military command and not told anything about the course of the war, much less permitted to participate in its direction. Granted, there were historical and constitutional differences between the two countries, but the situation in Japan was such that even Prime Minister Fumimaro Konoe, who had the goodwill of the army, was still at a complete loss as to what the military's intentions or plans were, and was obliged to find out the necessary information through the Emperor.

The underground facility, which became Churchill's fortress as it were, was safer than Number 10, Downing Street. Moreover, it was a very fitting setting for a premier who faced the advancing Germans head-on and directed the war effort while passionately calling for do-or-die resistance from the people, first along the coast, then in the fields, and finally in the towns and cities. He was advised to move to a safe location in the suburbs, but he insisted that he could not abandon the people of London. He refused to leave the capital, except to visit the victims in other cities devastated by bombings or to tour military facilities and factories on his private train that included a restaurant car and a sleeper.

The Battle of Britain reached its peak between mid-August and mid-September. This is indicated clearly in the numbers of enemy sorties by day: 9,310 in August, 12,095 in September, 8,035 in October and 5,130 in November. With such numbers, even the formidable RAF temporarily fell into serious difficulty at the start of September, mainly due to the concentrated attacks on their bases. Goering, who believed the overestimated results he received without question, even jumped to the conclusion that he had finally won. However, the resilient RAF recovered swiftly and promptly turned the tables, forcing Hitler finally to give up the invasion of Britain, for which the latest deadline, with the approach of winter, had been set as 17 September.

On 11 September, Churchill announced to the nation over the radio that, despite not having gained control of the skies, the Germans were progressing preparations for their invasion as planned. He warned that, considering the weather conditions, the population must be most on guard over the coming week or so. However, a subtle increase in confidence and relaxation in tone could already be detected in his voice.

While the war was gradually unfolding in Britain's favour, Churchill also knew, from decoded German communications, that the staff of the Luftwaffe communication centres in Belgium and northern France were to be redeployed to other fronts. He had, therefore, judged that Hitler had given up invading Britain, his interest had started to shift to the east, and that the worst was already over.

Germany's losses were 1,887 aircraft and 2,662 pilots; Britain lost 1,023 aircraft and 537 pilots. This was the final toll of the Battle of Britain, which, like the Battle of Midway and the Battle of Stalingrad, became one of the determining conflicts of the Second World War.

Churchill and Hitler

Churchill praised the remarkable feat of the RAF pilots, who had rushed to save their country in her hour of need, with his famed fine words: 'Never in the field of human conflict was so much owed by so many to so few.' However, his own contribution was by no means insignificant.

Specifically, following the retreat from Dunkirk he had held off France's repeated appeals for support in the form of RAF fighters and preserved the twenty-five squadrons (approximately 600 aircraft), enabling him to seize the opportunity for victory when the turning point came. While persuading the French Prime Minister, Paul Reynaud, that the German occupation of France was by no means the end of the struggle, and that the Allies could certainly defeat Germany by gaining aerial superiority over the Strait of Dover, he had been no less distressed and troubled by his counterpart's predicament. Nevertheless, having taken on board Dowding's unyielding opposition to sending aircraft to France, on which he even staked his career, there was no way that Churchill would change the decision made in order to achieve victory. His astuteness in foreseeing future developments and his resulting sound strategies amply demonstrate that his qualities as a leader, refined through his extensive experience as a politician and as a Cabinet Minister, were indeed exceptional.

From the beginning it had been the German Army, which formed the main pillar of the Third Reich's forces, which had advocated an invasion of Britain. The navy and the air force had always been pessimistic and doubtful of their own ability to establish control of the seas and skies as demanded by the army. Hitler himself was indecisive; he frequently postponed giving orders, and missed the opportunity to launch the invasion of Britain. Privately he was hesitating, and willing to compromise if Britain recognized the German expansion in continental Europe. When this hesitancy was combined with his defeat in the Battle of Britain, he went on to commit his greatest mistake and dig his own grave by switching his focus to the invasion of the Soviet Union.

In his memoir, Rear Admiral Hideo Kojima, the former Japanese Naval Attaché in Berlin, recalls Hitler's words back in November 1937, at a banquet hosted by Kintomo Mushakōji, the Japanese Ambassador to Germany, to mark the first anniversary of the Anti-Comintern Pact between Germany and Japan. Hitler had said to Kojima: 'In order to maintain the faith of the people, one must stage one visible triumph after another for them. I do this once or twice every year.' Kojima writes: 'This was exactly what he did, and we were always tense and on guard, wondering what he would do next.' He gives the example of the annexation of

Czechoslovakia, and adds that this prompted Britain's decision to go to war against Germany.[7] As a dictator, Hitler continuously needed to demonstrate his accomplishments to the German people, and his campaign against the Soviet Union was precisely driven by this need. Nothing remotely like Churchill's thoroughly considered stratagems could be seen here.

The Polish Pilots' Contribution to Victory

It should be noted that Poland's contribution to the Allied victory was not limited to the field of code-breaking. Many Polish air force pilots, having lost their homeland to Hitler, voluntarily moved to Britain. One-hundred-and-forty-five of them formed two fighter squadrons and repeatedly participated in the Battle of Britain, successfully taking on the Luftwaffe and playing a significant role in ensuring victory. The RAF was able to maintain sixty fighter squadrons during this period, but this was only possible when the Polish, Canadian and Czechoslovakian squadrons were created.

The Polish pilots reinstated their honour after failing to defend the skies of their own country and exacted revenge on Germany. Officially, the Battle of Britain lasted from 10 July to 31 October 1940. The number of Allied pilots involved in the fighting during this period was 2,917, of which the majority, 2,334, were, of course, British. The Poles were the second-largest nationality group with 145 pilots – more than the New Zealanders (126), the Canadians (98), the Czechoslovakians (88), the Australians (33) or the South Africans (25).

Though it was suppressed, the Hungarian uprising of October 1956, which saw the Hungarian army and civilians doggedly resist the Soviet forces, became one of the indirect causes of the collapse of communism. As we see here, sometimes the retaliation of the defeated becomes a sword of vengeance that remains in the body of the victor, and over time it becomes a factor that changes the trajectory of history substantially. The fact that, at a time when the training of RAF pilots was delayed and there was serious concern about the course of the battle, the Polish fighter pilots were very active and helped clinch victory could be said to possess a historical significance comparable to the Hungarian uprising, which lit a slow-match culminating in the fall of the Berlin Wall in the autumn of 1989.[8]

3

'Play for Time in Asia'

The Cabinet Meeting of 8 August 1940

FROM AUGUST TO September 1940, the British government's Cabinet meetings were dominated by the war situation, the damage caused by air raids and response measures, munitions production, maritime transport, and the formation and training of volunteer forces of Polish, Dutch and other nationals. Reflecting the pressing circumstances, Cabinet meetings took place frequently; urgent discussions persisted, surrounding the situation reports produced by the Cabinet Office, the General Staff of the army, navy and air force, the Foreign Office and the other government agencies. As ever, the three Chiefs of Staff were subjected to Churchill's unrelenting interrogations.

A top-secret document, which would eventually fall into the hands of the enemy through the capture of the *Automedon*, was presented to the Cabinet on 8 August 1940; the meeting was chaired by Churchill as usual. It was entitled 'The Situation in the Far East in the Event of Japanese Intervention Against Us'.[1]

Throughout that day there was intermittent fierce fighting between the Luftwaffe's Third Air Fleet of fighters and bombers, which had savagely attacked British escorted convoys in the Strait of Dover and in the waters around the Isle of Wight, and RAF fighters which responded intrepidly. The British lost twenty aircraft, the Germans twenty-eight. This episode, along with the action on the 11th, was a furious precursor to the full-scale battle that would begin on the 12th.

With such deadly aerial engagements taking place, on which British sovereignty depended, the Cabinet meeting of that day was permeated with an even greater sense of urgency than usual. It began at 11.30, in the Cabinet War Room. The details of the agenda, as laid out in the records of War Cabinet of that day,[2] were as follows:

1. Naval, Military and Air Operations
   Anti-invasion reconnaissances
   Loss of *Mohamed Ali-el-Kebir*
2. Japan
   Arrest of British subjects
   Japanese intentions in Indo-China
3. The Baltic States
   Attitude to be adopted towards Soviet absorption
4. The Far East
   Appreciation by the Chiefs of Staff
   Assistance to the Dutch in the event of Japanese aggression in the Netherlands East Indies
5. Home Defence
   Access to Protected Areas
6. The Allies
   Organization of Allied Naval, Army and Air contingents
7. Home Defence
   Effect on food production of military and air preparations
8. France
   Care of French Refugees in this country
9. Sweden
10. The Middle East
   Visit of the Commander-in-Chief to this country

The main focus of discussion that day was item Four, 'The Far East: Appreciation by the Chiefs of Staff, Assistance to the Dutch in the event of Japanese aggression in the Netherlands East Indies'. Two related papers were submitted, the Chiefs of Staff Committee report of 31 July entitled 'The Situation in the Far East in the

Event of Japanese Intervention Against Us' and that of 7 August entitled 'Assistance to the Dutch in the Event of Japanese Aggression in Netherlands East Indies'.[3] It was the Far-East situation report on which debate was concentrated, as it also covered the issues raised in the latter report.

'We Should Not Provoke Japan but Instead Buy Some Time'

The Chiefs of Staff Committee report, 'The Situation in the Far East in the Event of Japanese Intervention Against Us', was a very pessimistic one. It frankly admitted that the British defences in Asia were inadequate for thwarting a Japanese military expansion southwards, and that under the circumstances, it was difficult to improve the situation quickly since the British forces were fully occupied in the war against Germany. The British government's approach of that time, of heading off as much as possible Japan's southward expansion by not provoking her needlessly – even if war might ultimately be inevitable – faithfully reflected the analysis contained in this report.

As this was precisely the time when the aerial battles, pivotal to the nation's future, were intensifying, and it was still impossible to say anything definite about their outcome. All the Cabinet members were in agreement that Britain should dedicate every effort to winning the war against Germany as a priority, regardless of her weak position in the Far East. However, there remained the question of how to explain such a stance to convince Australia and New Zealand, and the discussions were mainly centred on this point. This was because, from around 1937, the two dominions had increasingly become nervous of Japan's growing military presence and the extension of her influence in Asia, and had frequently appealed to Britain to consolidate her defences in the region. The new Far-East appreciation by the Joint Chiefs of Staff was undertaken with an awareness of the need to respond to such petitions from the dominions.

Britain had last reviewed her defence situation in the Far East in June 1937. On that occasion it had been assumed that any Japanese threat to British interests would be seaborne. It had been concluded that Britain would be able to respond by sending a fleet of sufficient strength to protect the dominions and India and to defend British communications in the Indian Ocean within three months. However, by 1940, the Japanese had advanced into southern China and Hainan and developed communication facilities and aerodromes in Thailand. In addition, the situation in Indo-China had changed following the French defeat, and the range of Japanese aircraft had increased. It became apparent that, with these new factors, there was an increased possibility of a Japanese overland invasion of the Malayan Peninsula, and that a naval fleet alone could not respond adequately to this threat.

Moreover, owing to the collapse of France, the development of a direct threat to the British Isles, and the need to retain a fleet in European waters which matched the combined fleets of Germany and Italy, it had temporarily become impossible for Britain to despatch a fleet according to her original strategy, even if a crisis did occur in the Far East. Further, the British fleet in the Far East at that time was minimal, consisting of seven antiquated cruisers of small tonnage, two auxiliary cruisers and five old destroyers. All that could be done under such circumstances was to protect the trade route from the Cape of Good Hope to the Middle East by redeploying one battle cruiser and one aircraft carrier from the Mediterranean, where they could hardly be spared, and stationing them at Ceylon; this did not directly serve to strengthen defences in the Far East.

The report was a detailed document filling fifteen pages, comprehensively covering both the new appreciation of the situation, carried out on the premise that fundamental changes had taken place, and recommendations for the future. Its outline was as follows.[4]

Analysis of the Situation

1. 'Japan's ultimate aims are the exclusion of Western influence from the Far East and the control of Far Eastern resources of raw materials. . .Japan's immediate aim – in accordance with her traditional step-by-step policy – is likely to be the exclusion of British influence from China and Hong Kong.' 'A great deal of British capital is invested in the China trade, but this trade represents only about 2% of total British trade, and its cessation would not seriously affect the ability of the Empire to carry on the war.' 'Among the factors which may influence Japan in deciding whether to extend her interests southwards are: a) Her military and economic commitment in China, b) The Russian threat, c) The military strength by which she might be opposed, d) The fear of military

action by the United States, e) The economic consequences of war with the United States and the British Empire, on both of which she is largely dependent economically, and f) The prospect of achieving her aims at little or no cost in the event of the war in Europe going against us.' 'Although Russia is at present preoccupied in Europe, fear of Russian action will probably compel Japan to retain forces at home and in Manchuria. She must always be conscious of the probability that Russia would be quick to take advantage of the situation if Japan found herself in difficulties.'

2. 'We are advised that Japan is determined to bring the China war to an end, and that, with the closing of one after another of the arms routes into China, there is a distinct probability that the two countries will soon come to terms. The war in China cannot, therefore, be relied on for long to provide a serious deterrent to further Japanese activity, although its termination will bring no early economic relief to Japan.'

3. 'The defences of Singapore are formidable and their reduction would involve a combined operation of the first magnitude. Further, Japan must now reckon on the collaboration with the British of the substantial Dutch forces in the Netherlands East Indies against any southward thrust. On the other hand, the forces in Malaya are still far short of requirements, particularly in the air; and Japan must know that in present circumstances we should be unable to send an adequate fleet to the Far East.'

4. 'Japan may gamble on the assumption that – provided she takes no direct action against American citizens or American possessions – the United States is unlikely to be goaded to the point of armed opposition. She may foresee, also, that in the event of Great Britain's position in Europe deteriorating, it is probable that the United States would keep their fleet in the Atlantic. Although Manila is not comparable as a base to Singapore and the sea communications to the Philippines are more vulnerable to Japanese attack than those to Singapore, nevertheless Manila is a defended base and lies in the line of any Japanese advance to the south. The Japanese can never be certain that the United States will not intervene and send their fleet to the Philippines.'

5. 'One of the main influences must be the knowledge that further aggression may lead to a rupture of trade relations with the United States and Great Britain. The United States has already warned

Japan of her interest in the maintenance of the *status quo* in the Netherlands East Indies. On the long-term view, Japan's economic structure cannot stand the strain of a break with the British Empire and the Americas, upon whom she is dependent for markets and for essential raw materials. Only if she could rapidly gain complete control of the raw materials, especially oil, rubber and tin, of Malaya and the Dutch East Indies would she have a chance of withstanding British and American economic pressure.'

6. 'With the example of Italy before her, Japan may prefer to postpone any main advance until she sees more clearly the outcome of affairs in Europe. If Germany succeeds, Japan could achieve her aims quickly and without risk. On the other hand, she might abandon her traditional step-by-step policy and make a direct attack upon Singapore. We are advised that any steps Japan takes may be limited to local military action without resort to formal declaration of war, thus hoping to evade the far-reaching effects of war with the British Empire and possibly the United States. Such a policy would enable Japan to limit her action and "save face" if the local results or wider reactions were unfavourable.' 'We have, however, to consider the worst case, and to assume that Japan will not be deterred from her aim of dominating the whole of the Far East.'

7. 'The effort involved in war with the British Empire would be great for Japan, even in the absence of a British fleet, and for this reason we feel that Japan would hesitate to adopt this course unless she saw Great Britain so heavily committed in Europe as to be unable to resist her aggression, or until she was completely freed from the entanglement of the China campaign. Nevertheless, we must be prepared to resist an assault against Singapore, and by increasing our defences aim at deterring Japan from adopting this course.'

8. 'To sum up, it appears to us that, until the issue of the war in Europe becomes clearer, it is probable that Japan will confine her action to the elimination of British influence from China and Hong Kong to the greatest possible extent without incurring a rupture with the United States and the British Empire.'

Recommended Measures

1. 'Our own commitments in Europe are so great that our policy must be directed towards the avoidance of an open clash with Japan.

We have, in fact, to make a virtue of military necessity, and it is at least doubtful whether piecemeal concessions will ever have more than a temporarily alleviating effect, to be followed after an interval by further demands. It is most desirable that a wide settlement in the Far East – including economic concessions to Japan – should be concluded as early as possible, rather than that we should wait to be faced with a series of Japanese *faits accomplis*. The possibilities of obtaining such a settlement at the present time are doubtful; but we are convinced that every effort should be made to bring it about. Failing a general settlement on satisfactory terms with Japan, our general policy should be to play for time; to cede nothing until we must; and to build up our defences as soon as we can.'

2. 'The fact that our position in North China would be untenable in the event of war with Japan has already been recognized by the orders issued to troops at Peking, Tientsin and Shanghai to offer no forcible opposition to Japanese aggression. . . Although we should suffer some loss of prestige by withdrawing [these troops], the advantages of having them available elsewhere in the Far East would strengthen our military position.' 'Even if we had a strong fleet in the Far East, it is doubtful whether Hong Kong with its present defences could be held now that the Japanese are firmly established on the mainland of China. . .Should it be found possible to negotiate a general settlement in the Far East it would be in our best military interests to arrange to demilitarize Hong Kong, obtaining the best *quid pro quo* for this concession. Except as part of such [a] general settlement, demilitarization of Hong Kong is impracticable owing to the loss of prestige which it would entail. In the event of war, Hong Kong must be regarded as an outpost and held as long as possible. We should resist the inevitably strong pressure to reinforce Hong Kong and we should certainly be unable to relieve it.'

'The penetration of Indo-China or Thailand would give the Japanese bases from which to attack Malaya, and among other advantages would secure for them substantial rice supplies. An attack on Indo-China would not be a formidable undertaking for Japan, as her action would probably be confined to the limited objectives of seizing bases and aerodromes and controlling focal points in these countries. . .All the evidence goes to show that the Thai government would not oppose a Japanese penetration by force, while the French forces in Indo-China could not prevent a Japanese occupation of the ports and railways. We ourselves could not effectively assist in the defence of either Indo-China or Thailand.' 'A Japanese penetration of Thailand would thus threaten Singapore and unquestionably make the defence of Burma and Malaya far more difficult. Nevertheless, *under present conditions*, we do not consider that the threat to our vital interests would be sufficiently direct to justify us going to war with Japan with our present available resources.". . .for similar reasons we should not, under present conditions, go to war with Japan in the event of a Japanese attack on Indo-China.'

'The sea communications most likely to be threatened by Japanese action can be considered. . .a) The Indian Ocean (including the west coast of Australia), b) The South China Sea and Western Pacific (north of Australia), c) The seas east and south of Australia, including the Trans-Pacific routes.' 'The Indian Ocean would be the most fruitful field for Japanese action against our seaborne trade. . .Although the Malacca Straits might be denied to Japanese Naval Forces, these forces might use many other passages through the Netherlands East Indies for operations against our Indian Ocean trade. . .Although the distances from Japan are great, there are a number of potential fuelling bases in the Indian Ocean. . .A force of enemy cruisers, particularly if supported by one or more heavy ships, would constitute a most serious threat to our trade. . .' '[In defending the Indian Ocean and the seas around Australia] Dutch cooperation would, of course, be essential.'

Other recommended measures can be summarized as follows:[5]

3. In the event of Japanese aggression against British territory in the Far East, we will fight them. Since the Dutch East Indies are essential to the security of our sea communications in the Indian Ocean, if Japan attacks these islands we should go to war with her provided the Dutch also resist her. If the Dutch do not resist, we should concentrate on the defence of Malaya and Singapore. The Dutch forces in this region are stronger than ours and form a considerable deterrent. However there is no guarantee of Dutch cooperation in the event of Malaya coming under attack. Given that we lack the resources to support the Dutch, we cannot propose a plan of mutual assistance.

4. Our former plan was to counter any Japanese military expansion southwards with a fleet based at Singapore, but under present

circumstances in Europe it would be impossible for us to dispatch a fleet of sufficient strength to resist the Japanese Navy. In order to retain our route to the Middle East via the Cape of Good Hope and passage through the Indian Ocean, vital for communications with the Dutch East Indies, Australia and New Zealand, we shall send one aircraft carrier and one battle cruiser from the Mediterranean, to be based at Ceylon.

5. It is assumed the Japanese are likely to invade Malaya across her border with Thailand or from the coast of the Malayan Peninsula and proceed south. Therefore it is no longer sufficient to concentrate on the defence of Singapore alone and it is necessary to hold the whole of Malaya. In the present absence of a naval fleet as the principal force, we shall increase the aircraft stationed in the area from the current 88 to 336 by the end of 1941. We should simultaneously strengthen our land forces with Australian troops. It is highly unlikely that the Japanese will invade Australia or New Zealand and the threat is expected to be limited to that of seaborne air attacks on their ports.

6. Even if we cannot prevent Japanese aggression against British interests altogether, we must endeavour to retain a footing in the Far East for when the situation in Europe improves and we can afford to assume the offensive in the region.

7. The United States' forces stationed in the Philippines pose a threat to Japan in the event of her expansion into Malaya, Singapore and the Dutch East Indies. Therefore it is possible that the Japanese may first attack the Philippines with the aim of expelling the Americans. In the event of hostilities between Japan and the United States, we shall offer our naval base at Singapore to the American fleet.

Incidentally, as we have seen, the report admitted that it would be difficult to defend Hong Kong against Japanese aggression and concluded that Britain should resist reinforcing her forces there, but such an assessment was by no means a new one. Immediately after the First World War, the then First Lord of the Admiralty, John Rushworth Jellicoe, having visited Australia, Asia and the Pacific, had produced a report dated 21 August 1919. This report, while assuming that Japan was an imaginary enemy, had judged that, in an armed clash with Japan, the best that Britain could expect regarding the defence of Hong Kong would be to buy some time, and that it would be ultimately impossible to hold the colony.

Churchill's Letter

The discussions surrounding item four were not recorded in the general minutes of the Cabinet meeting of that day, but were entered in a separate confidential file labelled 'War Cabinet Conclusions' kept under lock and key at the Cabinet Office.

Let us study this record:

First, Churchill stated that he thought it was premature to make a decision on whether Britain would assist the Dutch in the event of Japanese aggression against the Dutch East Indies. Then the issue of whether a digest of the Far-Eastern appreciation should be sent to the dominion governments was raised, as a point on which an immediate decision was required. Viscount Caldecote, Secretary of State for Dominion Affairs, remarked that the conclusions of the report 'Assistance to the Dutch in the Event of Japanese Aggression in Netherlands East Indies' would sooner or later have to be shared with the dominion governments, but that he was concerned that the two documents together would give them a very pessimistic impression. He also pointed out that New Zealand was about to dispatch a brigade to Fiji, and that nothing should interfere with this plan. In response, Churchill suggested that if the conclusions were communicated to the dominion governments in the following manner, they might be inspired with a much greater degree of confidence:[6]

1. 'Our present policy was to beat the Italians in the Mediterranean for which purpose we [were] required to keep a considerable fleet there.'
2. 'We had been handling our relations with Japan very carefully and hoped to avoid war with her.'
3. 'Nevertheless we might at any moment become involved in war with Japan. It did not follow that we must abandon our operations in the Mediterranean immediately [when] Japan declared war. With China on her hands, it was unlikely that Japan's opening moves would be a full-scale invasion of Australia and New Zealand. Attacks on Hong Kong, Singapore and the Netherlands East Indies were more probable.'

4. 'If this appreciation of Japan's opening moves proved correct we should content ourselves with sending one battle cruiser and one aircraft carrier to the Indian Ocean, to be based on Ceylon, for the purpose of protecting our vital communications.'
5. 'We assumed that Australia and New Zealand would not ask us to modify our strategy on account of the presence of Japanese raiders on their trade routes, or of small-scale Japanese raids taking place on their coasts.'
6. 'If a full-scale invasion of either Australia or New Zealand was threatened the situation could be retrieved by the intervention of the United States. Indeed, if the United States had previously made it clear that they would not tolerate the invasion of Australia or New Zealand, the Japanese would never take the plunge.'
7. 'In the last resort, however, our course was clear. We could never stand by and see a British dominion overwhelmed by a yellow race, and we should at once come to the assistance of that dominion with all the forces we could make available. For this purpose we should be prepared, if necessary, to abandon our position in the Mediterranean and the Middle East.'

Viscount Caldecote commented that both dominions would be much reassured by such a declaration, and that they would see the Far-Eastern situation in a new light.

The First Lord of the Admiralty, Alexander, remarked that Britain should be cautious about renouncing her position in the Mediterranean. He warned that if this included withdrawing from Gibraltar, her trade route to the Cape of Good Hope would be threatened by Italian warships; she would have to reroute her shipping further west, and increase her naval strength in the Atlantic in order to protect the new route.

Viscount Caldecote and Viscount Halifax expressed their doubts regarding the probability, referred to in the Far-East report, of an early settlement between Japan and China. Viscount Halifax further remarked that, concerning the policy of avoiding war with Japan even if she invaded Indo-China, Britain should not make such a decision at this stage and should keep her options open.

Before bringing the meeting to a close, the War Cabinet: 1) deferred consideration of the strategic issues raised in the reports by the Chiefs of Staff, 2) asked the Secretary of State for Dominion Affairs to despatch telegrams to the dominion governments containing the aforementioned digest of the Far-Eastern appreciation, subject to the addition of a passage along the lines proposed by the Churchill, and 3) asked the Chiefs of Staff to verify, in consultation with the Foreign Office, the political assumptions made in the two reports. It was also decided to include in the aforementioned telegrams to the dominion governments the outcome of the verification to be done by the Chiefs of Staff as described above. [7]

There is another telegram, sent from Churchill to the prime ministers of Australia and New Zealand on 11 August. It is a most interesting document, which reveals how Churchill saw Anglo-Japanese relations, how he read the present and future course of the war and how adamant he was to see it through. As we shall see, in the March and April of that year, Churchill had actively coaxed the Japanese Ambassador to Britain, Mamoru Shigemitsu, and the Japanese Minister of Foreign Affairs, Yōsuke Matsuoka. He had believed that Japan had not yet reached the point of gambling all, and that there remained the possibility that she would make rational choices. We can see in this telegram that, even in August, this was still his assessment of the situation. Even Churchill had been unable entirely to decipher Japan's intentions.

The telegram read:[8]

> The combined Staffs are preparing a paper on the Pacific situation, but I venture to send you in advance a brief foreword. We are trying our best to avoid war with Japan, by both conceding on points where the Japanese military clique can perhaps force a rupture, and by standing up where the ground is less dangerous, as in arrests of individuals. I do not think myself that Japan will declare war unless Germany can make a successful invasion of Britain. Once Japan sees that Germany has either failed, or dares not try, I look for easier times in the Pacific. In adopting, against the grain, a yielding policy towards Japanese threats, we have always in mind your interests and safety.
>
> Should Japan nevertheless declare war on us, her first objective outside the Yellow Sea would probably be the Dutch East Indies. Evidently the United States would not like this. What they would do we cannot tell. They give no undertaking of support, but their main Fleet in the Pacific must be a grave preoccupation to [the] Japanese Admiralty. In this first phase of an Anglo-Japanese war, we should of course defend Singapore, which if attacked, which is unlikely, ought to stand a long siege. We should also be able to base on Ceylon a battle cruiser and a fast aircraft carrier, which, with the Australian and New Zealand ships which would return to you

would exercise a very powerful deterrent upon hostile raiding cruisers.

We are about to reinforce with more first-class units the Eastern Mediterranean Fleet. This Fleet could of course at any time be sent through the Canal into the Indian Ocean or to relieve Singapore. We do not want to do this, even if Japan declares war, until it is found to be vital to your safety. Such a transference would entail the complete loss of the Middle East, and all prospect of beating Italy in the Mediterranean would be gone. We must expect heavy attacks on Egypt in the near future, and the Eastern Mediterranean Fleet is needed to help in repelling them. If these attacks succeed, the Eastern Fleet would have to leave the Mediterranean either through the Canal or by Gibraltar. In either case a large part of it would be available for your protection. We hope however to maintain ourselves in Egypt, and to keep the Eastern Fleet at Alexandria during the first phase of an Anglo-Japanese war, should that occur. No-one can lay down beforehand what is going to happen. We must just weigh events from day to day, and use our available resources to the utmost.

A final question arises, whether Japan having declared war would attempt to invade Australia or New Zealand with a considerable army. We think this is very unlikely, because Japan is first absorbed in China, secondly would be gathering rich prizes in the Dutch East Indies, and thirdly would fear very much to send an important part of her fleet far to the southward leaving the American fleet between it and home. If, however, contrary to prudence and self-interest, Japan set about invading Australia or New Zealand on a large scale, I have the explicit authority of the Cabinet to assure you that we should then cut our losses in the Mediterranean and proceed to your aid, sacrificing every interest except only the defence and feeding of this Island on which all depends.

We hope, however, that events will take a different turn. By gaining time with Japan, the present dangerous situation may be got over. We are vastly stronger here at home than when I cabled to you on June 16. We have a large Army now beginning to be well-equipped. We have fortified our beaches. We have a strong reserve of mobile troops including our Regular Army and Australian, New Zealand, and Canadian contingents, with several armoured Divisions or Brigades ready to strike in counter-attack at the head of any successful lodgements. We have ferried over from the United States their grand aid of nearly a thousand guns and 600,000 rifles with ammunition complete. Relieved of the burden of defending France, our Army is becoming daily more powerful and munitions are gathering. Besides this we have the Home Guard of 1,500,000 men, many of them war veterans, and most with rifles or other arms.

The Royal Air Force continues to show the same individual superiority over the enemy on which I counted so much in my aforesaid cable to you. Yesterday's important air action in the Channel showed that we could attack against odds of 3 to 1, and inflict losses of 3.5 to 1. Astounding progress has been made by Lord Beaverbrook in output of the best machines. Our Fighter and Bomber strength is nearly double what it was when I cabled you, and we have a very large reserve of machines in hand. I do not think the German Air Force has the numbers or quality to overpower our Air defences.

The Navy increases in strength each month, and we are now beginning to receive the immense programme started at the declaration of war. Between June and December 1940, over 500 vessels, large and small, but many most important, will join the Fleet. The German Navy is weaker than it has ever been. SCHARNHORST and GNEISENAU are both in dock damaged. BISMARCK has not yet done her trials, TIRPITZ is three months behind BISMARCK. There are available now in this critical fortnight, after which the time for invasion is getting very late, only one pocket battleship, a couple of 8-inch HIPPERS, two light cruisers, and perhaps a score of destroyers. To try to transport a large army, as would now be needed for success, across the seas virtually without Naval escort in the face of our Navy and Air Force, only to meet our powerful military force on shore, still less to maintain such an army and nourish its lodgements with munitions and supplies would be a very unreasonable act. On the other hand, if Hitler fails to invade and conquer Britain before the weather breaks, he has received his first and probably his fatal check.

We therefore feel a sober and growing conviction of our power to defend ourselves and the Empire successfully, and to persevere through the year or two that may be necessary to gain victory.

The Automedon*'s Departure from Liverpool*

It was standard practice for most classified documents presented to the Cabinet to be sent to those in charge of the British government and military outposts and intelligence organizations in Asia. The top-secret papers from the Cabinet meeting of 8 August were placed in a large envelope addressed to the Commander-in-Chief of the Far East, Sir Robert Brooke-Popham. This was then contained in a strong, green canvas mailbag for special consignments, about 40cm long and 18cm wide. The mailbag contained a number of round holes, each fitted with a brass ring, so that it would sink immediately if it was disposed of in the sea. The mailbag was also marked: 'Classified: Destroy in an Emergency'. This confidential package was taken to Liverpool by an official who delivered it by hand to Captain Ewan of the *Automedon* in exchange for a signed receipt. Ewan kept the mailbag on the desk in the chart room so that it could be thrown into the sea at a moment's notice. Former Deck Boy Frank Walker, over sixty years later, can still clearly recall seeing it there on a few occasions. In fact, very few knew of its existence.

On her voyage from Liverpool to Shanghai via Penang, Singapore and Hong Kong which began on 24 September 1940, the *Automedon* was carrying 120 other mailbags. Among them were two bags of official documents, including highly sensitive material such as navy cipher tables, sailing orders, government papers, letters and memos. These mailbags were clearly marked: 'Safe Hand. British Master Only' in large writing. Like the classified mailbag kept in the chart room, they were made with several holes in them and were weighted so that they would sink instantly in an emergency.

At that time the Royal Navy was fully occupied with escorting convoys in the Atlantic and defending the English Channel. Therefore, it had no choice but to entrust merchant ships with the transport of top-secret paperwork. The merchant ships being inadequately defended as they were, the Royal Navy knew the risk that this entailed. Unusually for a time when there was an acute shortage of crewmen, on this particular voyage of the *Automedon*, T.G. Wilson was enlisted as an extra Second Officer. International maritime custom held that the Second Officer was in charge of the safekeeping of mail, so it must have been Wilson's role to ensure the security of the important consignments.

The *Automedon* was a passenger freighter built in 1923 by Palmer's Shipbuilding & Iron Company in Jarrow, in the Tyne and Wear region on the northeast coast of England. She was named after the nimble driver of Achilles' chariot in Homer's *Iliad*. Already seventeen years old, she was by no means new, but she was a first-class vessel, fully equipped and capable of speeds of over fourteen knots. The truly beautiful and elegant sight of her cutting through the waves certainly did her name justice.

The *Automedon* set sail for Shanghai with an assorted cargo including aircraft, cars, machine parts, microscopes, military uniforms, steel and copper plates, cameras, sewing machines, beer, whisky (550 cases), cigarettes (2.5 million Chesterfields) and foodstuffs.[9] This was about a month after she had returned from her previous voyage (on 22 August), that had begun at the end of March and had taken her to western Africa, Durban and Australia. Surely it could not have occurred to Captain Ewan or any of his crew that they had embarked on the *Automedon*'s last voyage from Liverpool.

Few vestiges remain of Liverpool's heyday as a port or as a city. Once there was a thriving traffic of ships from all over the world, including Japan, and emigrants, not only from Britain but from all over Europe, set sail from here, full of hope and trepidation, for the new world of North America. Now there are just a few ferries running to and from Dublin and the Isle of Man. It is said that Napoleon's troops captured during the Battle of Waterloo in 1815 were brought to Liverpool and made to help with the building of the port. Past glories are now only evoked through the many grand docks that still remain, bearing names like Albert Dock and Queen's Dock.

Liverpool was frequently bombed during the war, and in May 1940 the city had sustained particularly extensive damage. In September, the aerial battles were still continuing fiercely day and night and the number of attacking German sorties reached its peak of 12,095. However, the threat of a German invasion was already abating, and the British were increasingly confident that they had ridden the storm.

The *Automedon* left from the dock at Birkenhead, steamed the short stretch of the Mersey into the Irish Sea, and through St George's Channel into the Atlantic. She formed a convoy with a number of other ships for a while and then she steered a direct course to the coast of Africa, while remaining on guard for air raids and U-boat attacks. The U-boats had stepped up their activity since France's defeat and Italy's declaration of war against the Allies in June. In the period from July to October alone, Britain lost 144 vessels, and her supply routes – which were her lifeline – were seriously compromised. Even if she won the battle for her skies had she lost her ground at sea, especially in the Atlantic, victory would have been unlikely. The Battle of Britain was to be followed by the Battle of the Atlantic to protect the supply channels from the United States. Although their voyage was characterized by extreme vigilance, blackouts and restricted communication, among Harper, Parsons, Walker and the other crew members there was little real sense that they were facing the acute dangers of the war-ravaged seas. They did not worry about the dangers that might be in store for them over or under the sea. It was just another voyage.

The *Automedon* called at Freetown in Sierra Leone on 12 October before rounding the Cape of Good Hope and arriving at Durban on the east coast of South Africa on 29 October. There she refuelled, replenished water and other supplies and delivered some mail. There was an official mailbag for the Royal Navy Commander, Simonstown, which was handed to a naval officer who had come to collect it. Her tasks completed, the *Automedon* left Durban the same day. From here on her journey would be completely solitary. She sailed around Madagascar's southern tip and steered a course for Penang on the south coast of the Malayan Peninsula. By the time she had crossed the Indian Ocean and was approaching the waters southwest of Sumatra, it was over ten days into November.

The Tripartite Agreement that Sealed Japan's Fate

The Axis pact between Germany, Italy and Japan bolstered Japan's leaning towards a war with Britain and the United States. It had been signed in Berlin on 27 September, three days after the *Automedon* had set sail from Liverpool. By allying herself with Germany – whose first signs of demise could now be seen in the Battle of Britain – Japan had taken a major step on her road to doom. As we shall see, the secret British Cabinet papers aboard the *Automedon* would serve to lead her further down this road. Around this time, it is supposed, Captain Ewan constantly followed the international situation by listening to the BBC World Service. However, he could never have imagined that the contents of the green mailbag, placed on the desk in the chart room so that it could be jettisoned whenever it became necessary, were so precisely relevant to the current international situation, and, in particular, to Japan's strategy towards Britain and the United States.

Prior to the signing of the pact, public opinion in Japan had been divided on the issue. In particular, there had been deep-seated opposition to the alliance among business leaders, notably in the financial sector. A new Cabinet led by Prime Minister Kiichirō Hiranuma had taken over from the Konoe Cabinet in January 1939. The Prime Minister, Foreign Minister, Chancellor, Minister of War and Navy Minister had together held over seventy meetings between January and July. However, they had failed to reach a consensus on the pact: there had been a stand off between Seishirō Itagaki, the Minister of War, who had been in favour of signing it, and Admiral Mitsumasa Yonai who had been against. Then, on 23 August, a non-aggression pact had unexpectedly been signed between Germany and the Soviet Union, and this act of betrayal by Germany had caused turmoil within the Japanese government and among diplomats alike. Accused of misreading the international situation, Prime Minister Hiranuma had no choice but to resign five days later, with the famous exclamation: 'The situation in Europe is baffling and bizarre.'

Hiranuma had been replaced by General Nobuyuki Abe, but his Cabinet, too, had been short-lived, and a new Cabinet led by Yonai as Prime Minister had taken over in January 1940. Dazzled by the might of the German Blitzkrieg that swept through the Benelux countries and France between April and June, the pro-Axis movement headed by the army had rapidly gained strength, and brought about the collapse of the Yonai Cabinet on 16 July. Finally, the tripartite alliance had been signed by the succeeding administration formed on 22 July, the second Cabinet of Fumimaro Konoe. The strong pressure exerted by the army notwithstanding, Konoe had made the worst possible decision at a crucial crossroads in history which would be regretted for generations to come. This was his second great error, following his proclamation on 16 January 1938: 'The Japanese Government will cease henceforward to deal with the government of Chiang Kai-shek.'

When the tripartite agreement had been signed, Britain had responded by promptly deciding to reopen the supply route for Chiang Kai-shek through Burma to Chunking. Churchill had been holding on to the slim hope that the Japanese leaders would make the wise choice, and when it had become clear that Japan was aligning herself with his mortal enemy Hitler's Nazi Germany, and was complicit in the latter's ambition of world domination, he had despaired more than ever for the future of Anglo-Japanese relations. Even so, in talks with Ambassador Shigemitsu six months later on 4 March 1941, he urged Japanese prudence and did not abandon his efforts to avert the worst. Churchill's words, according to Shigemitsu's telegram[10] reporting on the talks, can be paraphrased thus:

> From now on there will be many difficult twists and turns in this war, and its peaks and troughs will continue until the end of 1942.

> However by the end of next year, Britain will have overpowered Germany with her air force. Bearing in mind our naval and aerial superiority and the American arms production, we will certainly win. When that time comes, we will extend our friendship to Japan, and our countries should collaborate on the political world stage. Japan and Britain should have a cooperative relationship, not an antagonistic one, especially considering our geographical similarities; we can both flourish as island-empires. In this war, inevitably the pendulum will swing to and fro. But do not let your vision be clouded by this; I ask you to look at the situation in the long term.

The war did indeed go on to develop exactly in the way that Churchill predicted. To make matters worse, in the middle of 1942 Japan suffered a major defeat at the Battle of Midway and her hopes of winning the war were completely dashed.

By the time of Churchill's meeting with Shigemitsu, the Battle of Britain was over and Hitler had given up on the invasion of Britain and was setting his sights on the Soviet Union. The United States' readiness to fight was also increasingly apparent, and an Axis defeat could now be predicted. The behaviour of the Japanese leaders, taking a great risk in such a climate and endangering their country, must have been unfathomable for Churchill, a politician who reacted so judiciously to any situation. He attempted to persuade Foreign Minister Matsuoka, who was at the forefront of the hard-line anti-Allies stance, one last time, to reflect on the consequences of joining the Axis. The resulting letter from Churchill to Matsuoka dated 2 April 1941,[11] was to be entrusted to Shigemitsu, who was due to meet with the Japanese Foreign Minister in Switzerland.

Shigemitsu was of the opinion that Japan should choose her moves very carefully, as the war in Europe was not progressing in Germany's favour as claimed by German propaganda. The Japanese Military Attaché in London, Captain Eiichi Tatsumi, shared this view. Shigemitsu undertook to arrange a meeting with Matsuoka during his visit to Europe and to persuade him to handle relations with Britain and the United States with the utmost caution. Matsuoka offered to meet Shigemitsu in Berlin, but he declined because of how this would have appeared to the British government. Instead, Shigemitsu attempted to meet up with Matsuoka in Vichy or somewhere in Switzerland and went to some lengths, such as requesting the British government to arrange a plane ticket to Lisbon for him. However, this meeting never materialized as Matsuoka, concerned about the domestic political situation back in Japan, cut his visit short.

Churchill's letter was eventually handed to Matsuoka by Sir Stafford Cripps, British Ambassador to the Soviet Union, at a theatre in Moscow on the night of 13 April: following his visits to Germany and Italy, Matsuoka was staying in the city for the signing of the Russo-Japanese neutrality pact. This meeting was arranged through Matsuoka's secretary, Toshikazu Kase, accepting the mediation of the American Ambassador to the Soviet Union, Lawrence Steinhardt, who acted on behalf of his British counterpart. It was set up in such a way as to attract as little press attention as possible. In a bar which had been cleared of its clientele, Matsuoka swiftly put the letter in his pocket without attempting to read it, and just talked at length about his tour of Europe and on the subject of foreign policy.[12]

There is no evidence that on his return to Japan Matsuoka brought this important letter to 'the attention of the Imperial Japanese Government and people' as Churchill would have hoped. When he visited the imperial palace on the night of 23 April and delivered his report to the Emperor, he did not once refer to the letter either, and instead he waxed lyrical about the welcome he had received in Moscow, Berlin and Rome, to the point of incurring the irritation of the Emperor. While in Moscow, Matsuoka had tried to engineer a direct meeting with Roosevelt through Steinhardt, and this was probably all he could think about. He was also intoxicated by his own inflated sense of importance, and so it appears that he did not pay any attention to what Churchill had to say. Meanwhile, Prime Minister Konoe, when asked for a meeting by the British Ambassador to Japan, Sir Robert Craigie, who was attempting to deliver the same letter, had refused to see him. He had given the incomprehensible excuse that he had been asked by Matsuoka not to meet with any ambassador, from any country, while he was away in Europe. Craigie had ended up giving the letter to Chūichi Ōhashi, the Deputy Minister for Foreign Affairs.[13] Thus, Japan once again missed an opportunity to avert her downfall.

The all-important American reaction to the tripartite alliance had been much more vehement than expected and, in contrast to Churchill's persuasive approach, it went straight to the point. Konoe, Matsuoka and the other Japanese leaders were both astonished and worried by the United States' forceful opposition.

Matsuoka's threatening language had no effect whatsoever on America. She increased her support for China, and emphasized more clearly than ever her intention to collaborate with the Allies to thwart Japan's ambitions. After 27 September, the antagonistic relationship between Japan and the Allies had become increasingly irreversible and began careering towards war. Japan held negotiations with France, from the latter half of 1940 through to the end of July the following year, on the acquisition of raw materials from, and the stationing of troops in, Indo-China. America was informed of the details of these talks. By the middle of 1941, she had concluded that these moves on the part of Japan were clear proof that the Axis countries had began their coordinated global strategy, that Japan could no longer be accommodated, and that war was inevitable. In his post-war hearing, Captain Katsuo Shiba, who was in the First Division of the Military Affairs Bureau of the Naval Ministry, stated that it was Article 3 in particular of the Tripartite Pact which had resulted in the stiff reaction of the United States. Her government interpreted the article as being targeted against America. In the article, the Axis powers agreed to assist one another with all political, economic and military means should any of them be attacked by a Power not taking part in the European War or the Japan-Chinese conflict. According to Shiba, at that time Japan considered the United States ill-prepared to take any drastic steps but actually Japan had been far too optimistic and had been indulging in wishful thinking.[14]

In the summer of 1940, Britain had been in the thick of defending her own skies and could not set out a clear policy regarding the defence of the Dutch East Indies, but by the following spring her attitude had hardened in alignment with that of the United States. She was determined not to allow a Japanese invasion of the Dutch East Indies because of the threat to her Far-Eastern interests that this posed; therefore she would equally not tolerate Japan's incursion into Indochina or Thailand, from where an attack on the Dutch East Indies could be launched. Britain and Australia seriously considered issuing a joint declaration with America, Holland and New Zealand to the effect that Japan's acts of aggression fulfilled the Allies' criteria for going to war against her. Such a change in approach was also spurred on by the US Congress passing a law on the loan of arms to her allies in February that year.

Even in this climate, Churchill did not give up working on the Japanese leaders. This indicates both the degree of confidence and the leeway afforded him by Britain's favourable situation at that time, and the long-standing goodwill which he retained towards Japan since the days of naval cooperation between Britain and Japan during the First World War. In his letter, dated 28 March 1915, to Rear Admiral Kōzaburō Oguri, the Japanese Naval Attaché in London, Churchill as First Lord of the Admiralty had written: 'When the history of this great war comes to be written, the ungrudging and whole-hearted assistance of Japan will furnish a striking chapter, and the cordial goodwill that has united the naval staffs of both countries will endure as one of our pleasantest recollections.'[15]

From the formation of the tripartite alliance to the Japanese occupation of southern Indo-China, the international climate became increasingly critical. Konoe was overwhelmed by the situation and deeply regretted appointing Matsuoka as Foreign Minister. In order to rid the Cabinet of Matsuoka he even had the entire Cabinet resign on 16 July, and then re-formed it with Admiral Teijirō Toyoda as the Foreign Minister. However, Konoe relinquished his position in less than three months and made way for a new Cabinet headed by General Hideki Tōjō, thereby driving Japan further down the road to destruction.

Konoe panicked over the rapid deterioration in relations with the United States, but it was too late. His Cabinet decided to dispatch troops to southern Indo-China on 2 July 1941. When he was warned, in no uncertain terms, by Baron Kijūrō Shidehara, former Ambassador to Washington, that this action would lead to war with the United States, Konoe was dismayed and reportedly turned pale.[16] Konoe had a habit of regretting his actions in retrospect. Matsuoka was the same in this regard. On 8 December 1941, Matsuoka heard on his sickbed that Japan had gone to war with America. He wept and said: 'It has really hit me, for the first time, that the Axis pact was the greatest blunder of my life.' The mass of the Japanese people conformed blindly and allowed men like Konoe and Matsuoka, who were devoid of foresight and strategy or reckless and emotionally unstable to occupy the heart of national government.[17] Moreover, they applauded these men, paving the way for their country's downfall, and suffered bitterly as a result. The people of Japan must reflect on the part they played, as well as denouncing their leaders. In the words of J.S. Mill: 'The worth of a State, in the long run, is the worth of the individuals composing it.'[18]

4

Atlantis, Predator of the Seas

The Atlantis's *Voyage Across the Seven Seas*

THE GERMAN RAIDER *Atlantis*, which attacked the *Automed*on off the west coast of Sumatra on 11 November 1940, had set out into the seas of war over seven months earlier. During the summer of 1939, when the air was thick with rumours of an impending war, Rogge was aboard the *Albert Leo Schlageter*,[1] a sailing ship built in 1937 used for naval training and exercises. He had set sail from the base at Kiel with some trainee petty officers and he was leading a practice mission in the Baltic. However, on 25 August, he received the order to end the expedition and to return to port immediately. He hurried back as, prior to his departing, he had been given secret orders to assume the command of a raider in the event of war breaking out. In consultation with naval engineers he immediately undertook the conversion of the vessel assigned to him into a commercial raider. This was the *Atlantis*.

Bernhard Rogge, who was to achieve great success as the Captain of the *Atlantis*, was born 4 November 1899 in a seaside village in the north of the Schleswig-Holstein region of Germany. It was a natural progression for him to develop an interest in the sea and in boats. Bernhard was only sixteen years of age when he joined the German Navy in 1915. His grandfather was a Lutheran scholar who had written many books and had considerable influence in Germany at the time. Judging from Bernhard's performance in the navy, it appears that his grandfather had little to do with his getting in the navy. It is believed, however, that his grandfather had a strong influence on Rogge's character development, and Rogge had grown into a man with boundless compassion and a deep sense of justice.[2]

The *Atlantis*'s keel had been laid in 1937 at the Bremer Vulkan shipyard, and she had been commissioned in 1939 as a Bremen Hansa Shipping Company freighter, the *Goldenfels*. As her specifications (7,862 tonnes, two 351 MANN diesel engines, 7,600 horsepower, maximum speed: sixteen knots, maximum continuous travel at ten knots: 60,000 miles) indicate, she had been designed with a future conversion to military use in mind. The name 'Atlantis' was derived from the legendary Utopia of the same name described in Plato's writings. It is said to have been an island to the west of the Straits of Gibraltar that sank in one night through divine retribution. It was as if the *Atlantis*'s name hinted at her fate that she, too, would eventually sink to the bottom of the sea.

Captain Rogge was extremely busy for several months. The procurement of all the essential supplies in sufficient quantities, including food, medicines and medical equipment, clothing and other daily necessities as well as arms and ammunition, required scrupulous planning and repeated checks. It would be too late to remedy any shortfalls once at sea. On a long-term naval mission, harmonious relationships between men were of the greatest importance, so Rogge paid particular attention to the recruitment of his crew, especially the senior officers. With the help of the navy's personnel department he was able to secure high-quality staff including Paul Kamenz and Ulrich Mohr. All the crewmen were either serving marines or reservists. By around Easter 1940, Rogge had completed all the preparations, and he was able to report to the Naval High Command.[3]

The *Atlantis* was armed with six 5.9-inch guns, four torpedo tubes, ninety-two mines, and machine guns. She also carried a Heinkel He144B seaplane, which could both search for prey and bomb and strafe suitable targets. It was installed in the No.2 hold fully assembled, so that it could be launched at any time, along with a reserve plane. The *Atlantis* was fitted with all kinds of devices to enable her quickly to disguise herself as vessels of various nationalities. For example, the height of her funnel could be adjusted, and she also had a false funnel which could freely be extended or retracted. The masts, too, were telescopic. In addition, her fire-control system was sophisticated and precise. A raider was typically a high-speed elite vessel like the *Atlantis* ingeniously mounted with concealable weapons including cannons, torpedoes and machine-guns.

The *Atlantis* moved around large areas stealthily and elusively. Her routine method was to alter her exterior to resemble a specific foreign vessel, such as a Japanese ship, to approach her target as closely as possible, and to attack her swiftly before she had the chance to raise the alarm. If her target did broadcast a message, she silenced her immediately by firing at her radio room and destroying it. In the case of British ships, they were instructed by the navy to send the emergency signal even if it invited an attack, and accordingly British losses tended to be higher.

The German Navy's ships, equipment and tactics for the disruption of maritime trade had developed rapidly during the First World War, as could be seen in the remarkable activities of vessels such as the light cruiser *Emden*. By the Second World War the ships ran on diesel and their operation was more efficient, so in the early days at least they wielded considerable power. In terms of its operations to disrupt commerce the German Navy achieved far greater results than that of Japan.

Once prepared for her mission, the *Atlantis* assumed the guise of a minesweeper along with two other raiders, the *Orion* and the *Widder*, and carried out gunnery drills in German waters. Then, on 23 March, she changed her appearance to that of the Norwegian merchant ship the *Knute Nelson* and flagrantly displayed the Norwegian flag. She entered a small inlet on the west coast of Schleswig-Holstein and awaited the go-ahead.

Finally, on 31 March, the *Atlantis* set sail into the North Sea and headed north. She was escorted by two torpedo boats and a few fighter planes until the evening. From the following morning she was guarded by a U-boat that travelled parallel to her a few miles away. Under the cover of darkness at dusk on that day, she removed her Norwegian façade and retracted the false funnel she had been displaying, leaving the real one only. She now feigned to be the Soviet Navy's auxiliary cruiser *Kim* heading for Murmansk. Following Norway's coastline, the *Atlantis* ploughed through the rough waves of the North Sea in poor visibility and under leaden clouds that hung low in the sky. Just in case they were picked up, Rogge even ensured some of the crew cut their hair in the style often sported by Russian sailors.

As time passed, the sea became increasingly rough. The submarine, which was travelling high in the water, could not increase her speed and began to struggle. If the *Atlantis* did not make the scheduled time to enter the danger zone between Bergen on the west coast of Norway and the Shetland Islands, her chances of being spotted by the enemy would increase. With this concern in mind, the *Atlantis* arranged to rendezvous with the U-boat at a fixed point near the Denmark Strait, and she made her way through the perilous waters alone at full speed and in one stretch. She continued to steam north, and to proceed on the route to Murmansk, even after she had entered the Arctic Circle at 9.00 on the third day. That night she made a sharp alteration of course to the west and followed the lane from Murmansk to Iceland. Eventually, she rejoined the U-boat which had been waiting at the agreed meeting point.

Then the *Atlantis*, with her crew keeping watch for icebergs, made her way through the ice floes of the Denmark Strait between Iceland and Greenland. Before she had reached the open waters of the North Atlantic it was decided that the U-boat should end the escort and return to Germany, as her conning tower and her hatch had become covered with ice, affecting her ability to proceed at speed. While she was steaming southwest along the coast of Greenland the *Atlantis* picked up a radio message sent from the U-boat to the Naval High Command: 'Parted from the *Atlantis* at Zone AD2957.' Thus the Naval High Command was able to confirm that its first raider of the Second World War had safely entered the Atlantic.

Once past the southernmost point of Greenland, the sea became warmer and much less hostile. The *Atlantis* now spotted many ships of different nationalities, including the occasional British warship. Every time there was a sighting the *Atlantis* changed course and distanced herself as much as possible. As she feared she might be seen by another vessel without realizing it, from time to time she made misleading moves, such as following the lane to Panama. On 15 April, she entered the stream of the trade wind. At this time British warships were gathering in response to the German attack on Norway. In order to distract their attention southwards, the

Atlantis was ordered by the Naval High Command to take the route from Freetown to Cape Town.

While his crew were merrily celebrating the *Atlantis*'s crossing of the equator, Rogge quietly left the party and shut himself away in his cabin; there was work to be done without delay in preparation for his next task. He had to decide which merchant ship the *Atlantis* should now disguise herself as. He and Adjutant Mohr combed through all the resources they had to hand, such as the Lloyd's Register of Shipping and collections of photographs of ships from the principal seafaring nations. Out of several candidates whose shape and tonnage were similar to that of the *Atlantis*, they decided she should impersonate the Japanese ship *Kashiimaru* (8,408 tonnes).[4]

On 27 April, the *Atlantis* hove to and all her crew hurriedly undertook the alteration work of repainting and refitting the ship. The painting of the hull down by the waterline proved difficult as the paint was repeatedly washed off by the waves. Rogge went so far as to have all the load and crew moved to one side of the ship so that the waterline on the other side was raised as much as possible. Eventually, there was a vessel resembling the *Kashiimaru* where the *Kim* had been before. Just to make sure, Rogge got into a motor launch and carefully checked the results from a distance with his own eyes. The *Atlantis* posed as the *Kashiimaru* for over three weeks, until 21 May when she transformed herself into the Dutch merchant ship the *Abbekerk*.

The *Kashiimaru* belonged to the Kokusai Kisen Kaisha, but she had been chartered by the Nippon Yūsen Kaisha (NYK) when the latter had opened a regular cargo service between Yokohama and Liverpool in May 1936. On 3 May that year she had become the first ship to leave Yokohama on this route. During the Pacific War, she was enlisted as a transport vessel for the fourth Special Attack Expedition to Leyte in the Philippines. She met her end on 10 November 1944 in Ormoc Bay on the west coast of Leyte Island, when she was attacked by American aircraft.

The Atlantis's *First Victim, the* Scientist

On 3 May, the *Atlantis* (disguised as the *Kashiimaru*) sank her first victim far off the coast of Namibia at latitude 19.53 degrees south, longitude 3.46 degrees east. It was the British freighter the *Scientist* (6,200 tonnes) belonging to the Harrison Steamship Company.

Rogge brought her crew aboard the *Atlantis* and segregated their living quarters between whites and non-whites. The accommodation for the whites was more cramped, but they were required to tolerate this until more space was created by the discharge of the mines. There was an Indian cook among the captives, and his extremely delicious curry was enjoyed by all. Once the *Atlantis*'s cooks were taught the recipe the dish became an enduringly popular item on the menu among the crew.

Following her encounter with the *Scientist*, the *Atlantis* increased her speed and continued further south. On 14 May, she laid her ninety-two mines at regular intervals in the waters from five miles to twenty-six miles off Cape Agulhas, the southernmost tip of Africa which divided the Indian and Atlantic oceans. The operation went well. As enemy vigilance was thought to be heightened at this time, the *Atlantis* first steamed a considerable distance into the Indian Ocean to appear as if she was heading for Australia, and then suddenly turned around and approached Cape Agulhas in the dark. It was a diversionary tactic with which they hoped to mislead the Allied surveillance, if only by a little. The *Scientist*'s Captain and officers were completely deceived by this. They were convinced that, from their experience and knowledge, they had calculated the *Atlantis*'s path, and that the mines were laid off the shore of Durban. Later, Rogge invited them to his cabin for drinks and subtly probed them as they drank whisky and joked together to discover that this was what they believed.

As the mining operation was carried out close to the coast, now and again the beam of a lighthouse swept over the *Atlantis*. Her crew could even clearly see many cars with their bright headlights coming and going along the coastal road. In order to conceal the fact that the mines were laid by a raider, the crew even soiled and marked a lifejacket, so that it resembled one belonging to U-boat 37, and threw it into the sea at a spot where, with the movement of the currents, it was likely to be picked up.

Having assumed the appearance of the *Abbekerk* on 21 May, the *Atlantis* entered the Indian Ocean at the start of June. Between then and the end of September she either captured or sank eight commercial vessels including: the *Tirranna* (7,230 tonnes) on 10 June, the *City of Baghdad* (7,506 tonnes) on 11 July, the *Kemmendine* (7,769 tonnes) on 13 July, the *Talleyrand* (6,731 tonnes) on 2 August, the *King City* (4,744 tonnes) on 24 August, the *Athelking* (9,557 tonnes) on 9 September, the *Benarty* (5,800 tonnes) on

10 September, and the *Commissaire Ramel* (10,061 tonnes) on 20 September.

Among these, the *Kemmendine* had a large passenger capacity, so Rogge wanted to acquire it undamaged, use it to detain the crew from the other ships and send it back to Germany. After the *Kemmendine* surrendered she launched a small boat. While it was approaching the *Atlantis* to obtain help for the injured, a tall gunner aboard the *Kemmendine*, for reasons unknown, ignored the Captain's orders, ran to the cannon on the stern, and fired a shot over the bridge of the *Atlantis*. The *Atlantis* replied ferociously and the *Kemmendine*'s stern was engulfed in flames, but the gunner fled the spot immediately and was unharmed. The fire soon spread as far as the bridge, and Rogge was forced to sink the ship after all. For a time he was furious with the reckless gunner. However, when he was told that the man had been a window cleaner in London until he had joined the *Kemmendine*, he decided against punishing him.

By then, the *Atlantis* had travelled the equivalent of once around the world and 10,000 kilometres more. Her victims totalled nine ships including the *Scientist*, with a combined tonnage of approximately 66,000. The *Atlantis* now lay low for a while in the waters west of Australia, at around latitude 22 degrees south, longitude 84 degrees east. There she replenished food stocks, water and fuel from a supply ship, and her crew rested. Then, in October, she set off again for her hunting grounds of enemy ships, which were gathering to pass through the Strait of Malacca and the Sunda Strait. On the 22nd, she took the Yugoslav freighter the *Durmitor* (5,623 tonnes) to the west of Java. This ship was loaded with 8,200 tonnes of salt from Spain, procured by the Japanese trading company Mitsui Bussan Kaisha, and was *en route* from Lourenço Marques to Hiroshima and Miike via Batavia. Rogge decided to seize the *Durmitor* partly because she gave him the excuse by ignoring his order and using her radio, and partly because she had previously transported coal from Cardiff to Oran in Algeria. He decided to transfer the prisoners aboard the *Atlantis* – who already numbered 260 – to the *Durmitor* and to send her to Somaliland under the guard of a prize crew of twelve, commanded by Sub Lieutenant Dehnel.

However, the *Durmitor* turned out to be very poorly maintained. One of the boilers leaked and was unusable and there were numerous other faults. She could only proceed at seven knots and she was overrun with cockroaches and mice. Furthermore, there was insufficient coal and drinking water, let alone any water for washing, for the journey to Somaliland. There was no berthing area for the prisoners, and apart from those over fifty years old who were issued with mattresses, there was no alternative to their sleeping directly on top of the salt in the holds. Rogge allocated them as much food, water and other essentials from the *Atlantis* as possible, but they fell far short of requirements. He explained the situation to the prisoners in advance, and while asking for their cooperation, he also made it clear that if there was any kind of revolt it would be suppressed without mercy. He addressed the Captain and the officers separately and obtained their promise to collaborate.

Unfortunately, it became apparent during the voyage that the *Durmitor* was even shorter of fuel than was initially thought. Fixtures, furniture and anything else that would burn were fed into the boiler. The crew even improvised a sail to compensate for the lack of speed. There was some unrest among the captives but with the help of the *Durmitor*'s Captain and officers a full-scale mutiny was averted. When the *Durmitor* arrived in Somaliland after almost a month, all aboard were dehydrated and thoroughly 'salted' from their sleeping arrangements. The prisoners' stories of their miserable journey were recounted time and again at the POW camp in Germany.

In November, the *Atlantis* switched her hunting grounds to the waters east of Ceylon instead of targeting ships in the Sunda Strait. She captured the *Teddy* on the 9th, followed by the *Ole Jacob* on the 10th. It was almost the 11th, the day when the *Automedon* met her end, just before her scheduled arrival into Penang. Whenever the *Atlantis* overpowered a vessel, a boarding party carried out a thorough search and confiscated important material such as Merchant Navy codes or Admiralty orders. The *Atlantis* had obtained particularly valuable secret information from the British freighter the *Benarty* which she had taken on 10 September. She effectively utilized the enemy data she acquired in this way when planning her strategies, and continued to be very successful in her operations. She terrorized the British merchant fleet while exasperating the Royal Navy.

5

The Trunks and the Cabinet Papers

The Sea of Tragedy

WE MUST NOW return to the story of the *Automedon*. When she was attacked by the *Atlantis* on the morning of 11 November 1940, 250 miles southwest of Achin Head, her Wireless Operator had desperately transmitted the emergency signal: 'RRR *Automedon*, latitude 4.18 degrees north. . .' This had been picked up by the *Macoma* (8,000 tonnes), a Dutch tanker of the Crown Petroleum Company, as well as the *Helenus* (7,366 tonnes) of the Blue Funnel Line, which was travelling with a general cargo from Penang to Durban.

Just after 8.20, the Captain of the *Helenus*, P.W. Savery, was told by his Wireless Operator that the *Automedon* had sent a distress call to the effect that she was being attacked by a raider. The Wireless Operator reported that the transmission had communicated the latitude of the *Automedon*'s position, but had been cut off before giving the longitude. This was indeed the case, as the *Automedon*'s radio mast had been severed and her emergency dynamo house destroyed by the first salvo fired by the *Atlantis*. According to the Wireless Operator, the *Automedon* was possibly within sight as her signal had been extremely strong. However, no matter how hard

Savery searched through his binoculars, the *Automedon* was nowhere to be seen.

Nevertheless, one thing was certain, that the site of the attack was very close. Captain Savery thought it would endanger his own ship to use the radio straight away. He instructed the Wireless Operator to listen out for a shore station retransmitting the *Automedon*'s distress call, and to report any new developments immediately. In this type of situation, the safest way to disseminate a warning to Allied ships in the region was to have a shore station, which would have picked up the original signal, retransmit the alert, and this was indeed the usual practice.

Savery waited until almost 9.00 but there was no repetition of the *Automedon*'s signal from anywhere, so he had to order his Wireless Operator to relay the alert to the Commander-in-Chief at Colombo. He had calculated the longitude of the *Automedon*'s position on the assumption that she had been following a particular course, and this, too, was conveyed to Colombo. The message was in code and it gave the *Helenus*'s secret call sign. However, this call sign had been allocated to the *Helenus* by the maritime authorities some time ago, and although the Commander-in-Chief should still have known it, he could not understand it and so required the *Helenus* to repeat the message twice. Captain Savery became increasingly worried that, with the *Helenus* communicating so frequently, her signals might be picked up by the raider and she too might invite disaster. For the sake of her own safety, that night just after 21.00 the *Helenus* changed her course from west-south-west to due south and fled at full speed. It was only after some time had passed that she returned to her original course.[1] In the wartime seas infested with enemy raiders, even if a merchant ship was armed to some extent, it was out of the question for her to rescue another ship. All she could do was to abandon the ship that had been caught and escape being attacked herself.

The concerns of Captain Savery, who played safe by taking evasive action that night, were certainly not groundless and his judgement was sound. Sure enough, the *Atlantis* had picked up the communication between the *Helenus* and Colombo. She had taken a bearing on the signals and ascertained that the *Helenus* was close and more or less parallel to the *Atlantis*, and that it was possible to launch an attack.[2] However, Mohr had not knocked on Rogge's door to inform him of this for a number of reasons. He had not wished to wake the Captain who was fast asleep after a hard day's work; sailors quickly gained the ability to sleep whenever they could. In addition, the *Atlantis* was now attempting to reach the meeting points where the *Ole Jacob* and the *Teddy* were still waiting as quickly as possible. Moreover, she had an important task to carry out, of despatching to Berlin via Tokyo without delay the top-secret documents recovered from the *Automedon*, which Rogge and Mohr had read earlier in the day and whose contents had astonished them. They were to be put aboard the *Ole Jacob*, which was to be sent to Japan under the command of a prize crew, along with her Norwegian crew currently held on the *Atlantis*. The next morning, when Rogge was told about the *Helenus*, she was already too far away to pursue but he did not upbraid anyone for this. The *Helenus* was lucky enough to survive this time, but she would be sunk off the coast of western Africa by U-boat 68 less than eighteen months later.

In the seas of war, there was no guarantee of survival for any ship regardless of which side she belonged to. During the Second World War the Allies and neutral countries together lost approximately 4,800 merchant vessels (twenty-one million tonnes). Thirty-two thousand crewmen lost their lives at sea and 5,000 went missing. The total number of merchant seamen was reduced by approximately 25%, which was a far greater rate of loss than that of the British Army, Navy or Royal Air Force. The Japanese statistics are even more gruesome. 2,500 merchant ships totalling eight million tonnes and 30,000 men were lost. The death rate was 43%, extraordinarily high compared to that of the Allies' merchant fleets. These figures, as might be expected, far surpassed the death rates within the Japanese Army (20%) and Navy (16%).[3] The tragic statistics clearly reveal how inadequate Japan's provision of escorted convoys was.

During the First World War, the Second Special Task Force of the Japanese Navy, under the banner of the Anglo-Japanese Alliance, had hoisted the Japanese Naval ensign and made significant contributions to the defence of Allied shipping in the Mediterranean. Its young officers and sailors had suffered extreme fatigue through the cold, hunger, rough seas and the sheer terror of death. They had learnt a valuable lesson on the importance of escorting civilian shipping, even while risking their lives. The fact that this was not upheld during the Second World War brought about such catastrophic results. Another lesson was related to the formidable military and industrial power of the United States.

When Admiral Chūichi Nagumo was an instructor at the Japanese naval academy he studied the military capabilities of the United States displayed during the First World War and lectured on the redoubtable might of the Americans. Yet he himself was killed in action in Saipan having experienced at first hand the overwhelming power of the US forces. If we do not learn correctly from history we bring fatal consequences upon ourselves. Japan is a very good example of this.[4]

The Boarding Party

The *Automedon* had been bombarded because she had sent a distress signal despite the *Atlantis*'s warning, and she was now a floating wreck. On her bridge, Second Officer Stewart gradually regained consciousness. He lifted his head, still feeling dazed, and looked around to see Captain Ewan lying to one side of him and the Third Officer, P.L. Whitaker, to the other. They were both dead. The Captain had always been strict where work and manners were concerned, but he had been a fine man of exceptional calibre. Stewart had always respected him and felt privileged to serve under his command. Miraculously, he had survived with only minor injuries, but he had no time to abandon himself to sentiment and grief over the Captain's death.

Stewart hoped that his colleagues, the extra Second Officer Wilson or the First Officer Evans, had long since thrown overboard the contents of the safe. 'Quick – the key,' he muttered to himself as he got up to go below deck. He ached all over and his legs felt weak. Just before the *Automedon* had come under intense fire, Evans, who had initially rushed to the bridge with Stewart, had gone to get the safe key kept in the Captain's cabin and to destroy the safe's contents. However Stewart found Evans lying across the threshold of what remained of the Captain's cabin, seriously injured and unconscious. As for Wilson, whom Stewart had woken when the attack had first started, it appeared he had been killed before he could leave his cabin. Although he had jumped out of bed immediately, he had lost two or three crucial minutes in getting dressed. Not even a body was found.

The *Automedon*'s bridge, the chart room and the Captain's and officers' quarters below them were decimated and did not bear looking at. If Stewart and Evans had been just a little slower to leave their cabins they would have met the same fate as Wilson.

Luckily, Stewart had run out of his cabin and up to the bridge without getting dressed, and so had survived by the skin of his teeth. He was doubly fortunate not to have then been killed on the bridge.

The Captain and five officers, including Wilson who had been in charge of the mailbags, had lost their lives in an instant, and twelve others were injured. One of the Chinese sailors on board, who were being repatriated to Singapore, is also said to have died. Most of the deck officers as well as the Captain – in other words the ship's leadership excluding Stewart – had perished. This along with the fact that the nucleus of the vessel had been thoroughly destroyed and the key to the strong room was lost rendered impossible the disposal of the mailbags of official documents marked 'Safe Hand. British Master Only'. The green mailbag of confidential papers kept on the desk in the chartroom was also missing as a result of the bombardment.

Stewart saw that a motor launch carrying the boarding party had already left the *Atlantis*, which had hove to on the *Automedon*'s starboard quarter. Having seen the state of the Captain's cabin he gave up hope of finding the key to the safe containing the ship's confidential papers. He now became anxious to throw the two mailbags of official documents into the sea. These were kept with all the other mailbags in the strong room below the forecastle. He was not particularly conscious of the presence in the same strong room of the passengers' luggage unwanted on voyage including that belonging to Mrs Violet Ferguson. Furthermore he was at this juncture ironically unaware that all his efforts to confuse the Germans would come to grief later by a whim of fate involving Mrs Ferguson's belongings. The key to the strong room was kept in Evans's cabin, but that had been obliterated without trace. Before Stewart had a chance to think about what he should do, the boarding party led by Mohr came aboard from the starboard side of the forward well deck. Walker too witnessed their arrival; astonished to see the German marines holding revolvers and with grenades crossed on their belts, for a while he just stared at them.

After the War, Mohr wrote in his memoirs that he was shocked by the extent of the devastation aboard the *Automedon*. The deck was scattered with clumps of severed hawsers and ropes and sharp pieces of steel which rolled with the ship. The sound of steam escaping from broken pipes broke the otherwise eerie silence. There were holes in the funnel and it was on the verge of collapse.

The stanchion posts were covered in scars made by shell splinters. The wireless room had caved in and was smouldering.[5] What he saw was manifestly the result of a series of direct hits. Walker remembers that the boarding party was dumbstruck by the aftermath of the attack, and that, far from treating it as a success, they looked around with sombre expressions. Mohr's first action was to have the twelve injured men transferred to the *Atlantis*.

In the *Automedon*'s engine room, the twenty-four-years-old Fourth Engineer, Samuel Harper, had done his utmost to deal with the crisis. This was his first voyage aboard the *Automedon*. Historically, many British seamen came from Scotland and northern England, and almost twenty per cent were from Liverpool, forming the largest portion alongside Londoners. Harper, too, was from Liverpool. His family had worked in marine engineering for generations, so it was no coincidence that both he and his brother Frank, who was two years younger than him, worked aboard ships as engineers.

Harper had been standing by the telegraph, feeling hungry and hoping that his relief would be early. Later, he recalled that as the clock had struck 8.20, he had been startled by a tremendous bang coming from the deck above. He had known something terrible was happening: steam and water had quickly started leaking from the pipes here and there in the engine room. Soon, the alarmed Chinese firemen had all come stampeding up the ladder. It has been claimed that they had descended into a state of panic, but Harper flatly denied this and suggested that anyone would have wished to escape in such a situation where 'pandemonium broke loose'.[6]

With one eye on these events, Harper had applied himself to carrying out the orders which had rung from the telegraph: 'Stand by' followed by 'Stop' two minutes later. Just as he had managed to stop the engines the Fifth Engineer, William Coventry, had come down, so Harper had him help change over the exhaust and fetch the life-jackets, while he had fed a little more fuel into the boiler. The Chief Engineer, James McNicol, had then arrived, his head streaming with blood. McNicol had asked Harper if he was hurt, and Harper had replied that he was fine. McNicol had then held his head as if in great pain and seemed unable to focus his eyes. He had doubled up into a stoop and remained so for a little while, before forcing himself to stand up straight and trudge up the ramp to see what was happening above deck. By 8.23 the bombardment had ceased. James Hendry, the Fourth Engineer, was lying on deck with his right leg severely damaged below the knee.

A little later, some of the boarding party came storming into the engine room. They ordered all the engineers apart from Harper to go on deck. They swiftly went about attaching time bombs to the ship's side valves. It seems that Rogge had originally intended to take the *Automedon* undamaged and use her as a supply ship: he would have studied his reference material for the details of her capabilities after receiving the tip-off, allegedly from the Italian intelligence service, and known that she was a relatively fast vessel, though she was old. However, Mohr had reported that the central section of the ship and her steering gear were damaged beyond repair, leaving Rogge with no choice but to sink her.

When Harper went on deck he was astonished to see the extent of the destruction caused by the attack. He saw how a large hole had been blown in the funnel and how the bridge and the officers' accommodation were in ruins; he also saw that all the lifeboats had been destroyed. He went to his own cabin to find that a shell had passed straight through it and exploded in the mess room opposite. Elsewhere, bulkheads had been demolished and small fires started. He found that Coventry had already thought to collect what remained of his belongings, his uniform and one shirt. This was indicative of how composed Coventry remained even in chaotic situations. Back on deck, Stewart, whose face was hurt, was deputizing for Evans, whose legs had been injured, and was supervising the transfer of the wounded to the *Atlantis*. According to Harper, Stewart was a quiet and fair man, who never uttered a bad word about anyone. He always dealt very effectively with difficult situations, such as dividing a small amount of food among the crew when there were shortages.[7]

Mohr did not have time to waste. He spotted Stewart and addressed him in English. His English was extremely fluent, enabling him to participate impromptu in the sketches staged by the captive English sailors, and single-handedly to deal with their various grievances. 'Who are you?' Mohr asked. 'Donald Stewart, the Second Officer,' Stewart replied. 'Where's the Captain?' Mohr asked. 'He's dead,' Stewart told him. Mohr replied: 'That is too bad. In that case I will ask you to accompany me around the ship.'

With these words, Mohr started walking towards the forecastle head. Stewart's heart sank as this was the worst possible place to start: the location of the strong room. He followed Mohr praying that it would not be discovered. Mohr pointed to the first steel door he came to and asked what was behind it. Stewart told him it was the windlass motor room and paint store. Mohr then asked what was behind the next door. This was the moment Stewart had been dreading. However, when he replied that it was the Bosun's store, Mohr seemed satisfied by this; he said nothing more and proceeded along the portside of the foredeck. Stewart breathed a deep sigh of relief. They continued as far as the stern and then returned to the No. 3 hatch located forward of the centrecastle.

While Mohr was being guided around the ship by Stewart, one of the other boarding officers discovered the green mailbag buried among the rubble that was the chart room. He also blew open the safe. He was searching, of course, for codes and other sensitive information, but all he found was a box containing a few shillings. Stewart started to feel confident that he would succeed in preventing the discovery of the strong room, but fortune would have it that it, too, was eventually found and opened.

Meanwhile, the *Automedon*'s other crew members were made to help with the trans-shipment of some of her cargo including frozen meat, whisky and cigarettes. They complained little, as they had been placated by being permitted to retain as many of their own belongings as they could carry. Rather, they voluntarily led the boarding party to the stores of whisky and cigarettes, since the alternative was that they would be sunk with the ship. The trans-shipment of cargo completed, all transferred to the *Atlantis*, carrying as many of their possessions as they could under their arms. They joined the forty-four prisoners from the *Teddy* and the *Ole Jacob*, and their lives as captives began.

Rogge's generosity regarding the prisoners' personal effects was not simply due to his kindness. It also reflected the German military command's view that it was preferable to facilitate the self-sufficiency of prisoners by allowing them to bring aboard as many of their belongings as circumstances permitted, since it was expected that under war conditions Germany would experience shortages of clothing and other essentials. The *Automedon*'s crew underwent medical examinations and their possessions were inspected. Their cigarettes and money were confiscated, in exchange for a receipt in the latter case.

Apart from top-secret information, acquisitions sought by German raiders included petroleum, rubber, tungsten, manganese, tin, biotite, opium and glycerol. Meanwhile, the appropriation of other materials and goods, such as crude oil, food, alcohol and cigarettes, was indispensable for German warships and civilian shipping alike to continue their operations while relying as little as possible on supplies from Germany. Thus considerable quantities of frozen meat, whisky and cigarettes were taken from the *Automedon*. As she had been outward bound to Asia, she was loaded with munitions and industrial products, but had she been on the return leg, the Germans could have hoped to seize much-needed raw materials such as rubber and tin.

The German diplomat and writer Erwin Wickert, who held a Secretary's post at the German embassy in Tokyo during the Second World War and spent eight years in Japan before returning to Germany after the defeat, wrote a book entitled *Tales of Courage and Daring from My Life*. According to this, not only the embassy staff but all German expatriates received a generous share of the spoils of the piracy conducted under the extraordinary circumstances of war. Examples of such booty included boxes of tinned sardines, tuna and sausages and barrels of lard, seized from an Australian cargo ship. After the war, when German nationals were detained in Japan and suffered an extreme shortage of food, they continued to be helped considerably by such looted goods.

The senior members of the Japanese Naval Staff and Navy Ministry would have gratefully received leftover whisky or cigarettes from the raiders' booty as gifts from the German embassy at Christmas and other special occasions. The year after the Pacific War broke out, the Japanese people were rationed to an extremely small quantity of sugar brought from the occupied South East Asia, but this was the first and last time. For the masses of Japanese people, who spent day after day hungry eating bitter pumpkins, tasteless potatoes and watery broth as defeat became increasingly probable, tinned meat and fish were luxuries they could only dream of.

The Search for the Trunks

Curiously, there are conflicting accounts as to how many passengers were aboard the *Automedon* and their true number cannot be definitively established. In the 11 November entry of the *Atlantis's* war diary it is recorded that the captives from the *Automedon* totalled thiry-seven British crewmen, fifty-six crewmen of other nationalities and three passengers, of which one was female. This is the most reliable official record but according to some, there were also a third man, a female nurse and an American woman, bringing the total of passengers to six. According to A. Parsons, the *Automedon*'s Assistant Steward, on the other hand, there were four passengers, Mr and Mrs Ferguson and Mr and Mrs McBride. These claims cannot be verified as the Department of Trade's passenger lists for ships which departed from Liverpool in September 1940, held at the British National Archives, do not include a list for the *Automedon*.

When interviewed, Harper did not recall the American woman or the third male passenger but he remembered the nurse, who he said was about twenty-years old and pretty. Some time after Harper's return to England on 26 June 1941, one of the Chinese firemen, who had escaped from a German POW camp, came to visit him in Liverpool and told him that the nurse had died from dysentery while interned in Germany.[8] Walker's version is that there were three passengers, Mr and Mrs Ferguson and Mr McBride. Apart from the puzzle of the number of passengers, there are a few other mysteries surrounding the *Automedon*, such as whether the Cabinet papers were put aboard as part of a secret plan hatched by the British secret services, and whether the *Automedon* was tracked by an Italian submarine. Today, sixty-five years later, these *Automedon* mysteries are even more shrouded in the veil of history.

Passenger Alan Ferguson was a Chief Engineer for the Straits Steamship Company, a subsidiary of the Blue Funnel Line based in Singapore which operated services all over South East Asia. He was born in Londonderry in Northern Ireland in 1906. He had two elder sisters and his father, John, worked for a seed and feed distributor. As he had loved the sea and boats since he was a child, Ferguson became a marine engineering apprentice at Brown's Foundry in Londonderry instead of going to a grammar school as his father wished. He became a junior marine engineer at twenty-one and began by working aboard ships on trans-Atlantic routes. Subsequently, he was recruited by the Straits Steamship Company as a senior engineer and moved to Singapore. In 1936, he married Violet Tyson, whom he had met while on holiday in the Isle of Man during his first leave from the Straits Steamship Company. The following January, he returned to Singapore with her. He and Violet were a well-matched couple, just one year apart in age. As a boy, Ferguson had played in the local rugby team and liked fishing. As an adult, he was very sociable. After the war, when the couple visited Britain on holiday, they always rented a house for a few months in a place where he could enjoy fishing and golf. He was a kind uncle to his sisters' children: when they came to stay at his holiday home, he would teach them fly-fishing and card games and enthral them with his stories.

Violet Ferguson was born in 1907 in St Albans to the north of London. She had two brothers and three sisters. Being the eldest daughter, she often took care of her siblings. She was a sweet-natured yet strong and self-assured girl. Her father, John, was a tailor and her mother, Rose, a dressmaker. Her parents had originally worked for the Nicholson clothes manufacturer in Cumbria in northwest England, and had moved to St Albans when the firm had relocated to this town. After leaving school Violet helped her family's finances by working in a local perfumery. She was a good correspondent and an accomplished seamstress, and her skills were to prove very useful when she came to be detained in Germany. Her younger sister, Madge Christmas, describes Violet as medium-height with black hair, and, as a young woman, a slender beauty who turned heads.

In May 1940, the Fergusons had been *en route* from Singapore to England for their first holiday together, when Violet had developed appendicitis and they had been forced to disembark at Marseilles. Violet had been pregnant and suffered a miscarriage while receiving treatment there. That month, Germany's invasion of France and Belgium had turned the two countries into battlefields and on the 27th, British and French troops had begun their evacuation from Dunkirk. Amidst the confusion, Ferguson had taken his convalescing wife to Bordeaux where the couple had been fortunate enough to catch the last ferry to England, and eventually reach their destination. When the couple left Liverpool aboard the *Automedon* at the end of their holiday, they could not have envisaged that they would end up returning to Bordeaux as prisoners in less than a year.[9] Though she had not forgotten the dangers that shadowed a wartime voyage, Violet had enjoyed those days travelling with her husband.

On the morning of 11 November, this very pleasant voyage came to an abrupt and violent end. The *Automedon*'s passengers were accommodated at the aft end of the upper deck, below the boat deck and the centrecastle where the damage was concentrated. They had, therefore, been safe from the bombardment and fortunately none of them had been injured. Before being rushed aboard the *Atlantis* ahead of the crew, the passengers had been told that they would be taken to cold regions and should bring suitable clothing. Violet had hurriedly grabbed those of her belongings which were in the immediate vicinity. Once aboard the *Atlantis*, what distressed Violet above all was the fact that she had to leave her two trunks and some packages behind on the *Automedon* as the so-called 'luggage unwanted on voyage'. These were packed with crockery, clothing and other items she had bought on holiday, as well as many objects of sentimental value such as photographs taken with her family and friends. However, there had been no possibility of asking anyone to bring her luggage from storage amidst the sudden chaos: Captain Ewan and the other officers were dead, and Stewart had been fully occupied as Mohr's unwilling guide. Even if she had asked Stewart, he never would have agreed to fetch her luggage from the very place he was desperately attempting to conceal from the boarding party.

Her panic grew when she heard that the *Automedon* would probably be sunk. Finally, she went to Captain Rogge and, without the slightest idea that this action would end up greatly helping the enemy, asked him to permit someone to look for her luggage which was in a storeroom somewhere. Though he was anxious to leave the site of the attack as soon as possible, Rogge agreed to get them for her. Rogge was compassionate by nature. He did not hide the fact that he felt an affinity for the English, perhaps because he had visited England on official duty and some of his close friends were English. He treated the prisoners fairly and his approach was to allow them as much freedom as possible: he even provided them with a small allowance and relaxed the regulations on the ship's shop, enabling them to buy daily sundries. Perhaps Rogge was chivalrous and willing to risk danger in a battlefield for the sake of a lady's request; or perhaps he was suddenly reminded of his wife who had died immediately prior to his departure on this dangerous mission of hunting Allied shipping.

Just as Mohr, increasingly conscious of the time, was thinking that he would soon bring the search to an end, he received Rogge's order: 'One of the passengers, Mrs Ferguson, is anxious to retrieve her luggage, which is in a storeroom somewhere. Will you have a look, but quickly, as we are running out of time.' He resumed the search immediately. Stewart was startled by this sudden and unexpected development because he knew, of course, that the luggage 'unwanted on voyage' was kept in the strong room with the mailbags. He also knew that among these were the official mailbags containing sensitive documents entrusted by the government and the military and a vast quantity of brand new Straits dollar notes. Mohr ordered Stewart to lead him to the room where the luggage was stored. Though he was at his wits' end, Stewart made his last attempt to obstruct Mohr's search, lining up one excuse after another as they occurred to him. In front of the door at the top of the stairs that led to the strong room he told Mohr: 'As I said before, this is just the Bosun's store so you'll be wasting your time.' Eventually, he began to stumble over his words and caused Mohr's suspicion to grow. Mohr lost his patience and dismissed Stewart, and shouted the order for the strong room to be inspected. As he saw the door being blown open Stewart suddenly felt the strength drain from his legs.

Mohr rushed down the ladder and entered the strong room. He gasped involuntarily on seeing the enormous number of mailbags tightly packed into several shelves all around the room. There were 125 in all. Every piece of Violet Ferguson's luggage was transferred onto the Atlantis immediately. National secrets were to fall into the hands of the enemy all because of a passenger's trunks which were supposed to be released to the owner only at destination, Singapore in this case. As he rocked on the motor launch fully loaded with a mountain of mailbags – including the classified consignments – and the trunks and packages so longed for by Violet Ferguson, Stewart could not stifle the sadness that swelled inside him.

6

A Gift from Hitler

A Thrilling Discovery

THE ELEGANT FORM of the *Automedon*, which had enchanted those who saw her in days gone by, had been thoroughly transformed by the *Atlantis's* merciless and accurate bombardment. The mangled *Automedon* was sunk by the explosives attached by the boarding party and a death-dealing torpedo at 15.07 on 11 November, about six hours after the attack. She slowly sank by the stern to the sea floor 325 metres (10,660 feet) below. According to the *Atlantis's* war diary the exact spot was latitude 4.19 degrees north, longitude 89.24 degrees east. The name 'Automedon' was revived seven years later, when it was given to a Malayan Airways passenger plane.[1]

In Walker's recollection the time of sinking was 15.15, which roughly coincides with the *Atlantis*'s record, 15.07. According to one account the *Automedon* was sunk before noon, but Walker is certain that she was sunk after lunch. He even recalls that this lunch consisted of some delicious bean soup and that it was served at around 13.00. The *Automedon*'s crew was invited to watch her final moments from the wing of the bridge but all the officers and engineers – including Harper – refused. Being just sixteen years old, Walker was rather indifferent to such principles and was curious to see anything out of the ordinary. With some crewmates, he watched the submergence of the ship that he had been aboard only that morning. As he witnessed her slow disappearance from beginning to end he felt an indescribable mixture of emotions.

The *Atlantis* then steamed at high speed to the meeting points where the *Teddy* and the *Ole Jacob* were waiting. Rogge and Mohr shut themselves away in the Captain's lounge and began examining the contents of the official mailbags and the classified mailbag, literally a treasure that had been dug out of the debris of the *Automedon*'s chart room. The din of the *Atlantis*'s engine, which was powering the ship at her maximum speed of seventeen knots, barely reached the lounge. The room was steeped in the calm that comes in the wake of engagement. The rays of the southern sun streamed through the gap in the chintz curtains onto the highly polished surface of the table and the cut crystal which sparkled in the cabinets.

At first Rogge and Mohr were incredulous as one secret document after another emerged from the mailbags. There were Merchant Navy codes and sailing orders which were familiar to them as similar documents had been confiscated in previous raids. There was also much material of kinds they had not seen before: directives, letters, administrative communications, sensitive information, reports and data sent from the British War Cabinet, military and secret services to their outposts in Singapore, Hong Kong, Shanghai and Tokyo. The jackpot, which delighted the two men above all, was contained in the long and narrow green mailbag marked: 'Classified: Destroy in an Emergency'. This, of course, was the confidential consignment for the Commander-in-Chief of the Far East. Rogge opened it straight away and read the papers without concealing his great excitement.

The document was the British Joint Chiefs of Staff Committee's Far East situation report dated 31 July that had been submitted to the War Cabinet on 8 August. It contained extremely detailed information on the Royal Navy's and the RAF's armaments and positions, the defence of Singapore and possible response measures to Japanese aggression, as well as an analysis of the roles of Australia and New Zealand. Rogge's reaction was hardly surprising. The two men agreed that the Japanese military was bound to show an interest in these papers and that they should be used to elicit a much greater degree of cooperation from Japan. Germany was frustrated by her Far-Eastern ally around this time, as she was behaving indecisively and insisting on upholding her neutrality.[2] Generally, the *Atlantis* restricted her communication for security reasons but on this occasion Rogge did not hesitate to send a telegram to Berlin, to inform the authorities that he would be sending without delay some seized documents of the highest importance.

On 13 November the *Atlantis* rejoined the *Teddy*. Captain Lütken was permitted to return to the *Teddy* to collect his belongings, and also to instruct his crew who still remained on board to gather their and their colleagues' possessions and to transfer to the *Atlantis*. At 13.00 on the 15th the *Teddy* was sunk by explosives and gunfire, but not before the *Atlantis* had transferred all of the *Teddy*'s oil into her tanks.

On the same day, the *Atlantis* rendezvoused with the *Ole Jacob*. The following day the sixty-one Norwegian and Swedish crew of the *Teddy* (twenty-eight) and the *Ole Jacob* (thirty-three) were ordered aboard the *Ole Jacob*. Under a prize crew of seven commanded by Lieutenant Kamenz she set off for Japan. She avoided the Strait of Malacca and instead took a longer route south of Sumatra. Rogge had decided that if the *Ole Jacob* sailed directly to Germany by the Cape of Good Hope she risked being caught by a British warship, and that the best way to send the precious top-secret documents safely to Germany was via Japan, where a favourable reception could be expected.

In order to prevent any disobedience or rebellion *en route* to Japan, Rogge took a signed pledge to follow Kamenz' orders from each of the Scandinavian crewmen, in exchange for an assurance that they would be released once they reached their destination. He told them that if they refused to pledge their obedience, all but the engine room crew would be kept behind on the *Atlantis*. Rogge always took this kind of measure in order to avert a revolt or sabotage when sending a prize ship to Germany or to a neutral territory.

Stewart was just as canny as Rogge. He thought the *Ole Jacob* would almost certainly head for a neutral port like Yokohama or Kōbe and attempted to use that opportunity to communicate the fate of the *Automedon* back to Britain. From among the Norwegian sailors whom he had met aboard the *Atlantis*, he picked out a man who was pro-British and appeared reliable, and discreetly asked him to report the sinking of the *Automedon* to the British consul at the first neutral port he arrived at. McNicol asked the same favour of a different Norwegian crewman, though it is not clear whether Stewart and McNicol had colluded. McNicol also gave the Norwegian a letter addressed to the Registry of Shipping and Seamen in Cardiff.

However, the British Admiralty's intelligence bureau had already received a telegram from the Chief of Intelligence Staff based in Singapore, sent at 17.26 on 14 November. The telegram read: 'Raider attacked Norwegian tanker *Ole Jacob* and British *Automedon* between Colombo and Achin Head. Subsequent search so far unsuccessful.'[3]

In addition, the Chief of Staff of Naval Command at Singapore sent the following telegram to the Admiralty on 30 December:

> Following capture of *Automedon* 11 November some sixty packages described as small mailbags were seen by Norwegian prisoner being transferred to raider. From statements later by officer of raider that six million dollars in notes had been taken it appears possible that entire contents of strong room were transferred to raider. Local agents have not details of contents but confirm large quantity of unissued Malayan currency was amongst cargo.[4]

By early 1941, the Royal Navy had deduced that the German raider that had sunk the *Automedon* was called the *Atlantis*, and that she had also attacked the *Tirranna* and the *Benarty* and laid mines off the shore of South Africa. Rogge had been unable to keep the crew of the *Teddy* and the *Ole Jacob* in the dark entirely, while the Germans' plan to prevent them from coming into contact with the British authorities in Kōbe failed through a lack of Japanese cooperation, as we shall see.

The Collaboration between the German and Japanese Navies

As soon as war had broken out in Europe, on 1 September 1939, Admiral Erich Raeder, Commander of the German Navy, had asked Captain Hideo Kojima of the Japanese Naval General Staff, who was accompanying Admiral Mineo Ōsumi on a visit to Germany, how Japan understood her status as a neutral state. He had then requested that Japan show as much favour to Germany as possible. Commander Schulte Mentteling, an adjutant in the German Naval High Command, had spoken in much more specific terms, and told Kojima that Germany sought to receive fuel and materials from Japan and wished to know the likelihood of such an arrangement. He had then explicitly revealed to Kojima that the German Navy was intent on actively undertaking trade disruption operations and on dispatching warships to distant foreign waters for this purpose. Precisely at this time Rogge had been in Bremen, busy converting the merchant ship *Goldenfels* into the raider *Atlantis* that he had been ordered to command.

In November that year Raedar had formally made the following three requests to the Japanese Navy through Rear Admiral Kiichi Endo, Naval Attaché in Berlin:

1. That Japan turns over some of her submarines, including those under construction, to Germany.
2. That Japan makes provision for German warships operating in the Pacific to use her ports and islands in order that they can covertly receive supplies or carry out repairs.
3. That Japan supplies information on British and French naval and civilian shipping in order to aid German operations in the Pacific and Indian oceans.

Having considered these proposals, the Japanese Navy had initially replied from the standpoint of preserving Japan's neutrality and refusing to intervene in the European war, that it could not comply with 1) and 2). Regarding the third request, its response had been that, though it feared this, too, undermined Japanese neutrality, it was willing to consider it further.[5]

Originally, it had been the Japanese Army which was eager for close collaboration with Germany. The navy had considered it desirable to maintain friendly relations with Germany and to expand the exchange of information and technology between the two countries, but remained wary of committing fully to cooperation with the German Navy, as it had not wished to provoke Britain or the United States. However, as a practical response to the German requests the navy had subsequently pursued a flexible approach which contained certain implications. Regarding item 2), it had stated that it could not allow specific ports to become supply bases for German warships, but that it was willing to make provision for them to receive supplies to the extent that this did not compromise Japan's neutrality. Concerning item 3), it had offered to discuss more effective methods for the sharing of intelligence which had already been taking place. The navy had instructed its attaché in Berlin to relay these policies as he saw fit.

The Germans had had little time to spare, and in mid-December had demanded that Japan select and indicate suitable harbours for the trans-shipment of provisions and for maintenance work. Their requirements had been specific: sites that were uninhabited as far as possible, were far from any cable or wireless stations and general shipping routes, were accessible to armoured cruisers and had sheltered bays and good anchoring facilities.

The Senior Adjutant to the Japanese Navy Minister, Captain Yoshiyuki Ichimiya, and the German Naval Attaché had held private talks, without even an interpreter present, on this issue until January 1940. One of the five locations proposed to Germany during these talks had been the Lamotrek Atoll[6] in the Caroline Islands. The others had been Oroluk Lagoon (one of the Caroline Islands), Ailinglapalap Reef (one of the Marshall Islands), Atka Island (one of the Aleutian Islands), and Amchitka Island. Lamotrek Atoll, which came to be referred to as 'Sheltering Place Y',[7] is situated approximately midway between the islands of Palau and Truk.

According to the Japanese Navy Ministry, anchorage was possible anywhere within the Lamotrek Atoll and there was almost no maritime traffic in its vicinity. However, in reality Lamotrek Atoll was located close to the shipping lane from Hawaii to the Philippines, and it was unlikely to remain a clandestine sheltering place for long. Soon after it had begun using this site, the German Navy had become concerned that its vessels were being spotted by civilian shipping and had attempted to find an alternative base.

Japan and Germany's relationship had grown stronger since their signing of the Anti-Comintern Pact on 25 November 1936. After Italy had joined the Pact a year later, it had increasingly taken on the aspect of an anti-British military alliance: Hitler had turned against Britain when the overtures he had made through Joachim von Ribbentrop, his Ambassador in London, to obtain Britain's approval for his acquisition of *Lebensraum* had been rejected. He sought to appropriate territories to the east, Poland, the Ukraine, Belarus and the Danzig Corridor, but, of course, there was no possibility that Britain would agree to such expansionism.

With the signing of the tripartite alliance between Japan, Germany and Italy in September 1940, military collaboration between the three countries had been stepped up. Though hesitantly, the Japanese Navy began catering to German warships operating in Asian waters by harbouring them and facilitating their repairs and their taking on of supplies on the nominal condition that this did not undermine Japan's neutral status. The ports of Yokohama and Kōbe as well as the Marshall and Caroline islands, which Japan ruled at that time under a mandate from the League of Nations, came to be utilized for this purpose. Shipyards and factories in the Osaka and Kōbe regions undertook the repair and maintenance of German supply ships and the procurement of equipment, materials and parts for German raiders. German supply ships, such as the tanker *Winnetou*, the freighter the *Regensburg*, the *Elsa Essberger* and the *Annelise Essberger*, used Yokohama and Kōbe as bases and made deliveries of food, equipment, materials and fuel to the raiders the *Orion*, the *Thor* and the *Komet* anchored at the Marshall and Caroline islands.

As the southern islands formed part of Japan's territory, her making them available to the German military contravened international regulations and her mandate agreement with the League of Nations. In particular, such collaboration with Germany was a serious breach of the neutrality demanded of Japan by international law, and it enraged the British. Unsurprisingly, the British Naval Attaché and secret services doggedly strove to catch Japan and Germany red-handed. Britain could not tolerate German raiders posing an even greater threat to her and her allies' shipping as a result of Japanese assistance. During the First World War there was amity between Britain and Japan in the form of the Anglo-Japanese Alliance, and Britain had supported Japan's occupation of the Marshall and Caroline islands, both prior to and during the drawing up of the Treaty of Versailles. It was bitterly ironic that twenty years later Britain was beleaguered by German warships using secret bases in those islands.

In order to gather intelligence on the collaboration between the German and Japanese navies, the entire British diplomatic establishment in Japan, led by the Military and Naval attachés, used all means both conventional and unconventional available to them. The assistance of the diplomatic representatives of the United States, the Commonwealth countries, and the anti-Axis states of Central and South America proved to be enormously helpful. The British also relied on information received from their secret agents and pro-British members of the Japanese public.

The round-the-clock reports supplied by the networks of British residents in the vicinity of ports set up to monitor the traffic of Axis shipping were particularly valuable. German ships using the ports of Kōbe and Yokohama were under constant surveillance. As well as their destinations and their dates and times of arrival and departure, the type of their cargo, whether relief raider crew were among those boarding and disembarking, and the levels of their waterline at the times of arrival and departure were all observed and analysed. These data were compared against the dates, times and locations of attacks on British and Norwegian merchant ships as well as the testimonies provided by their crewmen. Through this process, it was possible to make fairly accurate assumptions on which raiders the supply ships liaised with in the southern seas, what they supplied, and when. It was believed that among the German ships based in Kōbe and other Japanese ports the *Munsterland* supplied the *Atlantis*, the *Orion* and the *Komet* while the *Elsa Essberger* worked for the *Orion* and the *Regensburg* for the *Orion*, the *Thor* and the *Komet*, respectively.[8, 17]

From the autumn of 1940 to mid-1941, Sir Robert Craigie, the British Ambassador to Japan, scrupulously planned countermeasures to the collaboration in consultation with the British government. Armed with all manner of data and material, he uncompromisingly debated the issue with the Deputy Minister for Foreign Affairs, Chūichi Ōhashi, and sometimes with Foreign Minister Matsuoka. He pointed out that the collaboration contravened international law and repeatedly warned that, if the situation were not rectified, Britain would have no choice but to take action. In particular he threatened that, since there had been cases of German raiders pretending to be Japanese ships when carrying out their attacks, Britain would position her cruisers in the seas around Japan as she had done in the past and carry out patrols and inspections. This statement was quite a drastic one considering what had occurred about a year earlier. On 21 January 1940, the British light cruiser HMS *Liverpool* had stopped the Nippon Yūsen Kasisha's *Asamamaru* (16,975 tonnes), a regular service to San Francisco, in international waters thirty-five miles from Nojimazaki in Chiba Prefecture in Japan. The *Liverpool*'s officers had arrested twenty-one male German passengers aboard the *Asamamaru* on the grounds that they would potentially serve in the military once back in Germany, and the incident had exacerbated Anglo-Japanese relations.

Craigie also argued that, as long as Japan did not provide detailed information on the movements of German vessels which were repeatedly entering and leaving Kōbe and Yokohama, Britain could only conclude that these German vessels were engaged in military supply activity in the southern seas and would have to charge Japan with breaching her neutrality. Assailed in this way Ōhashi shrank from Craigie and could not produce any satisfactory answers. Judging by Ōhashi's reactions, Craigie ultimately became convinced, and reported to Britain accordingly, that the Japanese Navy had not informed its Foreign Ministry on the real state of affairs in any way, and that it was pursuing a coalition with the Germans without consulting the Foreign Ministry.[9]

At first, the Japanese Navy was sensitive to the British protests conveyed by the Foreign Ministry, and showed a tendency to worry over US and British reactions. However, as the strength of the pro-German camp within the Japanese Navy grew following the conclusion of the tripartite alliance, the navy accommodated Germany's ever-increasing demands. This was partly because, with the degeneration of Japan's relationship with Britain and America, it had no alternative but to obtain the most advanced military technology from Germany. Specifically for this purpose, a naval mission of twenty-two officers and technicians was despatched to Germany in February 1941 carrying a long shopping list. The mission was placed under the command of Vice Admiral Naokuni Nomura who was already there as the Japanese Navy representative. In his report of June 1941, however, Admiral Nomura expressed his disappointment in the result of the mission. German armed forces and private industries were not so enthusiastic about the exchange of technology with Japan. In conclusion, he had to stress the importance of Japan's own efforts and self-reliance.[10] Thus, the Japanese Navy became bound by its own words and rashly plummeted towards war. Of special note were the moves – of eloquent words and efficacious actions – made by the German Naval Attaché in Japan, Rear Admiral Paul Werner Wenneker, who played a significant role in bringing about this result. Meanwhile, according to the Japanese secret police report of 1939, the British Naval Attaché, Captain D.N.C. Tufnell, who had taken up his post on 11 February that year, had assisted Craigie alongside the Military Attaché, Major General F.S.G. Piggott, and had made every effort to persuade the Japanese military not to join an alliance with Germany and Italy.[11]

The surveillance by the Japanese secret police and military police of the intelligence-gathering operations of the foreign envoys in Japan – especially those of Britain, America, Germany and the USSR – was intensified. Such intelligence-gathering had become more active in the wake of the Manchurian Incident of 1931. Every single movement, not only of the British embassy staff but also of employees of British businesses such as Rising Sun Petroleum and Dunlop, and of British teachers, missionaries and sailors was observed. Their telegrams, telephone calls and mail became subject to interception, decoding and tapping. Various instances of British reconnaissance activity are recorded in the special high police's report of 1940. One such record states that at the start of May that year, the British Consul, Wilfred Cunningham, had visited Aichi Prefecture by car when attending the information committee meeting for the Kansai region and examined the condition of the roads using a map produced by the government's Land Survey Department. Another states that the British Trade Attaché, Oscar Morland (who would become the Ambassador to Japan after the war), while driving to the resort of Karuizawa with his wife on 23 August, had stopped on a hill near the town of Ōta in Gunma Prefecture and observed the Nakajima aircraft factory from a distance and made notes. It is also recorded that Tufnell was extremely active, citing the exchange of information between him and Lieutenant Commander Henri H. Smith-Hutton, the US Naval Attaché, on the movements of the Japanese Combined Fleet in May.[12] As Japanese counter-intelligence activity increased so did the cases of exposures and detentions of British subjects. Britain responded by arresting Japanese citizens living in England, and Anglo-Japanese relations became progressively more acrimonious.

Now even the British embassy, located at No. 1, Gobanchō, Kōjimachi Ward, Tokyo, was no longer a sanctuary. The secret police obtained innumerable and immensely varied documents and data through the Japanese employees at the embassy offices and residences. Among these were the minutes of the weekly information committee meetings, records of internal telephone conversations, incomplete or discarded draft documents and documents from the British embassy in Shanghai. The embassy's waste paper was promptly bought up by the awaiting secret police when it was brought out of the building. It was carefully analysed and became an important source of information. Even the intelligence on German covert operations obtained by the embassy passed into the hands of the secret police. The indiscreet chatter of embassy staff, fuelled by alcohol at the Tokyo Club or the

American Club, was listened to and recorded. It was only after the Pacific War broke out that the British Foreign Office realized that its embassy's security had been flawed and that secrets had been leaked to Japan.[13]

The Ole Jacob *Arrives in Kōebe*

The German embassy in Tokyo was located at No. 14, 1-Chōme, Nagatachō, Kōjimachi Ward, near the present-day site of the Diet Library. Its premises extended to over 4.4 acres, in a prime location not far from the Imperial Palace on high ground with a good view. It was also conveniently situated close to the Diet and government offices including the Army Ministry, the Navy Ministry, the Foreign Office and the Ministry of Industry and Commerce. The German Ambassador in 1940 was an ex-army man, Eugen Ott. He had worked as private secretary to Chancellor Kurt von Schleicher and had been posted to Japan in 1933 in order to monitor her army. The following year he had assumed the position of Military Attaché and in 1938 had been appointed Ambassador. He remained in this post until the end of 1942 when he was held responsible for the Sorge Incident[14] and was relieved of his duty.

The German Naval Attaché in Japan was the aforementioned Rear Admiral Wenneker. He was a man of mild character and balanced, impartial views. It was not unusual for his frank situation reports to incur the displeasure of the Nazi leadership. He was deeply trusted by the Japanese, as indeed was Ott. Within the Japanese Navy he had a good reputation as an unaffected character. Compared to the naval attachés of other nationalities his network of associates was much wider and much less superficial. He was always pessimistic about Japan's chances of winning the Pacific War.

The German Military Attaché, Lieutenant General Alfred Kretzschmer, on the other hand, was the archetypal military man whose interpretation of situations lacked Wenneker's flexibility. Even when the tide of the war in Europe turned against Germany he continued to pass biased and inaccurate military information from Berlin to the Japanese army, causing the latter to make increasingly erroneous decisions.[15]

On 27 November, Wenneker was informed by a telegram from Berlin that the *Ole Jacob*, which had been heading for Japan, would be diverted to 'Sheltering Place Y' – Lamotrek Atoll – and that it would undergo conversion to an escort tanker. Wenneker was ordered to have a tanker and a freighter ready at 'Sheltering Place Y' to retrieve the 9,000 tonnes of aviation fuel and the Scandinavian crewmen and to transfer provisions onto the *Ole Jacob*.

With the *Ole Jacob* now expected at 'Sheltering Place Y' Wenneker suddenly became busy, holding negotiations with Captain Katsuhei Nakamura, Senior Adjutant to the Navy Minister, choosing suitable vessels from those docked at Yokohama and Kōbe and loading them with the necessary provisions and selecting and preparing German crewmen to replace the Scandinavians. As for Nakamura, he had only taken over from his predecessor Captain Yoshiyuki Ichimiya on 5 November, and he struggled with the burden of the *Ole Jacob* situation so early in his new role. Nakamura had been in the year below Ichimiya at their naval academy, and he had spent about two years in the United States from the end of 1929. He had subsequently held posts in the command of the China-based fleet and as a lecturer at the naval academy. In February 1943, he joined the command of the Fifth Battle Unit and in March became the Captain of the cruiser *Myōkō* (10,000 tonnes). Following a spell as the attaché in Nanking, he was appointed Head of Administration of the General Navy Air Command in August 1944; this was the position he occupied when the war ended.

The *Ole Jacob* received the order to alter course and head for 'Sheltering Place Y', but Kamenz, who was hell-bent on delivering the prize documents to Berlin as soon as possible, ignored this and brought the *Ole Jacob*, flying the German naval ensign in full view, into the outer harbour of Kōbe at 10.00 on 4 December. It was a fine early winter day the temperature rising a little over 10°C. The sea was calm with a gentle, southeast-by-east breeze. Nakamura had told Wenneker that he objected to the *Ole Jacob* entering a Japanese port as this risked provoking an awkward international incident, and he had been relieved to hear that subsequently she had been diverted to the Lamotrek Atoll. When he heard that she had arrived at Kōbe two days ahead of schedule and moreover sporting an obvious naval guise he displayed 'visible consternation', according to Wenneker's diary.[16]

Nakamura had been at the point of making provision for German ships to go to the Lamotrek Atoll according to Wenneker's requests, even while worrying that he would incur the censure of the British and American Naval attachés for breach of neutrality; it was hardly surprising that he was overwhelmed by the sudden change of situation. Wenneker reasoned that if the *Ole Jacob* had gone to the Lamotrek Atoll, there would have been the risk of the Scandinavians realizing the German secret, and that it was wiser to release them in Kōbe as they had been promised. He also sought Nakamura's help in suppressing any press reports on the *Ole Jacob*'s arrival, arguing that this would be mutually beneficial to both Germany and Japan, but Nakamura refused to cooperate.

On the afternoon of 5 December, the sixty-one Scandinavian sailors who had kept their promise and had safely brought the *Ole Jacob* to port were transferred onto the German passenger ship the *Scharnhorst* (18,184 tonnes)[17] lying in Kōbe. On the 7th they were permitted to land, partly to honour Rogge's promise and partly because Japan demanded their release to comply with international law. Captain Krogh of the *Ole Jacob*, Captain Lütken of the *Teddy* and officers from both ships visited the Norwegian consulate for the Kōbe and Osaka regions the very same day and reported on the attacks. That day the Norwegian Minister in Tokyo, Alf Hassel, wired this report to the Norwegian legation in London, and this was immediately passed on to the British Foreign Office. McNicol's letter entrusted to one of the Norwegians also reached its destination in Cardiff postmarked 9 December. Through this, the British government came to know that the Fergusons were among the detainees.

The Scandinavian crewmen were placed under the custody of the Japanese police, and they divided into two groups according to where they wished to go: thirty-seven departed for Shanghai via Nagasaki on 10 December 1940; the remaining twenty-four headed home, sailing from Tsuruga on the Sea of Japan to Vladivostok from where they took the Trans-Siberian Railway. The latter's travel expenses were covered by the German government. Those travelling to Shanghai were required to pay for their own expenses, but it appears that the Norwegian Consulate met this cost. Craigie had consulted with the Commander-in-Chief at Singapore on ways of dealing with the Norwegians, and had initiated a policy of appealing to them not to accept Germany's invitation to return to their occupied homeland, but to support the Allied war effort instead. Craigie had set to work through the Norwegian consulate in Kōbe, and as a result thirty-seven crewmen who left for Shanghai had eventually gone to Hong Kong as arranged by the Norwegian Consul in Kōbe to join Norwegian vessels there. The American

Consul in Kōbe reported to the Department of State on 17 December that Thor Lütken, Captain of the *Teddy*, applied for a transit visa to enter the United States to proceed to a gulf port for the purpose of taking command of the motorship *Somerville* which also belonged to the owners of the *Teddy*. He intended to leave on the Japanese passenger liner *Nittamaru* for San Francisco on 11 January 1941. So it seems that Captain Lütken stayed behind in Japan for a while.[18]

Invoking international law, Nakamura had insisted that the *Ole Jacob* left Kōbe within twenty-four hours. So the *Ole Jacob*, though delayed by twelve hours having taken time to refuel, had brought aboard ten new German crew under cover of darkness and set sail for the Lamotrek Atoll on the 5th. Nakamura had imparted to Wenneker the Navy Ministry's official stance that on legal grounds it was not happy with this intake of crew either. However, since the Germans had been adamant that it would take place, he had ultimately let it be understood that he would turn a blind eye.

The *Ole Jacob*'s name was changed to the *Benno* and she was employed as a supply ship for the German raiders. The German Navy must have considered her a treasure as she had only been launched in April 1939, but she was to be short-lived and was never to return to Japan: on Christmas Eve 1941, she was sunk by British warplanes at Puerto Carino in northwest Spain.

On 4 December, Wenneker had been informed of the *Ole Jacob*'s arrival in Kōbe by a telephone call from the Chief Liaison Officer in the city, Kehrmann. Wenneker had sent his aide, Lieutenant Senior Grade Paul P. Wigand, to supervise the *Ole Jacob*. He had requested an aircraft for Wigand's use but the Japanese Navy had refused, so Wigand had travelled on the special express train *Kamome* ('Seagull') that had left Tokyo at 13.00 that day and arrived in Kōbe at 21.58. Wenneker had remained in Tokyo, and while negotiating with Nakamura, who was based at the Navy Ministry a short walk away, had given detailed instructions to Wigand over the telephone. Japanese telecommunications at that time were far inferior to those of the West. Stumped by being forced to wait two hours every time he wished to make a phone call to Kōbe, Wenneker had grumbled continuously. Though preoccupied with dealing with the *Ole Jacob*, Wenneker had still attended the state funeral of the last *genrō* (an elder statesman in the role of adviser to the emperor) in Japan, Prince Saionji, at Hibiya Park on the 5th. By doing so he had sought to demonstrate to Tufnell, who had also

1. The SS *Automedon* passing under Sydney Harbour Bridge – the first ship to do so following the bridge's official opening in March 1932. (Courtesy Heather Stewart whose grandfather Captain Donald Stewart was aboard the *Automedon* at the time.)

2. Alan and Violet Ferguson photographed in Singapore c.1950 (Courtesy Madge Christmas)

3. Violet Ferguson's tea-set, saved by the Germans before the *Automedon* was sunk, which in turn led to the discovery of the British Government's 'Most Secret' report on Japan's participation in the war (Author)

4. The German commerce raider *Atlantis*, also named *Tamesis*, as in this photograph (Courtesy Photograph Archive, Imperial War Museum, London, HU2348)

5. The *Atlantis* masquerading as the Japanese vessel SS *Kashiimaru* (Courtesy German Military Archives, Freiburg)

6. SS *Kashiimaru* (Courtesy Public Relations Office, Shōsen, Mitsui Kaisha)

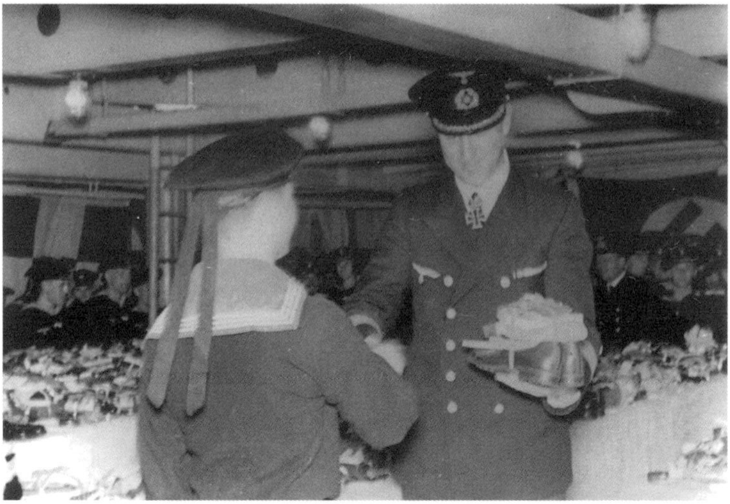

7. Captain Bernard Rogge distributing Christmas gifts to the crew of the *Atlantis*.
(Courtesy German Military Archives, Freiburg)

8. Rogge relaxing at sea on the *Atlantis* (Courtesy German Military Archives, Freiburg)

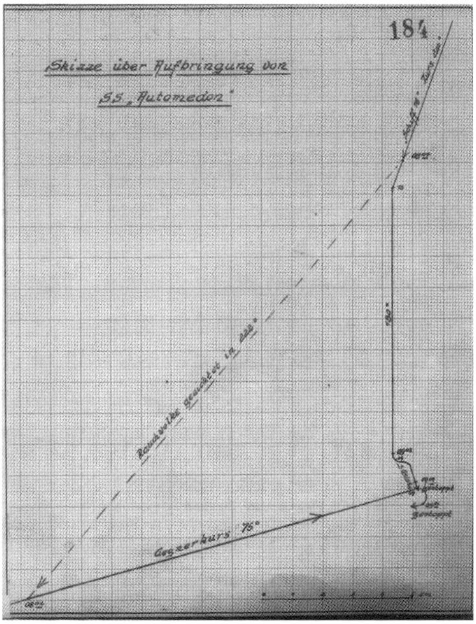

9. Sketch made by the *Atlantis* showing how the *Automedon* was captured. (Courtesy German Military Archives, Freiburg)

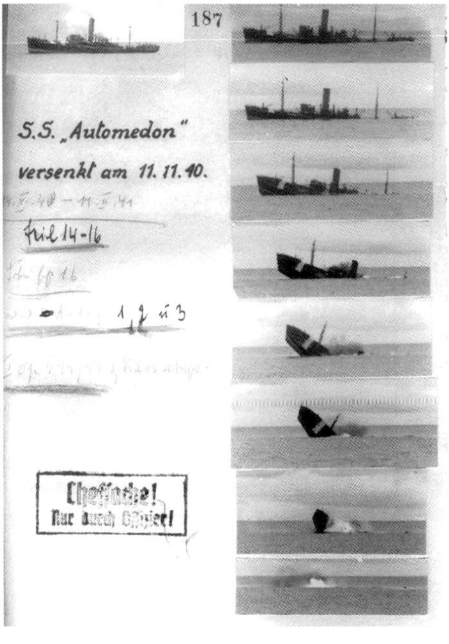

10. Last moments of the SS *Automedon* photographed on board the *Atlantis* (Courtesy German Military Archieves, Freiburg)

13. Overcrowded deck of the prison ship *Storstad* (Source not available)

14. Young Walker (far right) wearing an oversized military uniform, digging peat while in captivity in Germany (Courtesy Frank Walker)

15

16

15/16. Samuel Harper's friends, Ernest Howlett (left) and Robert Bellew (Courtesy Samuel Harper)

17

18

17. Recent picture of what was the Liebenau Women's Internment Camp (Author)

18. Violet Ferguson (left, front row) with her friends at Liebenau Internment Camp (Courtesy Madge Christmas)

19

20

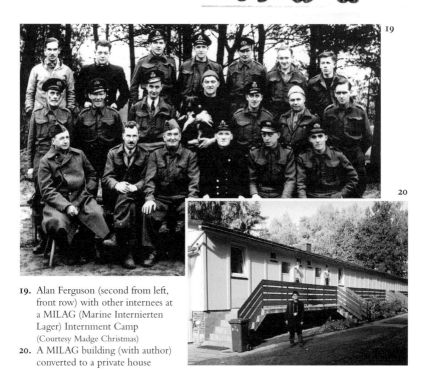

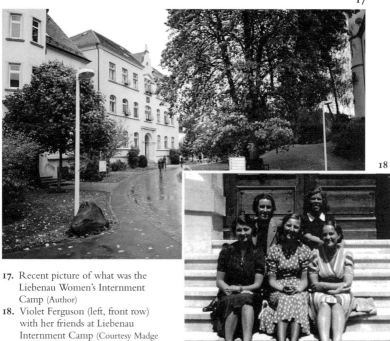

19. Alan Ferguson (second from left, front row) with other internees at a MILAG (Marine Internierten Lager) Internment Camp (Courtesy Madge Christmas)

20. A MILAG building (with author) converted to a private house

25

26

27

28

25. The German Embassy, Tokyo, August 1934 (Courtesy Mainichi Newspapers)

26. A view of the Diet building from the ruins of the German Embassy, 29 November 1945 (Courtesy Mainichi Newspapers)

27. Vice Admiral Nobutake Kondō (Courtesy Naval Historical Center, Washington D.C. NH 63696)

28. Vice Admiral Paul Wenneker (Courtesy German Military Archives, Frieburg)

29. HMS *Devonshire*, London class cruiser which shelled the *Atlantis* (Courtesy Photograph Archive, Imperial War Museum, London, A116)

30. The *Atlantis* on fire and sinking after being shelled by HMS *Devonshire*, South Atlantic, 23 November 1941. (Courtesy Photograph Archive, Imperial War Museum, London, HU62774)

31. British Embassy, Tokyo, on the day war was declared, 8 December 1941 (Courtesy Mainichi Newspapers)

32. Violet Ferguson with her family immediately after her repatriation in March 1943 (Courtesy Madge Christmas)

33. POW tags of Alan and Violet Ferguson (Courtesy Madge Christmas)

34. Samuel Harper with his mother, younger brother (standing) and younger sister before the war (Courtesy Samuel Harper)

35. Samuel Harper at his home, September 2002 (Author)

36. Frank Walker and his *Automedon* colleague, Alex Parsons, photographed by the author at Walker's house, 21 March 2006 (Author)

37. Inscribed in relief on bronze panels at the Tower Hill Memorial, London, the names of the SS *Automedon*'s crew who perished, and are among 'the twenty-four thousand who gave their lives for their country and have no grave but the sea' (Author)

been present, that the *Ole Jacob* was of no particular interest to him and indeed that he was not in Kōbe.

Tufnell had already begun watching the Japanese like a hawk to see whether they infringed their neutrality over the arrival of the *Ole Jacob*. On 15 December, Craigie visited Ōhashi and protested that the *Ole Jacob*'s thirty-hour stay in Kōbe had been too long for the sole purpose of taking on water and fuel, and that some issues such as the transport of the Scandinavian crewmen had not yet been resolved as claimed by Ōhashi. He announced that he would reserve judgement until he had consulted with the Norwegian envoy.

The Top-Secret Documents Arrive in Tokyo

Kehrmann had boarded the *Ole Jacob* as soon as she had docked and had taken charge of the prize documents. He had taken them to the German consulate and packed them in a large, sturdy chest. Two of the consulate staff had carefully taken it aboard the special express train *Tsubame* ('Swallow') that had left Kōbe at 12.20 and arrived in Tokyo at 21.00. The same night they had delivered it to Wenneker who had been waiting impatiently in his office at the embassy.

Wenneker had studied the contents of the chest from early the next morning, and focused his attention on the papers destined for the British Commander-in-Chief of the Far East. As he had read through them he had become excited by the profound significance of their contents and convinced that the confidential British Cabinet papers must be of the very highest interest to the Japanese. He had cabled a digest of the contents to the German Naval High Command and requested permission to share them with the Japanese. He had also had the foresight to take copies of the papers. The originals had been consigned to a diplomatic courier who had left Tokyo for Berlin via the Trans-Siberian Railway that day. Kamenz had accompanied this courier as a guard. He had other duties to carry out when he reached Berlin, such as reporting on the *Atlantis*'s activities to the Naval High Command, making requests for materials and food supplies, and consulting with the command of the submarine fleet on cipher communication, as concern was growing that it was increasingly being intercepted and decoded by the enemy.

Five days later, Wenneker received a telegram from Berlin granting him permission to pass on the confidential documents to the Japanese Navy. However, it came with a condition: he should not reveal the real course of events that led to Germany's possession of the documents and he must claim that they were obtained through elaborate manoeuvres on the part of the German secret services. It seems that Germany sought to propagate a reputation for the excellence of its intelligence agencies. The telegram also stated that the Japanese Naval Attaché in Berlin, Captain Tadao Yokoi, had been supplied with the information. Indeed, the telegram sent from Yokoi to Captain Minoru Maeda, the head of the Third Division of the Naval General Staff, on 12 December stated that he had received from the German Naval High Command the minutes of the British Cabinet meeting of 8 August and that he would send it with the next courier service to Japan. He also reported the key points of these minutes as follows:

1. Japan has long harboured an ambition to capture Singapore but under the present circumstances it is impossible for Britain to despatch a fleet to the Far East. Britain must defend Singapore by reinforcing her land and air forces in the region.
2. Japan will probably invade French Indochina or Thailand first, and then attack the Dutch East Indies. However, in the event of Japan's invasion of French Indochina or Thailand Britain will not declare war against Japan.
3. In the event of war against Japan, Britain will ultimately abandon Hong Kong, though she will continue to resist for as long as possible.
4. If the contest with the Italian navy in the Mediterranean progresses swiftly and in Britain's favour it will become possible to despatch a fleet to the Far East.
5. Britain should collaborate with the Dutch East Indies.
6. As it is thought that Japan will probably attempt to occupy Suva in Fiji, a brigade from New Zealand must be despatched.

It can be assumed that the British Cabinet papers sent from Tokyo to Berlin via the Trans-Siberian Railway had not yet arrived, and that Yokoi's summary of the report must have been copied from Wenneker's telegram. Incidentally, Yokoi's telegram was made public for the first time in January 1980 in the United States,[19] but it is not clear whether the British 'Ultra' code-breaking unit had intercepted and decoded it.

The Suspicion and Stupefaction of the Japanese Navy

While privately objecting to the aforementioned condition stipulated by Berlin, which he considered a cheap trick, Wenneker took the copies of the top-secret documents to the offices of the Japanese Naval Staff on 12 December, and with barely a greeting he handed them to Vice Admiral Nobutake Kondō, Deputy Chief of the Naval General Staff. Kondō took the substantial package with a wary expression, wondering what on earth it could be. As Wenneker looked on with an obvious interest in his reaction he turned the pages irritably. Without raising his head he then became absorbed in reading for some time.

Wenneker wrote in his diary: 'As anticipated, the contents were read with extraordinary interest.' This was the first that Kondō knew of the secret documents, as Yokoi's telegram was not sent until late that night. Wenneker reluctantly told Kondō how the documents had come into Germany's possession as instructed by Berlin. That evening Kondō invited Wenneker to an exclusive meal attended by his inner circle at a restaurant in the Akasaka district of Tokyo. It is not clear from Wenneker's diary whether this had been prearranged, but it was more likely a last-minute decision on the part of Kondō, who was astonished by the highly-sensitive content of the documents and wished to thank Wenneker without delay. Over this meal, Kondō repeatedly expressed his gratitude for the priceless information and remarked that: 'Such a significant weakening of the British Empire could not have been identified from outward appearances.'

These words were the first response from the Japanese Navy. However, subsequently some members of the Navy Ministry and the Naval Staff raised their doubts. Having reflected on Wenneker's explanation as to how Germany had acquired the documents, they realized that it was not feasible for any intelligence agency to obtain original material of such a calibre. They became sceptical and began to question whether there was a conspiracy by Hitler to entice Japan to attack Singapore. The German military's bid to present its secret services as highly advanced and effective generated unexpected repercussions in the corridors of power in Tokyo.

However, when the Japanese Navy spent some time analysing the documents in detail it found that the data on British armaments often matched those procured independently by the Japanese intelligence agencies whose activities were expanding in

South East Asia around this time. The navy came to regard the documents as highly reliable. Its initial suspicions gradually faded and gave way to astonishment. In time, this gift from Hitler would have the effect of hastening the Japanese military to war.

Intelligence Activity in South East Asia

As Japan's relations with the West became strained over her war on China, her interest in French Indochina and the Dutch East Indies grew stronger. The United States, Britain and the Commonwealth, plus Holland, whose survival depended on the former states, hoped that the Japanese forces would be fettered and exhausted in mainland China leaving them with no strength in reserve to direct southwards. They continued to support Chiang Kai-shek's regime by supplying munitions via the roads through Indo-China and Burma. Needless to say, the blockade of these routes became a major objective of the Japanese. Meanwhile, South East Asia was also a rich source of the key materials Japan needed in her war against China.

As the war in China became bogged down, a call to proceed south, with the aims of blocking Chiang Kai-shek's supply routes and procuring resources, rose within the Japanese military and gradually became influential. This strained Japan's relations with the Allies further. Both sides' intelligence-gathering in Asia became more vigorous, each avidly collecting military and economic data on the other. There was fierce competition to detect and obstruct the enemy's propaganda activities within each side's territories. Japan's political engineering as well as information-gathering was stepped up a gear, and her foreign legations – especially those in Bangkok, Hong Kong, Singapore and Manila – became important bases for such operations. Many secret agents, including military personnel, were sent all over South East Asia under the guises of attachés, Foreign Ministry secretaries or journalists. Japanese banks, businesses, shipping companies and the fishing and forestry industries were required to assist in the espionage activities.

There was a sizeable legation at the Japanese embassy in Bangkok around this time, a number of officers having been despatched there in addition to the Military Attaché and his aides. The British secret services in Thailand always focused their attention on the movements of the Military Attaché above all. They closely monitored his trips to the Malayan Peninsula and towards the Burmese border, and had their agents follow him and report back at every stage. He was Captain Hiroshi Tamura, and he occupied the post of Military Attaché in Thailand from April 1939 to February 1942. He was not only a talented linguist but was also able to use his personality to establish extensive connections reaching into the upper echelons of the Thai government. The British secret agents considered this proficient and smooth-talking man a key player and never failed to follow his movements.

Japanese offshore fishermen were asked for their cooperation in espionage. High-speed reconnaissance vessels, fitted with communications equipment and disguised as fishing boats, were mobilized to survey port defences, currents, water depths and coastal topographies in foreign territories. Britain and her allies were perturbed by the sharp rise in the number of Japanese fishing boats and in the requests for permission to enter, and unauthorized encroachments into, their ports and waters by suspicious vessels whose true purposes were unclear, and they strove to regulate their activity. The telegrams and letters sent between employees of Japanese companies based in Burma, the Malayan Peninsula and Borneo and their relatives in Japan were systematically intercepted and read by the British secret services. They were attempting to decipher the intentions and objectives of the Japanese intelligence agents from their requests for assistance made to the private sector.

Japan pursued the direct incitement of independence movements in Burma, Malaya and India and harboured their leaders within Japan. This was of particular concern to the British government. In Burma, two units were established for this purpose. One was headed by Captain Keiji Suzuki. The other, headed by Major Iwaichi Fujiwara, implemented 'Operation Harimau' and other operations targeting Malayan youth organizations, expatriate Chinese and Indian soldiers.

The Japanese military installations in Taiwan and Hainan were the bases that supported the secret service activities. Taiwan was a crucial foothold for any southward campaign. There the Japanese army and navy conducted research into the strategies and the armaments required for such a campaign, and increasingly developed airbases, port facilities, barracks and fuel stores. Notably, an important military compound was established in southern Taiwan. The British intelligence agencies focused on these projects and eagerly collected information on them. As travel to southern Taiwan was heavily restricted they could not easily procure data, but they were able to form a picture of the situation to some degree through published economics articles, on subjects such as the severe shortage of materials in the civilian construction sector and the skyrocketing inflation, as well as through the accounts of the ordinary people of Taiwan.

This is a digression, but there is a booklet entitled: *Koredake Yomeba Ikusawa Kateru* ('Read This And We Will Win')[20] compiled mainly by Masanobu Tsuji, an army staff officer based in Taiwan who was researching for a potential southern campaign around this time. It is said that a copy of this booklet was handed to every single soldier aboard southbound troopships immediately prior to the advent of the Pacific War. How must those soldiers have felt reading this flimsy booklet as they imminently faced the battlefields where they might meet their deaths? The booklet gives advice on matters such as sunstroke and tropical diseases, but it also presents a series of practices which evoke *ninja* period pieces, for instance: 'It serves well to bind heavy equipment such as machine guns and mortars to a buoyant object in the event of an amphibious landing.' The booklet repeatedly exhorts self-reliance in the field. While reading through it a strange feeling came over this author and he was filled with pity for the soldiers who staked their lives armed with such limited resources and information. The British military acquired and translated a copy of the booklet shortly after war broke out. It is recorded, somewhat inexplicably, that the British were impressed by the extent of the Japanese preparedness as embodied in this booklet, which is praise indeed for Tsuji.

It was not only the Japanese military that underestimated the opposition; the British forces, too, committed this error. In the wake of the First World War the Royal Navy had noted that the Japanese Navy was developing its air force at the Kasumigaura base, but judging by the perceived level of competence of the Japanese and their industrial standards, it had assumed that this would not evolve into a force of any significance and had attached little importance to it. In the British embassy's annual report of 1920 it is stated that, as pilot training was extremely dangerous there were few applicants, and that the general opinion among foreigners living in Japan was that the Japanese physique and character were unsuited to using aircraft or other machinery.[21]

The British forces looked down upon the Japanese intelligence-gathering activities as amateurish. However, with the advent of war, Japan rapidly overran Hong Kong, the Malayan Peninsula,

Burma and the Dutch East Indies, and the British realized that the Japanese plans of attack had been underpinned by careful research and accurate information. Churchill was deeply shocked when Singapore unexpectedly fell and was furious that the pride of the Great British Empire had been wounded. He learnt from what he called 'the worst disaster and largest capitulation in British history', promptly ordered detailed research into defensive operations for the Malayan Peninsula, and prepared for retaliation. He could not deny that the quantity and quality of intelligence amassed by the Japanese were impressive. However, the Japanese military undervalued the collection of data through code-breaking and the development of radio technology and were completely surpassed by Britain and the United Sates in these areas. It also neglected to protect its secret information adequately and ultimately met with defeat.

The Japanese Military Leaders' Error

As we have seen, the seized Joint Chiefs of Staff Committee report was written at the end of July 1940 in response to the demands made by Australia and New Zealand for a reassessment of the military situation in Asia and British response measures to it. At the time, as we have seen, Britain was engaged in the Battle of Britain upon which her very survival as a nation depended, and an armed clash with Japan was out of the question. It is notable in this report that the British military accepted this hard fact without contention and advised on countermeasures accordingly. Moreover, it is evident in the report that the only prerequisite as far as Britain was concerned was the continuation of military and economic aid from the United States: she did not even see Dutch support, let alone America entering the War or China's capacity to continue fighting, as determining factors when drawing up her strategies. She focused solely on the defence of her home territory and the Commonwealth. Defeating Germany was her priority, and she pursued reconciliation with Japan. She reasoned that even if such reconciliation failed, a war against Japan was of secondary importance for the present, and that she could ultimately attain victory in the Far East by gradually assuming the offensive and regaining lost territory as the war in Europe progressed in her favour and her forces were freed up. The reality of the 'the A-B-C-D encirclement of Japan' (by America, Britain, China and Holland), loudly proclaimed by the Japanese military to the people of Japan, was rather insubstantial. However, Japan's ensuing southward expansion inflamed the British, the Dutch and the Americans, and led to their stepping up preparations for a war against her.

In its report, the Joint Chiefs of Staff Committee judged that Japan would invade other countries according to her traditional step-by-step method while assessing the enemy's reaction at every stage, but it was mistaken. At this time, Japan's relationship with America had not yet deteriorated to the point where open hostilities were feared. It was not until the summer of 1941 that British and American diplomats in Japan began to fear that Japan might make a wild move that could not be predicted by the rational and results-oriented minds of Westerners, and began giving warnings to this effect.

The analysis of Japan's economy that accompanied the report estimated that Japan's oil reserves would be exhausted in a year and that her stocks of other key war materials would be depleted in just six months. It concluded that with the acute decline in overseas trade and shortage of vital supplies, the Japanese economy would collapse after six months at war. This point in time was to coincide precisely with the disheartening defeat that Japan suffered at the Battle of Midway in June 1942 and her loss of the initiative in the Pacific. When America entered the war following Japan's attack on Pearl Harbor the situation progressed more favourably for the Allies than had been predicted in the report, culminating in Japan's final defeat.

The written records needed in order to consider what effect the British Cabinet papers, supplied to Japan by special order of the Führer, had on the policies of the Japanese military and government cannot be found anywhere.[22] Such records would include documents relating to meetings held by the Naval Staff and the Navy Ministry, military appreciations, the journal of the Navy Minister's office, or war diaries. This type of official material produced after 1940 was all destroyed upon Japan's defeat. Moreover, the most important key figure, Kondō, subsequently never spoke publicly or wrote on this subject.

There is no alternative to theorizing on the contemporary situation on the basis of peripheral material. Two sources are worth highlighting. One is the General Staff Office's 'Sugiyama Memo' of 27 December 1940. The other is the situation report produced by Captain Shigetada Horiuchi, the Head of Division Eight of Section

Three of the Naval General Staff, included in the 21 January 1941 entry of the Army Staff Office's 'Classified War Diary'. Here Horiuchi asserts: 'In the event of Japan's invasion of French Indochina Britain will not declare war on us.' We can safely assume that this statement was derived from the British Cabinet papers.[23]

However, more important are the remarks by the Navy Minister, Admiral Koshirō Oikawa, found in the 'Sugiyama Memo', which is a record of the third liaison meeting held between the government and the military command at the Prime Minister's residence on 27 December 1940. Around the time that this meeting was held, Japan blamed her failure to clinch victory in China entirely on Britain, the United States and France, and was strengthening her posture towards a showdown with them through a southern campaign. At the meeting, Foreign Minister Matsuoka declared his hard-line view that Japan should not rule out an invasion of Indo-China. Oikawa responded by questioning whether Japan could still obtain her supplies if she displayed such aggression, and whether it was preferable to avoid provoking Britain and the United States and to proceed much more cautiously. Then, prefacing his statement with 'According to intelligence documentation. . .' he asserted that Britain did not intend to go to war against Japan so long as her expansionism ended with Indo-China, but that war with Britain would be inevitable if Japan encroached on the Dutch East Indies. Kondō was present at this meeting on behalf of the Chief of the Naval Staff.

Considering its timing and content, it is clear that Oikawa's declaration reflected the conclusions of the Joint Chiefs of Staff Committee's report that had been discussed at the British War Cabinet meeting of 8 August. While countering Matsuoka effectively by arguing that Japan must provoke neither the United States nor Britain by pursuing a heavy-handed policy towards Indo-China, Oikawa undermined his own argument by referring to the Cabinet papers which revealed that Britain would tolerate a Japanese occupation of that country. Given that he was strongly advocating a cautious approach, it was a blunder for Oikawa to have cited the 'intelligence documentation' that in fact bolstered the case for an aggressive incursion into Indo-China. All present at the meeting would have no doubt understood that there would be no adverse consequences to a southern campaign that was limited to Indo-China. However, it was the American reaction to such a move that was, in fact, most pivotal at this time.

As we know, when Kondō had first read the top-secret British documents he had remarked to Wenneker: 'Such a significant weakening of the British Empire could not have been identified from outward appearances.' This comment was an early betrayal of the Japanese Navy's misreading or lack of understanding of the documents. The Naval Staff became gripped by a fixed notion that a war with Britain and the United States would not materialize, and became absorbed in preparing bases for a southern campaign. It did not pay careful attention to America's reaction to the extension of its influence into Indo-China and Thailand. There was no longer any hope that it would read between the lines of the documents and react appropriately.

By accepting without question a report produced by the British several months earlier, and moreover during the period when the outcome of the Battle of Britain was unclear and the British had no leeway to focus on the Far East, Kondō committed a major error in evaluating the strength of the British forces. In December 1940, when he made the aforementioned comment to Wenneker, the Battle of Britain had already been won. The number of attacking German sorties had decreased dramatically from 12,095 at its peak in September to 2,335. Going ahead in time a little, Vice Admiral Naokuni Nomura, Chief of the Japanese Naval Mission in Germany, sent an expert team headed by Rear Admiral Katsuo Abe accompanied by two officers and one civilian technician on a study tour of German air bases, fortifications and other military installations on the north coast of France in February 1941. The findings brought back by the mission were sent to Tokyo by Nomura on 28 February. The report[24] also clearly suggested that the war was by no means progressing in Germany's favour, especially in the crucial battle for air supremacy against British fighters which performed well. Furthermore, the German air force, though large in number, lacked the competency required for attacking naval vessels and ships because they simply did not have sufficient time to accumulate the experience after they started rearmament in the early 1930s. If they studied this report in detail it would not have been difficult for the Japanese commanders back home, who claimed to be experts on military matters, to infer that the tide was turning in the contest between Britain and Germany. It is not known how men like Kondō of the Naval General Staff or Admiral Isoroku Yamamoto, the Commander-in-Chief of the Combined Fleet, interpreted the report. It was practically impossible for the Japanese military, who were in the grip of the intense anti-British/American fever that swept Japan at this time, to assess the situation calmly and rationally.

It was clear from the Cabinet papers that Britain would not regard Japan's occupation of southern Indo-China as a reason to go to war with her, but this policy was not one that had been decided in conjunction with the United States and the latter's reaction was something to be considered entirely separately. Furthermore, the British stand as reflected in the documents was becoming outdated and more hardened against Japan's southward push in Indo-China. The secret documents served to cloud the Japanese leadership's perception of Britain's military capabilities and the war in Europe, and the Japanese military's inclination towards war only strengthened further. The error of judgement committed by the Japanese political and military leaders proved fatal. Around the time when the Cabinet papers fell into German hands, Admiral Isoroku Yamamoto, Commander-in-Chief of the Japanese Combined Fleet, was formulating a plan to destroy the American Pacific Fleet at Pearl Harbor. He had been ambushed and brought down by eighteen American twin-engined P-38 Fighters whilst on an inspection tour of the Solomon Islands on 18 April 1943 being escorted by six Zero Fighters. He did not mention anything about the Cabinet papers, but it can be assumed that the intelligence gleaned from these British documents had encouraged him to promote the plan without worrying about being stabbed in the back. But the fact still remains that he, too, committed the fundamental error of strategic judgement, namely underrating the British potential and her chances for victory.[25]

The US Secretary of State, Cordell Hull, perceived Japan's occupation of southern Indo-China as a prelude to comprehensive Japanese expansionism into the southwest Pacific region. When Japan invaded Indo-China during negotiations with the United States, he deemed that the basis for continuing the negotiations were lost. As predicted, America responded with the tough measure of a financial embargo. Britain and Holland followed her example, and at once the climate of hostility intensified. Prime Minister Konoe was dismayed when he was warned by Kijūrō Shidehara, an influential figure in the diplomatic world, that war now looked certain. Konoe had been misled by the Japanese military, which had accepted the British report without attempting to understand it fully in an objective light. Captain

Shiba stated, at the same hearing in 1961 as mentioned in Chapter 3, that both the Ministry and the Naval General Staff undertook a rather perfunctory study of the repercussions that Japan's armed advance into southern Indo-China might have on the United States and Britain. They concluded that the United States would not be ready to have recourse to such a drastic measure as a total embargo due to her internal situations, let alone the United Kingdom. In retrospect, he said, there had been no alternative for the United States but the stiff response against Japan.[26]

The Japanese military leadership lost sight of the fact that Japan depended on Britain and the United States for most of her economic building blocks, such as capital, natural resources and technology. It factored the access to resources from conquered territories into its fundamental plan, when this should have been discounted as an uncertainty. It rushed to war, setting a cut-off point for negotiations with America, so that neither she nor Britain would have a chance to prepare. This was truly a case of counting one's chickens before they have hatched. The Japanese had not realized that Britain was confident of victory even while frankly admitting her lack of preparedness, and that this confidence was underpinned by the facts that Britain and the United States firmly controlled the majority of war resources and that Britain had the vast industrial strength of the United States on her side. The gift from Hitler, which only served to hasten Japan's progression to war, was nothing other than a gift of doom. There are British historians who contend that the top-secret papers formed a trap set by Churchill to draw Japan into the conflict and that Japan completely fell into this trap, which is of course an over-speculation. How could this really be the case? There are a number of points which cannot be explained by such a conspiracy theory.

First, around that time, Churchill was attempting to prevent Japan from entering the war, taking every opportunity to explain to her that the Empire on its own could win with the support of America's industrial production. He was concerned that if America entered the war she would no longer supply Britain with the munitions she needed; he had declared that Britain could finish the job if she was given the tools. Whether Churchill truly wished for America to join the war while knowing that by doing so she would assume the supreme position in the post-war international community is open to debate, and would require further investigation.

Second, it is certain that the classified mailbag would have been disposed of in the sea, had the *Atlantis*'s first salvo not struck the *Automedon*'s bridge and killed all the senior officers from the Captain down. Surely the Captain, who was responsible for the lives of his crew and passengers, would not have participated in a conspiracy in the full knowledge of its risks. If he was not a part of a conspiracy, needless to say he would have destroyed the mailbag himself or ordered one of his men to do so.

Moreover, judging by prior activities it cannot be claimed that Rogge knew of the existence of the top-secret documents through the work of the British secret services. It was possible for the *Atlantis*'s plans to fall apart as she pursued three ships in succession – the *Teddy*, the *Ole Jacob* and the *Automedon* – in a period of just two or three days, and for her to fail to capture the crucial prize. There was no way that Rogge would have run this risk if he had known about the documents. He would have made the *Automedon* his primary target and planned accordingly. In short, there were too many uncontrollable factors leading up to the attack on the *Automedon* for a conspiracy theory to hold.

Japan drove herself into a corner with her failure to settle the conflict in China and her alignment with the Axis powers. Her military and political leaders alike no longer had any psychological margin or the courage to voice their individual views to one another. They did not opt to conserve and nurture Japan's national strength while distancing her from the war in Europe. It had long been clear that a new international order would be formulated in the wake of the European war, but they failed to realize that, in that event, there would be opportunities to promote the principles of the self-determination of peoples, racial equality and fair trade. They lacked any sense of history or understanding of what was taking place around the world. They did not possess the wisdom to pursue tangible economic benefits for Japan instead of empty slogans. As we have seen, around 1941, Churchill was appealing to Japan that if she remained neutral by not joining the war in Europe the Allies would invite her to take part in the building of a post-war world order.

7

The Days of Captivity

The Prison Ship

THE AUTOMEDON'S CREW and passengers who were taken prisoner on the morning of 11 November spent the next month or so aboard the *Atlantis*. Owing to Rogge's generous policies their conditions were far better than anticipated. They were allowed to relax on deck for three hours each morning and afternoon. They were given the same meals as the German sailors, which were adequate both in quality and quantity. They were also given an allowance of forty pfennigs a day, and with it they could purchase small items such as tobacco, lemonade and toothbrushes in the ship's shops. The medical care was very good. Typed news reports apparently compiled from broadcasts from San Francisco, Manila and London were handed out to the prisoners every day. Some of the articles were clearly anti-German but this did not seem to concern Rogge in the slightest.

For the first three or four days the prisoners from the *Automedon* were held with the Scandinavian crewmen of the *Ole Jacob* and the *Teddy*. A few of them, including the *Teddy*'s Chief Engineer, were pro-British and agreed to report the sinking of the *Automedon* to the British authorities at the first neutral country they arrived in as McNicol and Stewart had requested.

The prisoners' life aboard the *Atlantis*, which was relatively free and more or less acceptable, though never could it be called comfortable, did not last for long. After the *Ole Jacob* had departed for Japan, on 9 December at 21.00, the prisoners were transferred onto a Norwegian tanker, the *Storstad*, at a secret rendezvous point codenamed 'Tulip' southeast of Madagascar at latitude 34 degrees south, longitude 59.55 degrees east. Among the transferred were of course Violet Ferguson, carrying her precious luggage, Harper the Fourth Engineer and Walker the Deck Boy. Parsons the Assistant Steward was kept aboard the *Atlantis* with James Hendry and one other POW as they were all seriously wounded. It was Rogge's policy to keep the wounded and sick POWs on his ship for as long as possible so they could receive the best available medical treatment and recuperate.

The *Storstad* had been captured by another German raider, the *Pinguin*, on 7 October 1940. She had subsequently been rigged with a dummy gun aft and disguised as a British ship; in fact she was unarmed. She was already carrying prisoners from eight other vessels, including the *Port Brisbane*, the *Benavon*, the *Domingo de Llarinaga*, the *British Commander*, the *Nowshera* and the *Maimoa*. As soon as the prisoners from the *Automedon* had been brought aboard and she had refuelled the *Atlantis*, the *Storstad* headed for Bordeaux, by then under German occupation.

The conditions aboard the *Storstad* were far worse than those on the *Atlantis* in every respect. The *Storstad* was originally a tanker so her living quarters were limited and 500 prisoners, about 400 of whom were British, were crammed like sardines into these areas. According to Harper's memoirs the eighty officers were accommodated in the forecastle and the floor space to each man was just $0.84m^2$.

The lavatory arrangements were entirely primitive, consisting only of a bucket placed on the floor, so sanitary conditions became extremely poor. Pills, which were apparently vitamins, were handed out every eleventh day but the food fell far short of requirements and only one cup a day of drinking water was permitted per person. The most recent arrivals before the *Automedon*'s captives joined the ship had been on board three days. The appalling conditions had already affected their attitudes and behaviour in that short period. When Stewart began supervising the distribution of food and water, however, the atmosphere became more amicable and the behaviour of all the captives became more reasonable. On Christmas Day each man received a bottle of beer but no extra rations of food.

The guards were extremely vigilant. When the prisoners were first brought aboard they had all undergone a physical examination and been photographed, and their possessions had been inspected. They had then been warned that if they attempted to take over the ship it would immediately be blown up. There were indeed explosives placed on the ship's cofferdam and wired to a trigger on the bridge. There were also two machine-guns fixed on the bridge and the twenty-seven German crewmen were armed with rifles and revolvers. When a hijack plan, hatched in spite of this, was exposed, the plotters were incarcerated in an isolated section.

In order to evade Allied warships and aircraft, the *Storstad* rounded the Cape of Good Hope 600 miles south of the coast and steamed north in mid-Atlantic. When she travelled close to the Antarctic Circle the cold became extremely severe and one of the prisoners died of pneumonia. The *Storstad* refuelled a few German vessels *en route* in the Atlantic. Her course took her close to the Azores and into the Bay of Biscay. The German crew then periodically threw grenades overboard and the prisoners assumed these to be some kind of signal. They later found out that they were signals to an Italian submarine that was escorting their ship. On the morning of 4 February the submarine surfaced and piloted the *Storstad* up the river Gironde in southwest France. She travelled about 100 km upstream and entered the port of Bordeaux.

That night all the men were sent to a holding camp at St Médard-en-Jalles northwest of Bordeaux. It was known as 'Front Stalag 221'. Violet Ferguson and the other women were detained in a convent about three miles away. Once the prisoners at these facilities reached a certain number they were transferred to camps in Germany by train.

The conditions at Front Stalag 221 were much worse even than those aboard the *Storstad*. The prisoners slept directly on plank bunks, and any straw handed out was scrambled over and gone in no time as they tried to make their beds even a little more comfortable. They were only fed 200g of unpalatable bread and some watery vegetable soup every day, and one after another they suffered digestive problems. Some even caught and ate mice. There were long queues for the toilet, which consisted of a plank placed over a hole in the ground in a shack. Its acrid odour and indescribable filth would be recounted by the detainees even after the war.

Even under such harsh circumstances the prisoners began to tutor each other in navigation, engineering and foreign languages. Their lives would have been unbearable without undertaking some kind of meaningful activity, however small. Stewart, for example, taught navigation. Even during these tough times of extreme privation, young men like Walker were presented with an opportunity to learn about a variety of subjects.

The Escape Plan

On the *Storstad*, some of the younger captives had formed covert networks and had schemed to take over the ship or make an opportunistic escape. Harper had been one of them, and he had hatched a hijack plan with W. Pascoe, one of the *Automedon*'s crew, her surgeon Dr Karel Sperber and Ernest Howlett, the Fourth Engineer of the *Maimoa*. However, the senior officers had rebuked them, saying that it was they who would make a decision on such matters. For this and other reasons the plan had been abandoned.

Dr Sperber had sought asylum in England following Germany's annexation of Czechoslovakia. His licence did not allow him to practise medicine in England, so he had taken employment with the Blue Funnel Line instead, as a valued crewmember with medical expertise. The presence of a doctor was invaluable both on the prison ship and at the internment camp.

Though the escape plan had been dropped, watches had been formed with the hope of encountering a British ship. However, the opportunity to make contact with one had never presented itself. The prisoners had also thrown overboard sealed bottles and cans containing messages, including the *Storstad*'s position and drawings of the raiders that had captured them, while the Germans were not looking. The Second Officer of the Port Wellington, P. Buchan, had ingeniously plotted the *Storstad*'s course throughout the journey and had kept the others informed. Eventually, he had declared that the ship's destination was Bordeaux and accurately predicted the arrival date and time within just a few hours.

Once landed, Harper and the others had known there would be more opportunities to escape and their urge to flee had grown even stronger. They had also known that such opportunities would vanish once they were interned in Germany, so they began to plan in earnest to escape while still in France, preferably in or near unoccupied territory. Plans were formed to cut through the double barbed-wire fence that surrounded the camp or to dig a tunnel under it but neither was realized. Harper was asked to join the tunnel plot, but this was one invitation he had to decline because of his claustrophobic tendencies.

When asked, years later, why he had been eager to escape to the point of risking his life, Harper smiled and replied that it was because there was no way that he could have endured a life without any freedom or pleasure for years on end. He assumed that he would remain at St Médard for some time, and as he was concerned about being on the run in the cold, he decided to make his escape in the spring and began gradual preparations. In his letters to his family in Liverpool he asked them to send him civilian clothes and foodstuff that would be easy to carry. However, on the night of 11 March the prisoners were suddenly told that they would be taken to Germany at 6.00 the following morning and his scheme of preparations was ruined. He had, however, put aside some dates and biscuits that the French Red Cross had distributed and had accumulated a reasonable stockpile of food.

At 6.00 on the morning of 12 March 500 prisoners were marched through the gates of the camp and to the station over three kilometres away. Dressed in few clothes, they were made to wait for the train alongside the tracks for two hours in the blustery cold wind. The Ober Lieutenant told them that the journey would take seven days, and that anyone attempting to escape would be shot. The prisoners were handed three days' rations of bread and meat. Eventually, they boarded the train and by the time it reached Bordeaux their bodies had warmed up and they felt slightly more comfortable.

Harper strengthened his resolve to escape in the very near future. He decided to find an opportunity after midnight that night. The clothes he had asked his family to send had not arrived in time and he was still in his Merchant Navy uniform. He pleaded with his colleague Holden, who was wearing a dinner jacket, to swap clothes with him and eventually he agreed. Harper then packed his food and belongings as tightly and neatly as he could into a sack that Stewart had found him so that they could be carried easily. Finally, he prepared for the coming days by eating the three days' rations he had received.

There were others who planned to escape that night and Harper was in contact with them. They were Howlett and Ross Dunshea, also of the *Maimoa*, and Robert Bellew of the *Nowshera*. Howlett and Dunshea were Australian and they were strong swimmers.

Bellew was born in 1914 in northwest Spain, in the port town of El Ferrol on the northern shore of the Bay of El Ferrol. His father was Irish, his mother Spanish. Naturally he spoke Spanish having grown up in Spain, but he could also speak French. How useful his French was soon to be! He played football and hockey and was a good boxer: at the age of fifteen he had fought opponents of twenty-six and twenty-seven years old. He was very proud of the fact that he had been baptized aboard the British warship HMS *Cochrane* when he was a child.

With the outbreak of the Spanish Civil War in July 1936 the Bellew family had decided to flee to England. Bellew had swum out to a British destroyer anchored in the Bay and asked for his family to be taken on board. He had ended up arranging not only for his family but also for all the local British residents to be evacuated by the destroyer. Bellew had settled with his family near Liverpool and worked on the assembly line at the Vickers plant. He longed to see the world and so had joined the crew of the *Nowshera* of the British India Steam Navigation Company as an engineer in 1940. On 18 November that year the *Nowshera* had been captured in the Indian Ocean near Australia and he had been taken prisoner.

For a group of people to risk their lives escaping in a foreign land together, first and foremost all must be physically fit and quick-witted. A command of the language would be a bonus. Harper, who was one to consider matters carefully, was naturally cautious in selecting his escape companions. Although no doubt luck was on his side, the other conditions for success were also all in place.

One aspect in which Harper and the other escapees were fortunate was that, whether by chance or by some deliberate policy, they were accommodated in a passenger carriage along with the prisoners of officer rank. The other ratings were treated like cattle or worse, crammed into box-like wagons with no windows. As Walker points out, it would have been impossible for anyone to escape from one of those wagons. Conditions in the wagons were appalling. The toilet consisted of a hole in the boards and the prisoners withstood the bitter cold by all huddling together. Walker attempted to escape from the German POW camp but was soon caught and as a result squandered his right as a minor to an early repatriation.

The Escape Over the Pyrenees

Let us now refer to Harper's memoirs to trace in detail his 1000-kilometres escape through France and over the Pyrenees.

There were forty German guards on the train. They were extremely vigilant, patrolling up and down the train whenever it stopped and putting their heads out of the windows and standing on the running boards whenever it slowed down. It was clear that an escape would be difficult. Harper and the other three took it in turns to discreetly keep watch. They considered the positions of the guards, the speed of the train, the surrounding landscape, and the distance to unoccupied territory in order to determine the optimum spot to jump off the train.

At around 1.30, the train dropped its speed to about fifty kilometres per hour apparently to take a bend. Harper nudged Howlett, whose head was out of the window, and urged, 'Now or never.' Howlett just replied, 'OK,' and opened the door and dived out. Harper jumped out next, and Dunshea and Bellew followed. Harper's head struck a large stone, and his whole body temporarily felt numb. He lay still on the ballast by the track until the train's tail-lights disappeared from view. He then moved his limbs and found that, thankfully, he had not broken any bones. The other three were bruised all over and felt considerable pain, but they had not sustained any broken bones or other injuries that would impede their movement. It seems that they were at a spot about forty kilometres north-north-east of Tours in central France.

Another train came from the opposite direction so the men lay flat until it had passed and was out of sight. Then they rushed up the railway bank and cut across fields heading due east. Presently they spotted a forest and walked towards it with the intention of sleeping there for a while, only to find that there was a German military camp there. They quickly hid in the shadow of a hedge and then crawled to the main road. After walking along the road for some time they came to a house in front of which were two German soldiers on sentry duty. By the time they had noticed the soldiers it was too late to flee or hide but somehow they were able to pass them without being challenged. Later, they learnt that a curfew was in force from 22.00 to 6.00 so they were extremely lucky – quite bafflingly so – not to have been apprehended. A little later they found another wood and slept there fitfully until dawn.

When the group awoke at 5.00 their whole bodies were stiff and cold, their clothes were rigid from the frost, and they were thoroughly uncomfortable. They ate a little of their food and then proceeded in a southeasterly direction. They were sure that by doing so they would cross the boundary into unoccupied territory, which would be their first definite step towards freedom. As they walked through Blois, a tourist town surrounded by chateaux on the river Loire, a German officer greeted them in French. They started momentarily but Bellew managed a reply, also in French. The men continued past St Gervais-la-Forêt and towards a village named Cellettes. Just outside this village a local farmer stopped Harper and Bellew and said that from their gaunt faces he recognized them as prisoners of war on the run. He told them that if they continued along the same road they would reach St Aignan which was on the frontier.

The men walked on through Cormery and to Contres. On the way they encountered hundreds of German soldiers. One German vehicle passed the men three times and its driver was looking at them suspiciously, so they hid among some trees until he had gone. Just before they reached Contres they were stopped by two gendarmes who asked to see their papers. Bellew explained their situation truthfully, upon which the gendarmes asked for their autographs and released them without charge, having repeatedly impressed upon them that the next large river they would come to was the border. The men decided to spend the night in a wood between Contres and St Romain. They made a bed of spruce boughs and bracken and lay as close together as possible under a single blanket. They were warm and comfortable that night in spite of the heavy frost.

The following morning, the men rose at 8.00 and resumed their journey. They asked the way from a woman they met on the road and she told them to avoid St Aignan as the German command headquarters were based there. So after passing through St Romain the men took a country lane to their right which led them to the west of St Aignan. After walking a further two hours or so they reached the brow of a hill from where they could see the river in the distance. As far as they could tell it was not a very wide river and all apart from Harper were eager to cross it at once.

For some reason Harper felt they should proceed with great caution and eventually he persuaded the others to hide and wait until nightfall. They hid in a copse of spruce trees at the top of a nearby hill, amongst dense undergrowth of briar and bracken. They kept very still and quiet so as not to disturb the birds, which could have alerted an observant person. They nibbled on some biscuits and dozed, waiting until it was dark.

Thinking of his imminent freedom as the day passed, Harper's excitement rose to a level he had never before felt. He expected to experience many difficulties and worries even in unoccupied territory, but he knew that at least he would be free from the constant fear of recapture. He could not help but compare his position with that of his 500 fellow prisoners whom he had left behind on the train, which must have been by then well into Germany and close to its destination.

Late in the afternoon, Harper and the others prepared an eight-foot long spruce branch with which to determine the depth of the river. They placed their watches in a tin and made a watertight seal by melting an old inner tube, to avoid ruining them in the river as they depended on their sale to buy food. At last the sun set and they emerged from the thicket and crossed the fields towards the river. It appeared to be just over one-hundred-metres wide.

The water was extremely cold and its flow was very fast. Even Howlett and Dunshea, who were strong swimmers, deemed it too dangerous to swim across. Harper was anxious to cross the river that night no matter what, and was prepared to use any means to access a boat. There were a number of boatmen living nearby. The men asked one of them to take them across the river but he was too afraid of the German patrol to do so. All the boats were locked up in boathouses so the men could not casually borrow one either. They thought there was a chance that one of the Germans' boats might have been left unsecured somewhere and they searched but were disappointed.

As they continued to look around, the men found a small homemade punt by a waterlogged area, secured to a sapling with a chain and padlock. They worked in relays trying to cut the sapling down with a table knife. Suddenly, Bellew said, 'Look!' and the others started thinking that he had spotted a German. However, he was just holding a nail file that he had found in his pocket. Howlett used it to pick the padlock in just two or three minutes.

The men tore the planks from the foredeck of the punt and used them as paddles. When they came to a swamp thick with trees, it became extremely difficult to proceed and at times they sank up to their waists. It was a tremendous challenge to their fatigued bodies but after about five hours of struggle they arrived at a more open stretch of water. By the time they reached the river bank seven hours had passed since they had first found the punt. Dawn was approaching and the landscape was covered by a low mist that gave everything a sinister appearance. Every tree stump and bush seemed to take on the aspect of a German soldier. Once afloat on the river they were able to cross in about fifteen minutes. They did not feel any pangs of guilt for having stolen the punt; they were just overjoyed to have succeeded in crossing the frontier, at 4.00 on 15 March.

With their backs to the river the men began to walk. About two hours after sunrise their clothes had dried. By then they were all on the verge of collapse. They decided to ask for some food and a place to rest at the next farm they happened upon. Its owner proved to be one of life's natural gentlemen. He gave them a delicious breakfast of toasted bread with cream poured over it. Once they had eaten their fill, he gave them some strong brandy to help them on their way to a neighbouring village, where he said there was somebody who could assist them. He took them to this village, Orbigny, which was about twenty minutes walk away, and introduced them to the mayor.

The mayor was a very old woman and she was extremely kind. Both her husband and her son had been taken prisoner by the Germans and she had no idea where they were. She told the four men that someone who could speak English would arrive shortly. The man who arrived was a lawyer named André Aubier who had formerly lived in Paris. Prior to the occupation, he had held a senior position in the French Ministry of Colonies. He did not reveal much else of his background but the men noticed that he had considerable influence over both the civil and military authorities. He asked the men for all details such as their nationalities, occupations and the course of their escape, and arranged for them to stay in his care instead of going to the police station.

The mayor prepared a delicious meal for the four men, and then let them sleep in her orchard until the late afternoon. When they awoke, some children, who had been watching them with curiosity, scattered in every direction. The men took baths and shaved and felt very much refreshed. They dined at the mayor's house again that evening, this time joined by Aubier. Aubier then took them to the local wine shop and introduced them to the men of the village. That night they slept in beds for the first time in four months and relished their very comfortable rest. The following day, Aubier took them to a village named Montrésor. They received a very warm welcome from the residents with whom they drank and sang all evening. They were even presented with a gift of 400 francs.

The next morning, Aubier woke the four men early and took them to Loches by train. There he handed the men over to his friend who was an officer of the French secret service. This man provided them with train tickets to Marseilles, ration cards and eighty francs each. All he asked for was their word that they would report to the French military headquarters in Marseilles. They arrived on 18 March. They went to the military headquarters as instructed, where the Commandant listened to their accounts of their ordeals with great sympathy. They were accommodated in the officers' quarters and treated extremely well. After three days they were permitted to visit the American consulate, which at that time had charge of British interests in France. The consulate issued them with papers granting them freedom of movement within the city limits. It required written statements of their experiences which they duly submitted. Another fugitive, Harry Rabin, a trimmer of the Port Wellington, also happened to be in Marseilles at that time, and he too submitted a statement.

The five men's testaments dated 30 March 1941 documented both their first-hand experiences and what they had heard from their fellow captives aboard the *Atlantis* and the *Storstad*. Regarding them as information sources of great worth, the Consul General, Hugh S. Fullerton, sent the accounts to the American embassy in London. Its Naval Attaché, Captain C.A. Lockwood, Jr. analysed and edited them, and on 3 May reported their content to the Intelligence Division of the Office of Chief of Naval Operations at the Navy Department in Washington with a cover note pointing out their exceptionally interesting and valuable nature.[1]

This report included a multitude of detailed facts including the raiders' structure, armaments, means of camouflage and typical methods of attack. It also documented the nature of the damage inflicted by the raiders on several ships and the numbers of casualties and their names. These ships included the *Storstad*, the

Nowshera, the *Maimoa*, the *Port Brisbane*, the *Domingo de Llarinaga*, the *British Commander* and the *Benavon*. Much other information was incorporated in the report including details of conditions aboard the *Storstad*. It can be presumed that this valuable information was shared with the Royal Navy without delay. It seems that around this time the Royal Navy had already established with considerable accuracy the circumstances surrounding the sinking of the *Automedon* and the course of subsequent events through the information it had gathered independently combined with that supplied by the American forces.

A particularly notable inclusion in this report in relation to the *Automedon* is the fact that, had the *Automedon* changed course and attempted to escape the *Atlantis*, the latter would not have pursued her for long as she would have come too close to land. It is recorded that the surviving crew of the *Automedon* were sickened to hear this revelation from Rogge. It is said that Rogge frequently invited the captains and senior officers in his captivity to his cabin and liked to share a drink and chat with them. He must have let slip this information regarding the *Automedon* on one such occasion when Stewart was present.

Following their stay at the French military headquarters, the four fugitives were accommodated at the Seamen's Mission. Its minister, the Reverend Donald Caskie, was a man of remarkable character and he was very hospitable. They covered the cost of their stay at the Mission with money borrowed from the US consulate. During this period they became acquainted with a man who said he could help them cross the border into Spain. True to his diligent nature, Harper immediately began building up his strength by eating carefully and following a demanding exercise regime, as he knew the crossing of the Pyrenees would not be easy.

The men needed to decide who would make the journey over the Pyrenees first. Bellew said he was happy to be the last, so the others tossed a coin and it was decided that Harper and Dunshea would leave first, followed by Howlett. They did not hear from their contact for some time, but then on 9 April they received a message to go to the railway station for 11.30. When Harper and Dunshea arrived, a complete stranger handed them train tickets. As they boarded the train they felt great relief to be another step closer to freedom. Harper put his ticket inside the lining of his hat as all his pockets had holes in them. When they changed trains at Tarascon his hat was blown under the incoming train. He had no money to buy a new ticket so he dived under the train and retrieved his hat moments before it started to move. With the alarmed station staff and police shouting at him, he leaped onto the train as it pulled away.

Harper and Dunshea alighted from the train at its terminus, Perpignan. There they made contact with their guide. He took them to a wood of cork trees in the foothills of the Pyrenees, where four British soldiers were also waiting to be taken across the border. A team of smugglers arrived and led the climb over the mountains. The party walked all night, and at dawn they went to sleep in a pigsty in a windswept valley of stunted oak trees. It was extremely cold and had it not been for the cover afforded by the pigsty some of the group would have certainly died of exposure. They rose at 17.00 and resumed their journey, walking through the night until 6.00. This time they slept in a small shed. The pace set by the leader was gruelling and all the fugitives apart from Harper were almost completely exhausted. Thanks to the training he had subjected himself to Harper had surprising levels of energy in reserve. The men saw on a map that they had climbed 4,000 feet to cross the mountains. On the morning of 13 April they finally entered Spain. Harper believed that his 1000-kilometres escape had brought him to freedom at last.

The Continuing Days of Hardship

Howlett left Marseilles two weeks after Harper and Dunshea had reached Spain. Finally, Bellew, armed with a cycling map, embarked on the mountain trek alone. He travelled by train to Perpignan where he spent the night, and took a bus to a village in the foothills the following day. He traversed the mountains enduring hunger, a fall into a river and a thunderstorm that soaked him through.

Returning to the Reverend Caskie of the Seamen's Mission, he had been sent to Marseilles by the Church of Scotland. The man who helped the fugitives cross the border into Spain almost certainly belonged to an organization based in Marseilles led by Captain C.P. Murchie of the British army. This organization's purpose was to extricate British servicemen who had been stranded in France following the evacuation from Dunkirk or who had been taken prisoner and had subsequently escaped, and it possessed considerable funds. Harper and Bellew recall that the organization had formed a highly-effective rescue network through contacts in the French

Resistance and the Vichy government. However its activities were eventually detected by the Gestapo which then applied pressure on the Vichy government. As a result the group was forced to withdraw from Marseilles in April 1941. It seems that Howlett accompanied them on this occasion.

The first settlement in Spain all the fugitives stopped at was the old town of Figueras, the birthplace of the artist Salvador Dali who produced many famous works such as *Prémonition de la Guerre*. Here they were all promptly arrested for entering the country illegally. Barely had they had the chance to savour their freedom when once again they found themselves in captivity. Spain at this time was under the dictatorship of General Franco that followed her civil war. The Spanish Civil War had been triggered in 1936 by uprisings of the army led by Franco and other right-wing forces against the newly-formed Popular Front government. It had ended in 1939 with the victory of Franco's forces which had received the support of Hitler and Mussolini.

In this political context relations between Spain and the Allies were strained. However, the latter sought to prevent Spain aligning herself with Germany as Italy had done, and with this agenda provided her with economic aid. Already debilitated by the civil war, Spain was economically hard-hit by the war in Europe and was in need of wheat and other food supplies. Britain, which governed Gibraltar, the strategically vital gateway to the Mediterranean, and which wished Spain to remain neutral to facilitate her intelligence activities against Germany, could not afford to take her eyes off Franco's regime. Using both the carrot and the stick, she struggled to tune her relationship with Spain. One course of action open to Britain was to pre-empt Germany's influence by occupying Spain. The British Ambassador in Madrid urged London to appoint a commander and undertake preparations for this operation as soon as possible.

Spain, like its neutral neighbour Portugal, was a battleground for the Allied and Axis secret services. The Gestapo was of course very active. In particular, it constantly requested that the Spanish security forces clamp down on the illegal entry into Spain of fugitive British prisoners from France and to arrest and deport undesirable Allied nationals. Under such circumstances many British were wrongfully detained or expelled. In particular, British secret agents sent to Barcelona and other cities under the guise of consulate staff were targeted.

Even if it was to be expected that Harper and the other escapees would be arrested for illegal entry as soon as they arrived in Spain, ordinarily the British consulate would have become involved and promptly resolved the situation. At this time, however, long periods of detention had become the norm, which turned out to be the case for the four fugitives. Harper and Dunshea were arrested by the Civil Guard as soon as they entered Figueras's railway station to board the 5.00 train to Barcelona as instructed by the smugglers, and were promptly imprisoned. All their money was taken from them, yet they were told that they would have to buy their own food.

After being imprisoned at Cervera to the west of Barcelona for fifteen days, Harper and Dunshea were transported for thirty-six hours in a cattle-truck to a concentration camp at Miranda de Ebro. There, using bribery and other means, the men managed to make contact with the British Naval Attaché, Captain A.H. Hillgarth in Madrid. The Attaché sent an official to the camp, who seemed disappointed to discover that Harper and Dunshea were merchant seamen and not naval personnel. However, he had brought with him a briefcase full of cash, which he used to bribe the camp's governor and staff before leaving. Spain's economy was severely damaged by the civil war immediately followed by the war in Europe and her people were struggling to live. As a result, everywhere the smallest bribes were openly offered and accepted and proved highly effective.

Through the mediation of the British embassy Harper and Dunshea were at last released on 29 May. They reported to the embassy where they were thoroughly deloused before being taken to Gibraltar in the embassy's minibus the following day. They arrived on the 31st, and were provided with new clothes and asked to report on their experiences of the preceding months. They travelled to Glasgow on a liner and finally arrived on 26 June. Their epic voyage of trials and hardship following the sinking of the *Automedon* had lasted 228 days.

MILAG: The Prison Camp for Merchant Seamen

On 18 March 1941, the 500 or so prisoners including the thirty-five crew and passengers of the *Automedon* arrived at a concentration camp at Sandbostel approximately fifteen kilometres south of Bremervörde to the west of Hamburg. This was the time that

Harper and the other three fugitives were aboard the train to Marseilles having successfully escaped from the prison train just past Tours. The prisoners' long days of captivity, which would last over four years until the camp was liberated by British forces on 28 April 1945, had begun.

The Sandbostel camp had been built to inter civilian prisoners from Eastern Europe, and the naval captives were detained alongside them. Within the site there were two sailors' compounds, MARLAG, which held Royal Navy personnel, and MILAG, which housed merchant seamen. They were adjacent but were two distinct prisons. They were both segregated from the rest of the camp by barbed-wire fencing. The Germans' treatment of the East Europeans was far worse than that of the seamen: their aim was to starve them to death. The British prisoners, who witnessed the barbarity across the fence, threw over pieces of bread and whatever else they could offer while the guards were not looking. Though their own food was far from plentiful they could not bear the sight of the blank-eyed Russians and Poles crippled with hunger and slumped on the ground.

Following complaints from the US (which represented British interests) and the International Red Cross about the conditions at MARLAG and MILAG, the German authorities moved these two compounds to the village of Westertimke about twenty kilometres away between the autumn of 1941 and the following spring. Westertimke lies on the road from Bremen to Hamburg between Tarmstadt and Zeven and is one of several villages in the area whose names end with '-timke'. The land in this region is generally an infertile mixture of sand and clay, and peat is also found beneath the surface. There was a disused Luftwaffe camp at Westertimke but this was inadequate for accommodating the Allied seamen. The buildings of the Sandbostel compounds were therefore dismantled and rebuilt on the site of the Luftwaffe camp. As the construction progressed, the prisoners were gradually transferred. At this new camp dedicated to British prisoners, the Royal Navy and Merchant Navy personnel were again clearly segregated. By February 1942, the camp, consisting of thirty barrack blocks, a medical facility, recreation rooms, kitchens, wash blocks, toilets and a sports field, was complete.

During the Second World War, approximately 5,000 Allied merchant seamen were captured by the German Navy and, of these, around 4,500 were interned at MILAG in Westertimke. The majority were of course British, but many nationalities were found among the prisoners reflecting the traditions of the British Empire's merchant fleet. Almost thirty countries were represented, including Norway, Brazil, Canada, China, Malaya, India, the Philippines and Poland. Interestingly there were four Japanese among the detainees. One of them, Kenji Takaki, had been a crewmember of the *Domingo de Llarinaga* captured by the raider *Pinguin*. In the evenings, the MILAG's classroom block was transformed into a casino. Those fond of gambling hired tables from the Entertainments Committee and ran poker and roulette tables among many other games, and earned money (in *campgeld*). The most well-known and highly regarded of these gambling entrepreneurs was Takaki. He earned a vast amount of *campgeld* but when he heard that the POW Exchange Commission would only honour £30 worth of it he is said to have divided the remainder of his fortune among many of his fellow prisoners.

Takaki was born in Fukuoka Prefecture in Japan. When he was still young, he had been inspired by the success story of his friend's older brother who had moved abroad, and decided to follow his example. Eventually, he had reached Liverpool and had attempted to get work on British ships as a machine operator but had failed. He had liked England and had found it an easy place to find work and to live, so he had taken the major step of obtaining a British passport. He had lived in Liverpool and worked on various ships until he was taken prisoner. On his return to England after the war he moved to London and spent the rest of his life appearing in West End shows and in films. He is no longer alive but his wife still lives in London. Even all those years ago there were Japanese of humble origin like Takaki, albeit rare, who made a success of themselves overseas through their audacity, wit and character. The other three Japanese nationals who were held at MILAG have also since died.

There was much sporting activity at the camp, in the form of football, cricket, boxing and ice skating. From 1942 onwards, American seamen joined the camp and consequently baseball boomed. The Red Cross sent the necessary equipment, and it became a popular sport even among the British prisoners. A number of teams were created and friendly matches were played accompanied by lively support from the spectators. Ferguson, meanwhile, belonged to the cricket club. An orchestra was formed and performed concerts, while the prison theatre staged plays.

These activities provided some comfort to the captives. A library was also set up with books donated from Britain and America via the Red Cross. The prisoners also contributed the books sent by their families once they had read them. The library even had a designated librarian and a repairer and binder of books.

The camp was also like a large school. The senior officers ran various courses following official syllabuses to help those wishing to pursue their seafaring careers in the future to pass the Board of Trade examinations for advancement. Stewart was again the navigation teacher. He constructed a Deviascope from materials he had to hand, to teach the principles of adjusting and boxing a compass. A fine working model of a 'Jumbo derrick', a mast and heavy lifting boom, was created with the help of the carpenters to teach cargo handling. Other subjects taught included algebra, geometry and languages. Again, with the help of the Red Cross, the prisoners were able to obtain textbooks and receive the examination papers from the Board of Trade in London, and to sit the examinations at the camp. In 1944, 106 candidates took the exams for the grades of Captain and Mate. All those who took the captaincy exam were successful. The overall pass rate was 75%, which was a testament to the efforts of both the teachers and the students.

These insights into life at MILAG reveal that the treatment of the merchant seamen was relatively liberal compared to that meted out to the Jews, Russians, Poles and criminals in the concentration camps established elsewhere in Germany and the territories under her occupation such as the Channel Islands, and that there were few cases of abuse or violence on the part of the German soldiers running the camp. In a large collection of humanity under the control of German guards, it was natural for rules to be broken and for incidents of theft or fighting to occur. It was common for prisoners to steal food from delivery vehicles, and it was not unusual for them to pilfer Red Cross relief parcels from storage.

The Hague and Geneva conventions, which were concerned with the treatment of prisoners of war, had been ratified in 1907 and 1929 respectively. They also addressed the treatment of captured merchant seamen: in principle, they were to be released provided they pledged in writing not to participate in combat. However, during the Second World War, Germany deemed this principle impossible to apply under the actual circumstances and interned merchant seamen in POW camps while treating them as civilian prisoners. This meant that the captive officers were not paid, but prison meals were chargeable, and that there was no forced labour for the ratings and any work they undertook was paid for. The British, on the other hand, treated enemy merchant seamen as prisoners of war and accordingly held them in POW camps. The British Ministry of Transport sent, via the International Red Cross, monthly pocket money to the value of £2 to every officer, £1 to every European rating and 10 (old) pence to every non-European crewman held in Germany.

Officially the prisoners at MILAG were not obliged to work against their will, but in reality the younger ratings were more or less coerced into cleaning and waste-disposal work, peat-digging, timber-felling and farm work. This was especially the case in winter when there were few volunteers. As they were considered to require little supervision, the Chinese prisoners were sent to work in Hamburg and other cities where there was a shortage of labour. Young Walker was often forced to dig peat for ten hours a day and he missed out on the various classes held at the prison that he wanted to attend.

In spite of the chronic malnutrition, overcrowding and poor sanitation, overall the prisoners' health was relatively good. The ten or so military and Merchant Navy doctors and other helpers contributed to maintaining this standard of health. The greatest threat was from tuberculosis. Its incidence had always been high on board the poorly-ventilated ships and also in the barracks where it spread rapidly for the same reason. The German authorities became concerned and dispatched extra doctors to the camp as well as implementing an X-ray screening programme for 3,000 men and taking other preventative measures. As a result the epidemic was brought under control. Thanks to a highly skilled surgeon, Major Robert Harvey of the Royal Army Medical Corps, being among the prisoners, operations for hernias and other ailments could be carried out at the camp's hospital. As he had done at Sandbostel, Dr Sperber of the *Automedon* worked hard to prevent and treat contagious diseases in the early days when there was a dearth of medicines and sanitation materials. The camp also had a dental treatment facility to which there was a constant stream of patients.

There was a chronic shortage of food at the camp and inevitably prisoners frequently fell ill as their immune systems were weakened by malnourishment. It was owing to Britain, Canada, India and other countries supplying food in the form of Red Cross parcels that the shortages did not lead to actual starvation. It is thought that up to 80% of the prisoners' food was provided in this way and the parcels were evidently crucial to their survival. Between 1939 and 1945, the British Red Cross alone dispatched more than nineteen million food parcels and 1,600,000 parcels for the sick from twenty-three packaging centres around Britain.

Though in theory they expected prisoners to pay for their own food, it seems the German authorities could not deny the importance of the Red Cross food supplies. Although disruptions to their transportation occurred at times due to wider circumstances, it seems the Germans did not obstruct the delivery of the Red Cross parcels or tamper with their contents. In any case, in reality, it was impossible for prisoners to pay for their own meals and the German authorities did provide them with fixed quantities of food. Parcels from the prisoners' families also reached the camp, though not always without hitches. Needless to say, they fulfilled an important function in boosting the morale of the detainees, and equally they were a crucial source of clothes and daily sundries. The Germans scrutinized these parcels to ensure they were not being misused but on occasions all manner of escape equipment was contained in them. The prisoners were always very pleased to receive chocolate and tobacco as they were coveted items when bartering with the local farmers and prison guards for other food and goods.

In terms of clothing, there were as many different outfits as there were prisoners. Many detainees were in the clothes they had been wearing the day their ships had been attacked. The prisoners used anything they could get hold of that would protect their bodies and keep them warm. Sometimes they were given military uniforms and boots from various countries riddled with bullet holes, presumably recovered from the battlefields. Walker searched for any garment among these that might just be small enough to fit him. On one occasion this was a Yugoslavian army uniform that was full of holes and falling apart. It was still too big for him, as were his shoes, but he had no choice but to make do with them. The prisoners often turned the blankets sent by the Red Cross into overcoats. For those planning to escape in particular, an overcoat was indispensable.

A shop was established at the camp and it was managed by a committee independently formed by some of the prisoners. The committee was permitted to buy in supplies from the surrounding towns and villages and its members were allowed to leave the camp in one of the German lorries in order to procure their stock. When they obtained luxury items like eggs, ham and fruit they were then able to make a profit on them in the shop. The committee kept full accounts and carried out audits, and the shop was regarded as a business and its profits were subject to tax.

It is natural for a prolonged period in an abnormal environment to put a man under severe psychological strain, especially one that allows virtually no personal freedoms and forces a large group of people with diverse ideas, interests, personalities and habits to live together, as well as the forced separation from home, family and friends. Added to this was the harsh reality that there was no guarantee even of the food needed to stay alive and healthy. Inevitably, many could not withstand life at MILAG and lost their mental and physical balance in all kinds of ways. Very few who escaped actually made it home. Without exception, for the prisoners the day of their release could not come too soon.

The Liebenau Internment Camp for Women

Violet Ferguson was taken from Bordeaux to the Sandbostel concentration camp on the prison train along with her husband Alan. However, she was promptly separated from him and during the following months, endured being transferred eight times between different prison facilities. In the late autumn, she was taken to a women's internment camp at Liebenau approximately eight kilometres south of Ravensburg in southwestern Germany, where she could settle for the first time. In a press interview[2] she gave following her repatriation in March 1943, she revealed that the most unpleasant and difficult period was that prior to her arrival at Liebenau. Perhaps the bad experiences took their toll, for it seems Violet Ferguson did not harbour much fondness for German people and rarely spoke of her life in Germany to her family.

The institution at Liebenau was a Catholic care home for the elderly and the disabled, including children, with a long and proud history. Run by the Liebenau Foundation it still fulfils its mission today. In the autumn of 1939 approximately half of its inmates, a few hundred non-Jewish German men and women, had been taken away in buses over a period of four or five days, to a camp near Stuttgart where they had been killed. Their clothes had been sent back to Liebenau. Their relatives had been sent notifications of their deaths that cited various illnesses as the cause and offered to send their ashes if desired. The victims, who included children, had been carrying out all manner of jobs at Liebenau. It is said that some had had a foreboding of the fate that awaited them and had been terrified. They were casualties of the Nazis' pursuit of racial perfection.

When the first buses had arrived many of the inmates had had little idea of where they were going or what was going to happen and they had not been particularly anxious, but their fear had soon grown and turned into terror. The nuns had realized what was taking place and wept with heartfelt sorrow.[3] As a result of this tragedy there was room at Liebenau to accommodate the Allied prisoners. About forty nuns, who had come from Poland to work at the institution, took care of the detainees. Violet Ferguson would have probably heard from the nuns about the tragic event that had taken place there two years previously. Incidentally, the nuns' altruistic service continued to be deeply appreciated long after the war, not only by the internees but also by their children and grandchildren. Two or three of those nuns are alive and well in convents today. It would seem that Violet Ferguson became involved in social work once back in England largely as a result of seeing the work of the nuns at Liebenau.

At any time during the Second World War, 300 to 500 women and children from Allied countries were held at the Liebenau camp. Today, there are a number of buildings both old and new in extensive grounds. During the war, animals were reared and vegetables and fruit trees were cultivated on site, enabling the facility to be self-sufficient. Thanks to the nuns' agricultural work, Liebenau was never plagued by serious food shortages. In the inspection report published by the International Red Cross on 12 June 1942, it is stated that the meals at Liebenau, like its medical care, were very satisfactory. Aside from suffering the separation from their families and being afflicted with homesickness, the internees were able to lead a relatively peaceful life that was comfortable by wartime standards. This can immediately be detected in the photographs of Mrs Ferguson and her friends at the camp. There was one occasion when the German authorities crammed all the British detainees into the cellar in response to what they alleged was the sub-standard treatment of German women and children at a British camp in the Caribbean, but this did not last long.

In spring and summer, the grounds of Liebenau were full of riotously blooming flowers painstakingly grown by the nuns. The internees could walk freely amongst them and exercise in their own way and keep fit. Though they were accompanied by guards they were also allowed to go out in groups, for walks in the hills and fields around the camp or to shop in the nearby town of Ravensburg. Dental treatment was available at the camp but the waiting time was very long, during which all that the women could do was read. There was also a shoe repair man onsite. No matter how hard he worked there was always a waiting list of at least three months to have any footwear fixed. About six detainees shared one room. There were communal toilets and bathrooms, which were supplied with hot water four hours of the day, on each floor of each block. Each internee was permitted to take one bath in two weeks. They were required to do their own washing and were rationed with one bar of soap a month each for this purpose.[4]

The women were allowed to send three letters and four postcards a month. There was a library within the facility and a range of courses was run, on subjects including English, German, French, English literature, the sciences, shorthand, handicrafts and folk dancing. The internees distracted themselves from their loneliness by joining interest groups, or organizing concerts or nativity plays. They even produced a Theatre Variety show under the direction of a professional actress from the London stage who happened to be among them. Violet Ferguson's name is included in one of the nativity play programmes, as she was in charge of the costumes. With her needlework expertise, she made garments from all kinds of materials. For the detainees who only had a few clothes, she made coats out of blankets and undertook repairs. She herself wanted for little in terms of clothes, including warm garments essential for the cold German winters, or other personal items, thanks to having had her trunks safely recovered from the *Automedon*. There was no way that she could have known at this time that secret British Cabinet papers had fallen into the hands of the enemy because of these trunks.

There is an old manor house in the centre of the grounds at Liebenau. One of its wings has been rebuilt and is of a modern design, but the rest is a heavy and sedate stone structure that still evokes the 1930s and 1940s. Violet Ferguson's room was on one of the floors of this old building. The interior is predominantly wooden, which gives a solid and settled atmosphere, and features fine pieces of furniture. A solemn air fills the magnificent chapel, whose ceiling is covered with a Fuger painting. One can easily picture the detainees uttering their prayers during the masses held here.

There are hills at the back of the Liebenau estate, and at the front the land gently slopes downwards to give a view of the Bodensee on a fine day. As stated in the reports produced by the Red Cross and the American embassy staff at the time, the camp was in an idyllic environment where the scenery is beautiful and the soul is soothed. There is something about the tone of the church bells, which are still tolled here everyday, that calms the heart. How must those bells have comforted the women as they bore their loneliness and their yearning for home.

8

The *Atlantis* Meets Her End in the South Atlantic

The Atlantis's *Last Christmas*

AFTER DISPATCHING THE *Automedon* and sending the *Ole Jacob* to Japan the *Atlantis's* condition deteriorated. She was now running low on drinking water and her engines were in need of an extensive overhaul. To find a place where he could take on fresh water and carry out maintenance work, while giving his men some rest over Christmas, Rogge carefully analysed the seized sailing orders, the information he had gained from the captains he had taken prisoner and the topography of various areas. He decided on the Kerguélens, a group of French islands close to the Antarctic Ocean at latitude 49.15 degrees south, longitude 69.10 degrees east. The Kerguélen Islands are extremely cold and they were not an ideal place for rest and recuperation, but there was no alternative safe refuge in the area. The islands had been discovered by a Frenchman in 1772 and they had only ever been visited by explorers, whalers and seal hunters. Past attempts at establishing a settlement there by one adventurer or another had failed and the islands were completely uninhabited.

From the secret meeting place 'Tulip' the *Atlantis* steamed non-stop in a southeasterly direction with Parsons, Hendry and one other POW on board. Hendry was convalescing from the amputation of his right leg below the knee. On 14 December, her crew were able to make out the Kerguélens in the distance. By that time Parsons was able to get up and was allowed to walk around on deck. He remembers coming across Captain Rogge who was walking his dog 'Ferry'. They exchanged friendly greetings and each time Rogge did not fail to enquire how he was recovering. He does not hesitate to say that Rogge was a first-class gentleman. He also found his Adjutant Mohr, the doctors and other staff/crew well disciplined, fair and kind enough. They were well-trained professionals doing their duty for their country. They were different from those German soldiers whom he would meet later. Parsons recalls that the surgery was fully equipped and modern. There were two operating tables and in the adjoining sick ward there were six beds. He was looked after and fed very well with food from the nearby galley.

Once she reached the islands the *Atlantis* searched for a suitable anchorage. Her crew carefully sounded the water depths and marked her path as she proceeded slowly through a field of floating seaweed but suddenly she ran into a pinnacle of rock that jutted out from the sea floor. This caused a section at the bottom of the ship to be flooded. For a time the situation was extremely worrying and Rogge even donned a diving suit and after a short lesson in the art of diving went underwater to investigate the damage for himself. After a prolonged struggle, the *Atlantis* at last freed herself from the rock on 16 December. The relief was beyond expression. The crew forced out the seawater with compressed air, and repaired the damaged area by dint of sheer hard work in spite of the limited tools and materials at their disposal. This meant that the *Atlantis* was more vulnerable in rough seas than Rogge would have liked. He reported to the Naval Staff 'Maintenance of high speed possible except in bad weather.'[1] It seems that the Royal Navy eventually came to know about this structural weakness, perhaps through the shrewd observation or sharp ears of the prisoners on board.

The taking on of drinking water the *Atlantis* desperately needed was as challenging a task as the repair of the big hole in her hull. Through their inventiveness, resourcefulness and hard work the crewmen managed to connect hoses together over a distance of

900 metres from an inland waterfall to the ship anchored in Gazelle Bay, and to fill her tanks without pumps, relying on the force of gravity alone. They were then all able to celebrate Christmas at their leisure.

While the *Atlantis* took refuge in the Kerguélen Islands, Parsons and other POWs were confined to the sick ward. The Germans were at pains to hide their sheltering place from the prying eyes of the British. Parsons could guess, however, that the ship was at anchor somewhere for rest and supply. He was not aware of the serious accident of the *Atlantis* going aground as he was asleep when it happened. But he learned about it later through his conversation with some of the German crew. The Germans celebrated Christmas in a traditional but somewhat melancholic way in the semi-Antarctic region far away from the motherland. It was more so because of a tragic accident that happened on Christmas Eve. A rating fell to the deck while painting the funnel and sustained a fracture to both thighs. He died five days later. Captain Rogge read the story of the Nativity from the Gospel of St Luke. He played Santa Claus and distributed gifts which contained shoes, pencils, cigarettes and other items which were taken from the Christmas mail found on board the *Automedon*. Even POWs were not left out of this 'generosity'. Parsons remembers being presented with a lady's decorative silk scarf, Australian *Have-a-luck* cigarettes and a bottle of *Evening in Paris* perfume!

While at the Kerguélen Islands the *Atlantis* disguised herself as the *Tamesis* of the Wilhelmsen Line, as Rogge feared the Royal Navy now knew details about his ship through the accounts of the *Ole Jacob*'s crewmen. He picked the *Tamesis* because she was a new vessel built in 1939 whose appearance was not yet widely recognized and whose call sign was not included in the current Lloyd's Register of Shipping. As before, Rogge got into a motor launch and scrupulously inspected the disguise from a distance, and found it to be satisfactory. On 10 January 1941, the *Atlantis* left the Kerguélen Islands and steered north at seven knots later increasing to nine. She resumed hunting in the Indian Ocean on the Capetown-India route on 19 January.

On 24 January, to the east of the Seychelles, the *Atlantis* attacked the *Mandasor* (5,144 tonnes) which was travelling from Calcutta to England via Durban. The *Atlantis* obtained some precious cargo from her prey, including food and machine-guns, before sinking her. On the 31st, she captured the *Speybank* (5,144 tonnes), which was *en route* to New York loaded with raw materials such as teak, manganese, monazite and tea. On 2 February, she took the tanker the *Ketty Brøvig* (7,031 tonnes) with 4,000 tonnes of diesel oil and 6,000 tonnes of other fuel oil. This was the *Atlantis*'s last ever prize in the Indian Ocean.

On 10 February, the *Atlantis* accompanied by the *Speybank* and the *Ketty Brøvig* met the *Tannenfels* (7,800 tonnes) and the Italian submarine *Perla* at a secret rendezvous point east of Madagascar. They both came from Italian Somaliland. The *Tannenfels* was in a bad shape with her hull foul after languishing in Somaliland for many months suffering from every sort of obstacle from the Italian authorities. Built by the same shipbuilder Vulcan Bremen in the late 1930s, the *Atlantis* and the *Tannenfels* were sister ships belonging to the same Bremen Hansa shipping company. Rogge put the *Tannenfels* under his command in addition to the *Ketty Brøvig* and the *Speybank*. On 13 February, the little squadron of four ships commanded by Rogge got under way to meet the so-called pocket battleship *Admiral Scheer* (10,000 tonnes) and the commercial raider *Kormoran* (8,736 tonnes). Two days later, Parsons witnessed the rather impressive sight of a reunion of all these German ships in the area southeast of Madagascar. Soon after, Rogge had the *Tannenfels* sail for Europe with five men as guards over forty-two Englishmen including Parsons from the *Atlantis* as well as sixty-one others. The *Tannenfels* arrived safely at Bordeaux on 19 April. Thus Alex Parsons stepped into his new life as a POW in France and Germany.

On 21 February, towards the end of her operations in the Indian Ocean, to the east of Madagascar, the *Atlantis* pursued a merchant ship for nine hours thinking it to be a Blue Funnel Line vessel. She replied to Rogge's challenge by identifying herself as the Japanese ship *Afrika Maru* and so he let her go. The *Afrika Maru* (9,476 tonnes, 7,890 h.p., 16.3 kt.) had been built by the Japanese Osaka Shōsen Kaisha (OSK Line) at the Mitsubishi shipyard in Nagasaki in 1918 as the First World War was drawing to a close. Initially, she had served routes to North America but from 1931 she had sailed to the east coast of Africa. In 1941, she was requisitioned by the Japanese army and at the start of 1942 she was deployed in the invasion of Ambon and Timor. On 21 October, that year she was sunk by the American submarine *Finback* off the east coast of Taiwan when she and two other ships in convoy were heading for Moji, Japan, with a full load of rice and corn and thirty-eight passengers including some crew members from the NYK ship *Teibōmaru* (4,472 tonnes) sunk on 25 September by an American submarine. In their lifeboat, they survived machine-gun strafing by the attacking submarine, but they were doomed to experience the *Finback*'s attack on the *Afrika Maru*.[2]

The *Atlantis* then looped far south of the Cape of Good Hope and entered the South Atlantic once again. At 4.00 on 17 April, to the south of St Helena, she spotted a vessel that resembled a British merchant ship but which she suspected to be an auxiliary cruiser. The *Atlantis* cautiously tracked this vessel and when visibility began to improve with daybreak at around 6.00 she moved into gun range. To prevent her prey raising the alarm at any cost the *Atlantis* took pre-emptive action and fired a salvo without warning. However, when she approached her sinking victim her crew realized that she was the Egyptian passenger ship *Zamzam* (8,299 tonnes). She was travelling from New York via Baltimore to Alexandria. The majority of her 129 crewmembers were Egyptian and the Captain and the Chief Engineer were British. Among the 202 passengers were seventy-three women and thirty-five children. Of the passengers, 138 were American; they also included twenty-six Canadians, twenty-five British and four Belgians.

The Egyptian crewmembers concentrated on saving themselves and fled in the lifeboats, while many of the passengers were stranded on the deck of the sinking ship or were jumping into the shark-infested sea. Some had taken off their life jackets and floated their children on them, and were desperately trying to swim to the *Atlantis*'s motor launches. As this scene unfolded Rogge became extremely worried that the situation could turn into another *Lusitania* incident, which had directly led to the United States entering the First World War. He, therefore, applied every effort to the rescue of the passengers – especially the women and children – and the treatment of the injured. Miraculously not one life was lost.[3]

The *Atlantis*'s crew left the rescue of the Egyptians until last since they had abandoned the passengers. They ran from cabin to cabin gathering the passengers' possessions and threw them all onto the motor launches and brought them on board the *Atlantis*. There was even a child's tricycle among them. Soon, the *Atlantis*'s deck was covered with piles of clothes and other personal belongings and resembled a jumble sale. The women cried out with delight every time they spotted their own clothes.

In a public relations exercise to give a positive impression to the passengers and especially to the Americans, Rogge invited passengers' representatives to his cabin and explained in detail his perspective on, and reasoning during, the course of events leading to the attack and apologized for causing such trouble for citizens of a neutral country. Among the passengers there happened to be a well-known American journalist Charles Murphy, who was the editor of *Fortune* magazine and a contributor to *Time* and *Life* magazines, and *Life*'s photographer David Scherman. They had been travelling to Africa to cover the war, and had boarded the *Zamzam* at Recife in Brazil. Rogge endeavoured to improve the conditions of the passengers, even by a little, by transferring them all to the German supply ship the *Dresden* within twenty-four hours, and he promised their prompt release and repatriation. He sincerely dedicated all his efforts to deliver this promise.

The *Dresden* parted from the *Atlantis* on 26 April 1941 and steamed north. She rounded the Azores from the west and aimed for Cape Finisterre on Spain's northwest coast. In the small hours of 21 May she arrived at St Jean-de-Luz on the Bay of Biscay in southwest France. There the passengers were freed, and Murphy and Scherman travelled from nearby Biarritz to Lisbon from where they returned to America via Horta in the Azores on board a clipper. They arrived safely on 9 June. Murphy's article on the *Zamzam* incident, published in *Life* on the 23rd, was long, detailed and highly objective yet sympathetic.[4] It contributed to averting a crisis in relations between Germany and America; and how relieved Rogge must have been by this!

However, there was a major twist at the end of this story. Murphy's article was complemented by many of Scherman's vivid and powerful photographs. The large image which headed the feature was a full-length photograph of the *Atlantis*, which he had risked his safety to take from a lifeboat. This was an extremely valuable resource for the Royal Navy and one that the Kriegsmarine would have been desperate to suppress had it known of its existence. Needless to say, the image was sent from New York to London and distributed to the British warships on the frontline in no time.

When Scherman had been rescued by the *Atlantis* his camera had been confiscated and examined, but it had soon been returned intact. This must have been due to Rogge's kindness. Ironically, exactly five months later, the photograph taken by Scherman sealed the fate of the *Atlantis*. It was used by the pilot of the British cruiser HMS *Devonshire*'s spotter plane to identify the *Atlantis* prior to the *Devonshire* surprising her. In contrast to the occasion when he recovered Violet Ferguson's luggage, Rogge would pay dearly for his benevolence.

As we have seen, Lieutenant Kamenz, who had commanded the captured *Ole Jacob* and safely taken the British Cabinet papers to Kōbe, had left Tokyo for Berlin on 6 December 1940. Part of his duty had been to serve as a guard to the diplomatic courier delivering the Cabinet papers to the Nazi leadership. The Soviet authorities had been told in advance that a high-ranking German officer would be travelling on the Trans-Siberian Railway, and Kamenz had enjoyed the lavish hospitality they had laid on during his journey. When he had arrived in Germany for the first time in nine months, he had gone straight to the Naval High Command in Berlin. He had carried out the important tasks Rogge had charged him with, including presenting a detailed report on the *Atlantis*'s operations. He had also conveyed and negotiated on requests from the frontline concerning the schedule for the delivery of supplies, communications, and in particular the preservation of the latter's secrecy, among other matters.

In order to rejoin the *Atlantis*, Kamenz left Germany aboard a U-boat. He then transferred to the *Nordmark*, a supply ship to the raiders, which secretly rendezvoused with the U-boat in mid-Atlantic. The *Nordmark* eventually met with the *Atlantis* in the seas to the north of the Tristan da Cunha Islands in the South Atlantic, 2,800 kilometres to the west of the Cape of Good Hope. Kamenz was able to return to duty on the *Atlantis* on 27 April 1941, approximately five months after he had parted from Rogge and his colleagues. He had made a perilous journey of thousands of kilometres, spanning the Atlantic. However, just seven months later the *Atlantis* was caught and sunk by HMS *Devonshire*. Kamenz would make another epic voyage, aboard a lifeboat, then the supply ship the *Python*, and then on German and Italian submarines, finally arriving at St Nazaire in France at Christmas that year.

The Atlantis *Meets Her End in the South Atlantic*

The *Atlantis* continued to be very active following the *Zamzam* incident. In the South Atlantic she attacked the *Rabaul* (5,618 tonnes) on 14 May, the *Trafalgar* (4,530 tonnes) on 24 May, the *Tottenham* (4,640 tonnes) on 17 June, and the *Balzac* (5,372 tonnes) on 22 June. She then rounded Africa far south of the Cape of Good Hope and followed a long course, across the southern Indian Ocean and south of Australia, emerging into the South Pacific east of New Zealand in September. On the 10th of that month, far to the east of the Kermadec Islands, she took the *Silvaplana* (4,793 tonnes) which was *en route* from Singapore to New York, and seized 120 tonnes of raw rubber.

Rogge planned to end his campaign in the South Pacific on 19 October and to return to the South Atlantic by Cape Horn, where he intended to spend about ten days on engine maintenance and a further ten days hunting for prizes, before returning to Germany by 20 December, just in time for Christmas. Around this time Rogge had come to feel strongly that, faced with the increasing effectiveness of the Royal Navy's defence measures against German submarines and raiders, the *Atlantis*'s future security was far from guaranteed. His presentiment was not misplaced; even the *Atlantis*, mighty hunter of the seas, was nearing her demise.

At the end of October when the *Atlantis* was approaching Cape Horn at the southernmost point of South America, Rogge received news that a U-boat supply ship had sunk off Cape Town. Always willing to come to the rescue, he immediately volunteered the *Atlantis* to be her replacement. The waters around Cape Horn were calm, but it snowed continuously. Rogge considered attacking a whaling vessel but he decided against this as he did not have a chart of the local seas. Two or three days later the *Atlantis* rendezvoused with U-boat 68 as ordered by the Naval High Command, and the two vessels parted company after a few days.

U-boats frequently met with Allied surprise attacks but the surface fleet, including the raiders, had not yet suffered any. However, Rogge was extremely concerned that its codes might have been broken, so he never failed to remove the *Atlantis* to a significantly different location immediately following a meeting with another German vessel of any kind.

Rogge was next ordered to deliver supplies to U-boat 126 at the secret meeting point 'Lily 10' 350 miles northwest of Ascension Island. He was reluctant to carry out this order as the *Atlantis*'s engines were in need of an overhaul. In addition, the supply ship *Python* was shortly due to cross the equator and arrive at her assigned territory around St Helena, and it seemed better to him that she should undertake the duty of supplying the submarine. Perhaps Rogge felt an intuitive foreboding. His fear of being detected and captured by a British warship was soon to become reality. The Royal Navy's heavy cruiser HMS *Devonshire* (9,850 tonnes) refuelled at Simon's Town on the Cape of Good Hope on 12 November 1941. She put to sea after midnight on her patrol course to Freetown in Sierra Leone on the west coast of Africa. Her targets were of course German raiders and supply ships, and in particular the *Atlantis*.

In spite of his misgivings Rogge proceeded to 'Lily 10' as instructed. Before dawn on 22 November the *Atlantis* joined U-boat 126. Her crew immediately got underway with refuelling the submarine and repairing the *Atlantis*'s portside engine. Rogge considered playing safe by moving his ship to a different location using the remaining engine but decided against this, partly because his Chief Engineer Kielhorn reported that one of the pistons needed to be replaced without delay. This was to be a fatal decision, and one that Rogge regretted for years to come.

Once the refuelling pipe had connected the two vessels, Rogge invited the Captain of the U-boat, Lieutenant Commander Bauer, to breakfast. Mohr was still asleep in bed, tormented by his usual nightmare of an enemy attack. At 8.16 the alarm was raised as a three-funnelled silhouette had been sighted.

HMS *Devonshire* had located the *Atlantis* much earlier. At 5.20 that morning she had, as usual, launched her twin-engine seaplane Walrus, to patrol her course ahead and scout for U-boats. The Walrus's crew were forbidden to use the radio unless they spotted an enemy warship, so when they returned to ship at 7.10 they reported a vessel resembling a merchant vessel at latitude 4.21 degrees south, longitude 18.5 degrees west. This was suspected to be a German raider, so the *Devonshire* changed course at once and made haste, steaming at twenty-five knots, to the reported location. At 8.09 her crew sighted the ship and the Walrus was catapulted again at 8.18.[5]

Just a few minutes later, the *Atlantis* was being observed by the Walrus from above and she was cornered. The refuelling pipe and the lines were thrown into the sea instantly and the U-boat dived rapidly, leaving Bauer on the *Atlantis*. Rogge, ever the seasoned and consummate tactician, impersonated the Dutch merchant ship *Polyphemus* and transmitted a distress call. He was trying to buy time until the U-boat could launch an attack on the *Devonshire*.

However the Captain of the *Devonshire*, R.D. Oliver, saw through Rogge's canny strategy in his careful yet quick assessment of the situation. Oliver knew that the *Polyphemus* had been at Balboa near the Pacific entrance to the Panama Canal on 21 September, but he did not miss the fact that the *Atlantis*'s transmission did not follow the new system of tapping out that day's signal letters following 'RRR'. Oliver had the Walrus circle the *Atlantis* to confirm her identity. In due course, the pilot reported that, having carefully compared the suspect vessel against the photographs of known German raiders he had in his hand, he was certain that she was the *Atlantis*. It is safely assumed that the photograph used was precisely the one that had featured in the 23 June edition of *Life*.

The *Devonshire* kept her distance from the *Atlantis* while subjecting her to a concentrated bombardment. Oliver's strategy was to maintain a one-sided attack by remaining outside the *Atlantis*'s gun range and denying her the possibility of retaliation. Rogge realized his 5.9-inch guns were useless against a heavily armoured cruiser rigged with 8-inch guns of superior range, and decided not to hoist the battle ensign. This was also to persist with his claim to be a merchant ship. He ordered all crew to evacuate in the lifeboats. Even amidst the sudden chaos he did not forget to evacuate the injured prisoners first. The waters were full of sharks. Just after 10.00 the *Atlantis* was scuttled by her crew.

The *Devonshire*'s crew witnessed the complete submergence of the *Atlantis* at 10.16. The wind was gathering strength and the sea was becoming rough. They recovered their seaplane from the water at 10.40. Oliver was certain that a U-boat was in the vicinity as there was a patch of oil on the surface of the water. Moreover, the *Atlantis* seemed to have been constantly manoeuvring in such a way as to lure the *Devonshire*, and so Oliver judged a submarine attack to be highly likely. He decided to leave immediately, abandoning the *Atlantis*'s drifting lifeboats.

For a long time the Royal Navy had been unable to establish accurately the position of the *Atlantis* and had been continuously frustrated. However, the Enigma machine had become capable of decoding almost all the orders the U-boats received. The Royal Navy patiently persisted with its deciphering and investigations, and eventually gleaned the date, time and location of the *Atlantis*'s rendezvous with U-boat 126. This facilitated the *Devonshire*'s search considerably. The *Atlantis* herself used a completely separate cipher to that of the submarine fleet, which the Royal Navy never succeeded in breaking. The fact that the U-boat communications had been decoded by the Royal Navy placed Rogge in a great predicament. What he had long feared had become reality.

Once the *Devonshire* had departed, U-boat 126 surfaced. Her crew took on board the injured and rounded up the lifeboats. They tethered them together and the submarine began to tow them. The *Atlantis*'s officers and marines with experience or special expertise were placed aboard the U-boat since their loss would have directly led to a decline in the Kriegsmarine's capability. Some of the remaining crewmembers were divided between two motor launches and four cutters. The odd-looking convoy of small boats was rescued by the *Python*, which had rushed to the scene following orders from Admiral Karl Dönitz, the Commander-in-Chief of the U-boat fleet, between 24 and 25 November.

Before the war, the *Python* had been a merchant ship belonging to the African Fruits Company of Hamburg. Rogge had travelled aboard her before, when he had visited England for the coronation of King George VI in 1937. He was now given the same cabin that he had occupied on that occasion.

Dönitz had also sent U-boats 124 and 129 to rescue the *Atlantis*'s crew. The *Python* was sunk by the British cruiser HMS *Dorsetshire* on 1 December and subsequently the crew of the *Atlantis* and the *Python* totalling 414 men were towed by the two submarines in a train of eighteen lifeboats and rubber rafts. They initially headed for Brazil, but when they were met by two further submarines that had been urgently dispatched by the German Naval High Command, they changed course and made for France. They were picked up by four Italian submarines, which had also joined the rescue operation at the German Navy's request, at the Cape Verde Islands. The men were divided among the eight submarines. They endured all manner of difficulties during their ensuing voyage of 6,000 nautical miles, but one by one the submarines reached St Nazaire between 25 and 29 December that year. Rogge arrived on Christmas Day.

Rogge returned safely to Germany at the end of 1941. Once he had tied up the loose ends relating to the *Atlantis*, he became involved in the Kriegsmarine's training programmes. During that time he drew on his experiences to produce a training manual for captains and officers of merchant raiders. However, owing to the developments in communications and the evolution of shipping escorts, by then the commerce raider's heyday, which had begun during the First World War, was already coming to an end.

In August 1944, the advancing Soviet forces reached the shores of the Gulf of Riga, the deep bight on Latvia's Baltic coast. The Kriegsmarine's Second Battle Group, which consisted of large warships, fiercely bombarded the Soviet troops with its heavy artillery to aid the struggling German land forces, but it could not halt the Soviet advancement. The situation was deteriorating rapidly for Germany at the start of 1945, and Rogge, aboard his flagship the *Prinz Eugen* as Commander of the Third Battle Group, made haste to the battleground and supported the campaign during March and April. Linking up with the Second Battle Group, his fleet assisted the army enormously as well as fighting off the Soviet navy. Finland eventually capitulated to the Soviet forces and the situation continued to develop to Germany's disadvantage. From then until Germany's defeat, Rogge's fleet was heavily occupied with supplying the German Army on the eastern front and with extricating units that had become isolated. Rogge also shouldered much of the responsibility for rescuing civilian refugees from eastern Germany, and he implemented this operation over a prolonged period without respite, while subjected to attacks by British and Russian aircraft. He was forced to change his flagship from the *Prinz Eugen* to the *Admiral Scheer* at the height of the intense fighting, and finally to a transport ship towards the end of the war.

The German Trade Disruption Operations

Unlike the Kaiser, Hitler had never aimed to build a large navy to rival the Royal Navy. This was because he did not have much interest in the navy or any intention of vying with Britain for supremacy to the bitter end. He had dedicated all his efforts to training and strengthening his army and air force and neglected the navy. Therefore, by the late 1930s, when once again the cloud of war had loomed heavy over Europe, Germany's naval capability had been far inferior to that of Britain. At the outset of the war, the German surface fleet had only consisted of two outdated battleships which were fit for little else than cruising backwards and forwards in the Baltic, three pocket battleships, two battle cruisers, eight cruisers, twenty-two destroyers, and a number of torpedo boats. Worse, three cruisers and nine destroyers had been lost and two cruisers and one destroyer damaged in the Norway campaign in the early days of the war. Although the battleships *Bismarck* and *Tirpitz*, and the cruiser *Prinz Eugen* joined the fleet in 1941, it was never able to recover from its early losses. Germany attempted to build an aircraft carrier with technical support from the Japanese Navy but this did not materialize. As for Dönitz's submarine fleet, only thirty-seven of the fifty-seven cruise submarines had been seaworthy at the start of the war. For Dönitz, who had long advocated the creation of a 300-strong submarine fleet instead of large warships, this had been a very frustrating state of affairs. However, by 1941, the number of U-boats had increased to 120, and they had become a menace in the Atlantic and elsewhere.

Given her naval inferiority, the best means for Germany to defeat Britain was to destroy her air force and gain aerial supremacy while blocking her maritime trade routes and severing her supply of raw materials and foods. For this purpose, Admiral Raeder had concentrated on the build-up of the submarine fleet and the building of surface vessels for the obstruction of trade routes, and especially the formation of a commerce raider fleet. He had driven the pre-war project of the state subsidizing private merchant shipping companies to build superior, high-performance ships, which the navy would be able to requisition as transport ships or convert to auxiliary vessels once at war. The Japanese Navy had implemented a similar system. Examples of Japanese ships built under the subsidy scheme for the production of high-performance vessels were the Osaka Shōsen Kaisha's *Hōkoku Maru* and *Aikoku Maru*, both built in 1940.

When war had become imminent, Raeder had implemented the plan of converting merchant ships into commerce raiders. Three raiders had begun service by the end of 1939 and another three had joined them during the first half of 1940. The German Navy referred to these six raiders, the *Orion*, the *Komet*, the *Atlantis*, the *Widder*, the *Thor*[6] and the *Pinguin*, as the 'first wave', and the *Atlantis* had been at its forefront. A second wave, consisting of five raiders including the *Kormoran*, was subsequently launched. Out of these eleven vessels nine actually put to sea on expeditions. Four of these were sunk and only the *Thor* succeeded in making two expeditions. The Kriegsmarine also mobilized two small battleships, named the *Deutschland* and the *Admiral Graf Spee*, on trade disruption missions.

9

Conclusion

The Gunfire that Announced Freedom

BEING A PRISON camp for seamen, there were always internees skilled in communications technology at MILAG in Westertimke. They applied their wit and ingenuity, found the materials and built a receiver and even a transmitter. Among the materials collected was a device attached to a tank-operator's helmet which was picked up by some prisoners who had been sent out to work on a farm, and it proved very useful. Every day, the internees secretly listened to BBC broadcasts while the guards were not around. They listened to developments in the war, and in particular to the movements of the fronts, and marked them on a map. This map was stuck to the back of a door and was concealed when it was pushed open, so it was never found by the guards. One of the German camp staff did discover that the prisoners were listening to BBC broadcasts but he would just place himself nearby and listen to the transmissions in silence. He must have felt unable to trust German news broadcasts, and been worried about the progress of the war. There was of course no danger of his reporting on the prisoners' activities.[1]

The prisoners went one step further, and transmitted information to London. This type of clandestine activity may well have been more prevalent at MARLAG, the prison for RN personnel next door. The merchant seamen sent any information they thought might be of the slightest use, even if it was nothing more than hearsay, on the situation inside and outside the camp and on the daily lives of German civilians. This information was undeniably limited, but the prisoners are thought to have supplied some useful material to the British government and military, aiding their assessments of trends in the German economy and the level of morale among the military and the civilian population.

Mail, delivered by the International Red Cross, was of course utilized for the secret exchange of information. Objects that could be useful in the event of an escape were ingeniously concealed inside parcels. Apparently ordinary letters from girlfriends and relatives in England had in fact been carefully and elaborately written by the Ministry of Defence in London, embedding information and instructions. They included such messages as : *M. 23. Steal all -phoney parcels sent to Lt. R.S. Buck from Robert Winter and LT. Alan Baker from Ruth Pitt. Stop. Had your M.1. to M.5.* of 2 August 1944, *Strangers near Schaffhausen Salient are liable to arrest for questioning even if papers in order* of 11 November 1944 or *Beware of being incited by Huns to join rising Stop Tell all Camps they must not unless ordered by Eisenhower* of 9 December 1944.[2] Detailed records were made of these government letters, disguised as letters from family and fiancées, including the type of writing paper and envelopes used, the senders' names, and the places of posting, which extended all over Britain. Although they were written in perfect English, something unnatural can be detected in these 'official private letters'. However, it would have been nigh on impossible for the German inspectors to single them out from a large quantity of correspondence.

Towards the end of the war, between the lines of the letters of love and encouragement sent to the prisoners was the instruction to refrain from staging any revolts, even if the guards had relaxed or the prisoners were provoked as in the case of the aforementioned secret message. Here we can clearly see the care that the British military took to prevent any unnecessary casualties. However, elsewhere, some POWs met a pitiful fate. Two hundred and forty-seven Japanese POWs died during their attempt at a mass escape from the Cowra Camp in Australia in August 1944. Japan had not ratified the Geneva Convention of 1929 and when questioned by the United States on this matter during the war her only reply was that she would 'make the necessary amendments (*mutatis mutandis)* and then apply it'. The Japanese military did not even make public the existence of Japanese prisoners of war, let alone recognize, in any way, their achievements, individuality or human rights. It ordered its soldiers to die rather than be taken prisoner, and no doubt such an attitude affected its treatment of enemy POWs. The Japanese military had degenerated markedly since the Russo-Japanese War and the First World War, when it had meticulously adhered to the international laws of warfare including those relating to the treatment of prisoners. During the Second World War, it had a far-from-modern mindset and it was futile to expect it to deal with enemy prisoners in full observance of the Geneva Convention.

On 6 June 1944, Allied forces landed on the beaches of Normandy and on 15 August they arrived in southern France. They liberated Paris during August, and Brussels on 3 September. They continued to advance eastwards, and finally, in March 1945, American troops crossed the Rhine and marched into Germany. Meanwhile, Germany had failed to resist the Soviet advancement from the east and had retreated. By the spring of 1945, the Soviet army had overrun Hungary, Austria and Poland and was marching on Berlin. These dramatic developments were followed closely and with great hope at MILAG. The 21st Army Group, which was commanded by Field Marshal Bernard Montgomery and included British, Canadian and American troops, led the left flank of the Allied lines, sweeping from Belgium into western Germany. In mid-April, it subdued the area around Bremen, and looped in an unstoppable surge to cross the Elbe and take Hamburg. The battleground between the retreating German troops and the British forces which pursued them was moving ever nearer to Westertimke.

To avert bombings by Allied aircraft, the word 'prisoners' and a red cross were painted at a clearly visible size on the roof of the MILAG compound. The detainees dug trenches to dive into in an emergency here and there in the camp's grounds. In the latter half of April, an RAF reconnaissance aircraft came flying low over the camp to confirm the presence of the prisoners. A large group of prisoners had rushed outside, shouted and waved at the plane. They had begun to realize that the day of their liberation was very close. From around the 20th, the thunderous reverberations of heavy gunfire could be heard at the camp. Aerial battles took place overhead and stray bullets came flying into the compound. A battle also raged at the nearby village of Kirchtimke.

As the German forces retreated, the prison's guards and commanders became manifestly perturbed. Some even sneaked away unnoticed, perhaps fearing reprisals from the prisoners. There were in fact almost no instances of the prisoners exacting revenge on the guards. Suddenly the camp's security relaxed drastically and it was as good as being liberated. Some prisoners boldly walked back and forth through the main gate just to savour their freedom.

After subduing Bremen in mid-April, the Welsh and Scottish Guards Armoured Division split and one unit proceeded to occupy Sandbostel, the site of a large concentration camp, while the other headed for Zeven. It was the latter that liberated the camp at Westertimke, which lay on the route to Zeven. According to the division command's war diary, the liberation operation was launched before dawn on 26 April, but a German unit, which had retreated to the east and which was attempting to rejoin the main German lines, put up a fierce resistance all around the camp and the operation was stalled. The British reinforced their troops and relaunched their offensive. Between midnight and the early morning of the 27th, they succeeded in driving back the German troops from around the camp.

A Royal Navy contingent immediately headed for the camp in a convoy of ten vehicles led by an armoured car flying the white ensign. They were stalled on the way while mines were cleared, but then safely proceeded to liberate the camp. They reported that the camp was 'in good order, the inmates including at least 1,400 Merchant Navy and 200 Guardsmen . . .'.[3] The war diary for the following day records: 'The news which started the day for us was the final liberation of the Westertimke PW Camp. The Total number of PW which we freed has been mounting in the reports all day, but a definite figure of 8,000 has now been reached, of which half are US Merchant Navy within a separate camp and the other half, mostly British Merchant Navy with a good sprinkling of service personnel from many other countries. Forty-two nations were, in fact, represented. The conditions of the camp are fortunately said to have been fair with sanitation and accommodation good, and food eatable, though short in quantity. One of the favourite occupations of the inmates was, apparently, to sit on the roofs of their huts and watch German convoys moving along the main road. They would then point frantically into the sky, clamber down, and watch with delight the German drivers tumbling out of their vehs[*sic*] in dread and fear of yet another Spitfire attack.'[4]

It is recorded in the war diary that an 'escaped' German officer accompanied the convoy. He was in fact the Commandant of the camp, Captain Walter Rogge, who had presented himself at the headquarters of the Guards Armoured Division's 32nd Brigade to arrange the handover of the prisoners on the 25th, and he had been required to return to the camp with the British. He and his aide had arrived at the 32nd Brigade headquarters white flag in hand and the British officers who had received them had at first tried to treat them as prisoners. Rogge had protested vehemently that there were no grounds for him to be treated in this manner since he had come to negotiate on behalf of the German military. The British had soon softened their attitude, providing the two men with beds for the night and allowing them to eat in the officers' mess. This may have partly been due to Rogge's remonstrance but it was primarily owing to the intervention of Lieutenant Winn of the Royal Navy. He had formerly been a prisoner at MARLAG himself, but had succeeded in being repatriated by feigning illness and had returned to liberate the camp as a member of the 32nd Brigade. Winn knew Rogge, rated his character highly and was sympathetic towards him.[5]

An officer of the British Field Intelligence happened to be present when the two German officers, still in their uniforms and blindfolded, had been interrogated by staff at the Brigade headquarters. According to this officer's War Report, one of the Germans – Rogge – was thin and rather weary-looking, but was tall and handsome and spoke excellent English. The other is described as a typical Prussian, short with a stout neck. They had requested an eight-hour truce for the safe handover of the prisoners. The Brigadier had promptly rejected this proposal as he had suspected the Germans' true motive was to buy time to enable their withdrawal from Bremen and to lay mines in the path of the British.

By then the atrocities of the Nazi concentration camps had been uncovered and the British press had begun to report on them extensively, and anti-German sentiment was stronger than ever. When Rogge again protested at being treated as a prisoner, the Field Intelligence Officer had thrust at him a British newspaper which showed photographic evidence of Nazi brutality and demanded to know what right Rogge had to complain about his treatment when the Germans were capable of such things. The officer wrote that Rogge 'studied these pictures with interest and horror and thereafter had nothing to say'.

Disarmed by his character and curious, the British officers had begun to talk to Rogge. At the meal table they had been impressed by his manner of speaking, which had been compliant and to the point, when answering their questions. One conversation had gone something like this:

Q: Were you treated well when you were taken prisoner by the British during the First World War?
A: Most certainly. There was nothing to complain about except the boredom.
Q: Were you pleased at Germany's early victories in this war?
A: Of course, I was delighted.
Q: Why did Germany lose?
A: Because Hitler is a megalomaniac and he attacked Russia.
Q: Are you a Nazi?
A: Yes, not by inclination but by necessity. A businessman cannot trade in Germany unless he belongs to the Nazi Party, and it is the same for me.
Q: Did you know about the inhumane concentration camps?
A: Yes, but I didn't know the full truth. Everyone was afraid of the Gestapo. With one wrong word both you and your family would be taken away. Many of the victims were German.[6]

Walter Rogge, MILAG and MARLAG's last Commandant, was born on 5 March 1897 and was two years older than Bernhard Rogge. Both men had joined the navy in 1915. At the end of the First World War, Walter Rogge had been a crewmember of a torpedo boat. His vessel had been one of the German warships that had gathered at the Scottish naval port of Scapa Flow and simultaneously scuttled themselves rather than surrender. Subsequently Rogge had been held prisoner in England for fourteen months, which no doubt accounted for the good standard of his English. Walter Rogge spent the second half of the Second World War posted at Westertimke and for the last ten months he was Commandant of the camp as Korvettenkapitan.[7]

A fair and rational man, he was well-liked and seldom criticized by the prisoners. As we can see, the two Rogges had much in common apart from their family name: their ages, their appearance, their characters and their linguistic ability. Moreover, towards the end of the war both men were addressed as 'Captain' though

Bernhard Rogge, the junior by two years, was in fact two ranks above Walter as Vizeadmiral at the end of the war. This caused the two men to be confused even further. In the British war diaries and related records the two men are only referred to by their surname, which is misleading. Even among the captive British servicemen and merchant seamen a fair number were convinced that Commandant Rogge and the Captain of the *Atlantis* were the same man.

Early in the morning on 27 April 1945, the prison camp at Westertimke was liberated, taken over by British forces and placed under the command of Lieutenant Winn. The following day, the Union Jack was hoisted high and the liberation was formally declared. From then on, the internees were the responsibility of the POW Exchange unit. Several dozen lorries arrived a few days later, representing the captives' first step towards home. They were taken to an airport about eight miles south of Bremen from where they were airlifted group after group by Dakotas to Leighton Buzzard, Bedfordshire.

The Homecoming

The band of escapees – reduced to just Harper and Dunshea – were taken to Gibraltar on 31 May in a minibus belonging to the British embassy in Madrid. On 16 June, Harper parted company with Dunshea, with whom he had shared so many hardships and good times, and left Gibraltar on the troopship *Nea Hellas*. He arrived in Glasgow on the 25th. As soon as the ship berthed a man came aboard, found Harper and handed him a train ticket to Liverpool. Harper disembarked and stepped onto British soil for the first time in eight months. He was overcome by emotion as he looked back on the hard times aboard the prison ship, his perilous flight through France and his days of captivity in Spain. He was filled with gratitude at having been able to return to Britain safely.

Harper could not wait to get home and he made straight for the railway station. However, probably owing to air raids, none of the trains were running on schedule. After a long wait, he was at last able to board a crowded train to Liverpool. At midnight, the train finally reached the outskirts of Liverpool but came to a standstill for a long time as the city was experiencing an air raid. Eventually, the alert was lifted and the train pulled into Liverpool's main station. By then it was almost dawn on 26 June. The whole country observed the blackout at this time and the streets of Liverpool were also shrouded in darkness. There were just a few fires caused by the air raid glowing in the dark. Harper was startled by the extent of the damage the city had suffered; it was a grim sight to behold.

There was no public transport whatsoever, so Harper had to walk to his parents' house at 68 Holmfield Road in Aigburth, a southern suburb of Liverpool. When he arrived, the house was empty and steeped in silence. Later that day, his father came home. He told Harper with visible heartache that the merchant ship *Matina* (5,389 tonnes), with Harper's younger brother Frank on board, had been sunk by a German submarine on 24 October 1940, 500 miles west of the Outer Hebrides, and that there had not been a single survivor. As he heard the news, Harper, who had been very fond of his brother, tried to bear the grief that welled inside him; a grief which would never leave him for the rest of his life. Twenty-two-year-old Frank had been an apprentice engineer. The *Matina* had been attacked by U-boat 28 commanded by Captain Kühnke which itself was sunk in March 1944.

Harper's mother Jessie had been told that the *Automedon* had sunk and that it was not known whether there were any survivors. Believing she had lost her two beloved sons in succession she had been distraught, and when her husband's ship had not returned to port when expected, her anguish had been exacerbated. She had fallen ill and had been hospitalized.

As a child, Frank had been very attached to Samuel and had always followed him around wanting to be played with. He had joined in all of Samuel's activities and the two boys had done everything together: they had gone bird-watching and taken their eggs, caught fish for their aquarium, hunted for rabbits, played cricket and football, gone swimming, and boxed. They had also been boy scouts together. Frank had grown into a good-looking young man. As they grew older, Frank had become interested in ballroom dancing and tennis, while Samuel tended to spend his time with boats and go out drinking with his friends. Although they had developed different hobbies the brothers' closeness had never changed.

The following day, Harper presented himself at the Blue Funnel Line offices, relayed in detail the circumstances of the sinking of the *Automedon* to the legal department, and signed a report that was prepared from his account. This became the first detailed resource on the *Automedon* and continued to be regarded as valuable information. It was cited widely after the loss of the Cabinet papers became public in the aftermath of the war.

Even Harper, who had a strong constitution, had lost thirty kilogrammes through malnutrition and only weighed forty kilogrammes when he first returned to England. This fact on its own is testament to how trying his epic escape had been. He asked to be exempted from seagoing work and for a while worked in the offices of Alfred Holt & Co. Once his health recovered, he returned to sea, on ships serving as war transport to Colombo and Calcutta. He returned to Liverpool after his last voyage, from Australia via Ceylon, on 27 June 1946.

Just a few days after Germany's surrender, Harper had been sent to Kiel to recover and bring to England the merchant ship *Glengarry* that had been built in Denmark by Alfred Holt and which had been seized by the Germans at the start of the war. He had accomplished this major task to great success. It must have been a very emotional mission for him, as the *Glengarry* had been converted to a merchant raider just like the *Atlantis*, and called the *Hansa*.

The woman who married Harper in 1945, Severina, had moved to England from her native Spain with her family because of the civil war. Harper and Severina had known each other for a few years and were good friends. When Harper had been missing following the sinking of the *Automedon*, Severina had been working as a nurse for the RAF. They had met again after his return to Liverpool. They had married on 17 February 1945 and had a baby daughter. Life at sea as a marine engineer was arduous and physically demanding, and the work required frequent and long periods of separation from his beloved family, so Harper withdrew from the Merchant Services in 1947 to begin a new life. Initially, he worked as a Mechanical Design Draftsman in Liverpool, after which he was employed as Methods and Equipment Engineer at Dunlop's General Rubber Goods Division in Manchester. He was often sent to Germany, the United States, France and Romania to provide advice to Dunlop's overseas plants. In retirement, Harper and Severina moved to Sale on the outskirts of Manchester. Following Severina's death in January 1994, Harper spent his remaining years comfortable and content, cared for by his daughter Geraldine. In October 2003, Harper's life, characterized by such perilous events as being taken prisoner and escaping to freedom, drew to a close.[8]

Alex Parsons went home from Leighton Buzzard to New Brighton to enjoy freedom and to rebuild his life that had been torn asunder through years of captivity. To his regret he was unable to go back to sea again because of the physical infirmities resulting from the severe injuries and emaciation he suffered in the war. He worked on shore for the Blue Funnel till he turned fifty-six and then he was with its subsidiaries for some more years before retirement. Now eighty-three years old and in good health, he lives happily with his family in New Brighton.

As for Frank Walker, who had been the youngest member of the Automedon's crew when he joined at sixteen, he endured prison life for a full five years, until the camp's liberation on 27 April 1945. The Germans usually allowed the early repatriation of minors, but he had squandered this privilege when he had attempted to escape and failed. When he was freed he was already twenty-one years old, but due to malnourishment he only weighed forty kilogrammes. Once back in England, Walker wished to return to work at the Blue Funnel Line immediately. However, he was told by a doctor that his physical strength had not recovered sufficiently and was ordered to rest for four weeks. He was then able to join the crews of the Blue Funnel Line and he made around ten voyages to the ports of Japan. He continued his seafaring career until 1978 when he began working for a manufacturer of coaches. He retired in 2000 at the age of seventy-five. He now lives happily and in good health with his wife Vera in Wallasey, south of the Mersey, in a house with a view of the Irish Sea.[9]

The *Automedon*'s Chief Steward, P.J. Moseley, who sustained fatal injuries that nightmarish morning in November 1940 and was nursed by Walker as he died on the deck, had a son named John. Over half a century later, at the end of 1996, John Moseley was on holiday in Scotland and noticed a photograph of a Blue Funnel Line ship on the wall of his hotel room. He then discovered that the hotel's owner was a member of the Blue Funnel Line Association. As if he had been guided by an invisible hand, this encounter enabled John to make contact, in early January 1997, with the surviving witness to his father's death, Walker, for whom he had been searching for many years. Moseley visited Walker and asked for all the details of his father's last moments. In doing so, he could at last find some peace of mind over the violent death of his father.[10]

In the early 1990s, Walker and his friend from MILAG, Allan Cain, visited the site of the camp at Westertimke. All those barracks, bar one, had disappeared without trace. The two men were filled with disappointment, faced with a scene unrecognizable from their memories. However, the local residents were very welcoming, especially the older generation who remembered MILAG. The two men found the village of Westertimke and the surrounding countryside incredibly beautiful and peaceful. They realized that during their time at the camp they had never given a thought to the beauty of the nature around them.[11]

The Tea-set Recovered

Violet Ferguson spent about two years at the Liebenau internment camp, separated from her husband Alan who was held at MILAG, 300km to the north. She returned home safely in March 1943, at the height of the war, thanks to a mutual agreement between Germany and Britain, brokered by the International Red Cross, on the early repatriation of women, minors and the infirm. She was released from Liebenau and set off for Britain with thirty other women on 18 January. They travelled by train to Lisbon, where they were placed in the custody of the British embassy. They had to wait for about a month before they were put on an airplane to England.

Violet arrived in St Albans on 6 March, and had a joyful reunion with her family whom she had not seen for two-and-a-half years. However her happiness was mixed with sorrow: her father had died at around the time she had been taken prisoner by the *Atlantis*, and she had been informed of his death by mail months later, but this reality hit her all over again once she was home. This perhaps explains why she now stayed by her mother's side much of the time.

News of the St Albans girl who had returned after two-and-a-half years in a German prison spread like wildfire all over town. The local newspaper, *The Herts Advertiser & St Albans Times,* featured an article entitled 'Home from German Internment Camp' on 12 March.[12] The article read:

> Mrs Violet Ferguson, daughter of Mrs R. Tyson, of 45 Burnham Road, St Albans, is overjoyed to be home with her mother again after experiences that read like pages in an adventure story. They began when she and her husband, returning to Singapore in 1940, were on board a ship chased and sunk by a lone German raider. Wondering what their fate was going to be, the passengers were taken aboard the raider, were treated fairly well, and, after two and

a half months at sea, found themselves internees in Germany. Here the hardest blow for Mrs Ferguson was to be separated from her husband. The suspense of not knowing where he was or how he was faring was terrible, but later on they were allowed to correspond.

Mrs Ferguson's worst recollections are of the eight prisons through which she passed on her way to a women's internment camp in the heart of Germany. Once in the internment camp, she found conditions fairly good, and the chief problem for her and for the other 500 women in the camp was how to pass the time. They were not made to work. Mrs Ferguson is a good needlewoman and spent much time patching and mending for her companions, and innumerable shows and concert parties were arranged. Mrs Ferguson tried to learn French, but found concentration hard in her strange life, although she picked up a little German.

Potatoes were the main food in the camp and Mrs Ferguson declared: 'The Red Cross Parcels were a life-saver to all of us.' She herself was more fortunate than some of the women in one respect, for her own luggage had been saved and so she had her own supply of clothes. 'We were absolutely overjoyed when we knew we were going to be repatriated,' she said. Sick women and women taken prisoner on the sea were released - in all a total of thirty-one from her camp. They travelled to Lisbon and, after a month there, Mrs Ferguson was flown home. She had a happy reunion with her family on Saturday, and now awaits her husband's return. She is going to take a job in St Albans to help on the war effort.

Almost two years after Violet's repatriation, Alan Ferguson was also released early, for health reasons. On 5 February 1945, he arrived in England on board the merchant ship the *Arundel Castle*. After about four years apart, he was reunited with his wife and her family in St Albans.

Ferguson was called upon to help rebuild the Straits Steamship Company[13] which had suffered extensive damage in the war. He took the job right away, and before the year was out the couple relocated to Singapore, where the devastation caused by the war was everywhere to be seen.

Scheduled commercial shipping was not fully restored until 1947. At the end of 1945, it was out of the question to choose one's preferred route or ship. The couple would have just boarded whatever ship was heading for Asia. How emotional they must have felt when the ship passed near the area to the west of Sumatra, where the *Automedon* had sunk five years previously, and entered the Strait of Malacca heading for Penang and Singapore; and again when their life in Singapore resumed after being suspended during five years of war.

As the Straits Steamship Company had sustained extensive damage in the war a great deal of effort was required in every area to rebuild the business: in the procurement of new vessels, the re-establishment of a network of agents, the appointment of personnel, and the repairs to company buildings, including the employees' accommodation. The Fergusons, who were among the first to return to Singapore, initially had to endure many inconveniences in their daily life. Alan worked hard under difficult circumstances. Once the rebuilding of the company was on course and shipping was gradually returning to pre-war levels he worked as Chief Engineer of the *Kimanis*, the *Keningau*, the *Kunak* and other vessels serving the route between Singapore and Tawau in northeast Borneo. His work routine followed the service's schedule: he would spend five or six days checking and repairing the ships at Singapore, and then go to sea, returning three weeks later. His stays at Singapore were never long in this cycle. However, he did have holidays, though dependent on staffing, as well as leave to return to England every three years. He was able to work under relatively good conditions for a seafarer.

On 1 May 1947, Malayan Airways (now Singapore Airlines), which was created through joint investment by the Straits Steamship Company and the Ocean Steamship Company of Liverpool, opened routes linking Singapore, Kuala Lumpur, Ipoh and Penang using two Consul aircraft built by the British manufacturer Air Speed. One of these airplanes was named 'Automedon'. It was as if the steamship *Automedon*, which had sunk to the bottom of the sea seven years earlier, was reincarnated as a charioteer of the skies.[14] How would the Fergusons have felt hearing this news? It is not known whether the couple ever flew to Penang by the new *Automedon*, the destination the original *Automedon* had failed to reach. It is unusual to give the name of a ship that sank to another means of transporting the public, but those who made this decision must have wished to mourn the dead and honour the courage and endurance of those who were taken prisoner.

Ferguson was a quiet and very charming man of well-rounded character. He had many friends both inside and outside the Company and he was respected and well-liked by the local staff too. He was even popular among the passengers, and was thought of fondly by many of them.[15] He was born with hearing difficulties and he used a hearing aid, but this did not impinge on his daily work in any way. His hearing problem was limited to particular frequencies and he was in fact better able than his co-workers to hear orders from the bridge in the very noisy engine room.[16] Some of his colleagues even suspected that not only did Ferguson never feel restricted by his disability but that he actually exploited it, pretending not to have heard what he did not want to hear. However, at MILAG he had struggled as it had been difficult to obtain parts for his hearing aid.

The Fergusons enjoyed life in the tropical land, playing golf, bridge or mahjong with friends at weekends. As a senior Chief Engineer, he with his wife Violet occupied one of the Sommerville Estates flats owned by the Straits Steamship Co.[17] As a result of enduring the pain of separation while detained in Germany, their bond had grown stronger than ever, and their life together in Singapore was a very happy one for over twenty years. However, in 1968 Alan died suddenly from major heart failure.

The grieving Violet settled their affairs and left Singapore, which had become home and a place of so many happy memories, and returned to St Albans to live near her mother and younger sister, Madge Christmas. Perhaps motivated by the many tragic events she had seen and heard of during the war, Violet was interested in welfare work for the disabled, and she began working hard for this cause. For some reason, she was reluctant to talk about the wartime Germany and its people even when asked by her family. Her husband had been the same. Violet never travelled to Singapore again. She probably thought she could not bear the sadness of visiting on her own the place where her husband no longer was. On 24 April 2003, at number 335 The Ridgeway, St Albans, just a stone's throw from her sister's house, ninety-six-years-old Violet died peacefully in her sleep.[18]

As for Violet's belongings which had been retrieved from the *Automedon* that day in 1940, the trunk that contained a tea-set, among other items, had initially been sent to MILAG with Alan and kept there. However, as there had been a shortage of tableware at Liebenau the trunk had been transferred to this camp and its contents used for a time, after which they had been repacked and stored on site. When Violet had been sent back to England in 1943, this crockery along with her clothes and other possessions had been left behind.

On the eve of the couple's departure to Singapore in 1945 they had been informed by the British military authorities that they had received Violet's luggage from Germany. By the couple's request it had eventually been shipped to Singapore and safely delivered into their hands. The luggage had been kept in a large warehouse in Hamburg ever since Violet's repatriation and not a single item had been lost or broken. The Fergusons' friends and acquaintances who heard this story all agreed that it was nothing short of a miracle.

Professor K.G. Tregonning, former Raffles Professor of History at the University of Singapore, who wrote the history of the Straits Steamship Company, *Home Port Singapore*, in 1967 at the Company's request, interviewed the Fergusons in February 1965. He writes that he was served afternoon tea with that very tea-set from Violet's trunk; a tea-set with a story, one that had crossed the Indian Ocean three times.[19] This author visited Madge Christmas to interview her in the autumn of 2003, and when shown the same Taylor & Kent tea-set on that occasion, was deeply moved thinking of the many twists and turns it had followed with its owner over time; he was face to face with a silent witness to history.

As for the classified British Cabinet papers, it has been claimed that the British secret services recovered just a fraction of them from among German documents seized in Berlin in the aftermath of the war.[20]

Rogge's Life after the War

Following Germany's defeat Bernhard Rogge was confined in an internment camp for German officers near Heiligen-Holstein, east of Kiel, on 7 July 1945. He was cleared of any suspicion of war crimes and released on 17 September. The Commander of the British Eighth Army immediately appointed him to the committee charged with the rebuilding of the Schleswig-Holstein area. He was deeply trusted by the Allied authorities and for a time, in the aftermath of the war, the occupying British forces sought his advice and assistance. He went on to participate in the establishment of the Bundesmarine which he joined in June 1957. He held one important position after another, including Commander of the NATO forces responsible for defending northern Germany, until his retirement at the end of March 1962. Between 1962 and 1965 he was a civil defence consultant for the government of Schleswig-Holstein and Hamburg.

Rogge's accomplishments as a military man were remarkable. The *Atlantis* had covered 110,000 nautical miles (approx. 204,000km) and spent 655 days at sea; he had achieved unequalled results, sinking twenty-two enemy ships totalling 145,697 tonnes. On 31 December 1941, Rogge had been honoured with the Oak Leaves to the Knight's Cross, after receiving the Knight's Cross a year earlier.

Rogge had also been presented with a sword by a Japanese private organization on 27 April 1942. Western books and essays on the *Atlantis* and Rogge, as well as a television documentary aired on the British Channel Five, have claimed that Rogge, along with General Hermann Goering and Field Marshal Erwin Rommel, was given a sword by the Japanese emperor or government, but this was not the case.

According to the Japanese newspaper *Asahi Shinbun* of 28 April 1942, an award ceremony organized by a private sector organization, 'The Association for the Propagation of the Spirit of Imperial Edicts', in which outstanding members of the Italian, German and Thai armed forces were presented with Japanese swords, had been held at a banqueting hall, *Seiyōken*, in Ueno in Tokyo from 18.00 the previous evening. The Chairman of the Society, General Noriyuki Hayashi of the Japanese Army, had awarded three swords each to Germany and Italy, and two to Thailand. Over eighty guests had attended the ceremony, including the German Ambassador Ott, the Italian Ambassador Indelli, the Thai Military Attaché, Major General Phya Sorakich Pisal, General Shigeru Honjō of the Japanese Army and Admiral Eisuke Yamamoto of the Japanese Navy. Both of these officers had by then retired.

On this occasion Ott had revealed that the three swords would be allocated to Rommel, Rogge and an outstanding member of the Luftwaffe chosen by Goering. From this statement it appears that it had been left to each country to decide who should receive the swords. The selection of Rogge would have been down to a recommendation from Raeder. Rogge was little known in Japan at the time, so those presenting the sword must have wondered why he had been chosen. The fact that Rogge had obtained classified British documents from the *Automedon* had been a very closely-guarded secret between the Japanese and German navies and there was no way that anyone else could have known about it.

Rogge's sword, along with his award certificate, is now displayed at the Wissenschaftliches Institut für Schiffahrts und

Marinegeschichte in Hamburg. The certificate reads: 'It is my honour as representative of the Association to present you with this sword for your loyalty to your great country and your distinguished accomplishments in the field.'

In retirement Rogge lived at 26 Bahnsenallee in Reinbek in the southeastern outskirts of Hamburg. He continued to be active both in public roles and in his private life. On 29 June 1982 he died at the age of eighty-three. His obituary, printed in the 2 July edition of the *Frankfurter Allgemeine Zeitung*, is signed by his wife Elsbeth and Friedrich Karl Rogge, but whether he had any other family or their whereabouts has not been established. The villa where Rogge lived is located in an exclusive neighbourhood of Reinbek and its back garden overlooks a beautiful small lake. Rogge must have often cast his mind back to his past while looking out onto this lake.

It appears that Rogge had distanced himself from the Nazi Party before the war, and he had maintained his position as a true warrior of the seas. He was a man of excellent judgement and boundless kindness, and as such was respected and loved by his peers, seniors and juniors alike, but also by many people of former enemy countries. When, for a period after the war his life had become difficult, he had received gifts of comfort from such people.

Captain J. Armstrong White of the *City of Baghdad*, which was sunk by the *Atlantis*, provided the preface to Rogge's memoirs in 1957. In it he writes:

> That there is a camaraderie of the sea . . . there is no doubt. And Rogge proved this fully in his attitude and behaviour to the prisoners he took. From the moment that we found ourselves upon his ship the treatment he afforded us was correct and humane in every detail. His first thought and attention was always for those wounded in the attack and, secondly, to provide as much comfort for the remainder of his prisoners as the circumstances permitted. To the best of my knowledge and belief not one accusation has ever been levelled against him, either by his prisoners or by his crew . . . And that is why the greater majority of his prisoners first began to respect, and then to like him.[21]

Notes

Chapter One A Fateful Decision

1. Eiji Seki, *Destroy The Asakamaru*, Rekishi Kaidō (Historical Vista), PHP Institute monthly magazine, Tokyo, March-April 2000.
2. Alex Parsons, Interview with Author, 21 March 2006.
3. Peter Elphick, *Life Line: The Merchant Navy At War 1939–45*, London: Chatham Publishing, 1999, p. 46.
4. *Secret Reports of Naval Attachés, 1940 to 1946, of May 3rd 1941*, entry 98B, Record Group 38, file F-6-E, serial 22886A and 22886B, The National Archives at College Park (NACAP), Maryland, p. 14.
5. Peter Elphick, *Far Eastern File, The Intelligence War In The Far East 1930 – 45,* Coronet Books, page 256. Also Samuel Harper, Letter, 14 November 2002.
6. Bernhard Rogge, *Under Ten Flags,* Weidenfeld & Nicolson, 1957, pp. 99–103.
7. *Das Kriegstagebuch Atlantis*, Wissenschaftliches Institut für Schiffahrs-und Marinegeschichite GmbH, Hamburg, Monday 11 November 1940.

8. BBC Worldwide, television documentary, *Secrets of World War II, Nazi Pirates*, Nugus/Martin Productions Ltd.
9. Letter of Captain D. Stewart to Captain S.W. Roskill, R.N., 23 October 1961, manuscript, The Imperial War Museum (IWM), London.
10. Frank Walker, Interviews with Author, 29 October 2002 and Letters, Papers and Articles.
11. Samuel Harper, Interviews with Author, 27 October 2002 and Letter and Papers, 14 November 2002.

Chapter Two The Battle of Britain

1. Though Ronald Lewin explains in detail the Polish achievements in breaking the German military cipher system during the 1930s in his book *Ultra Goes To War*, Penguin, 2001, pp. 29–50, he refuses to give credence to the story of a German factory worker who allegedly contributed to the Polish construction of an Enigma machine by smuggling its parts into Poland.
2. Peter Calvocoressi, Guy Wint and John Pritchard, *The Penguin History of The Second World War*, p. 163. The authors state: 'The British cryptographers at Bletchley Park might have read Enigma ciphers through their own efforts but the timing of their first successes – and the timing can be crucial in war – owed much to the brilliance and ultimately the generosity of the Poles.' Also John Colville, *Downing Street Diaries 1939–55*, London: Hodder and Stoughton, 1985, p. 294.
3. Hugh Sebag-Montefiore, *Enigma*, Phoenix, 2001, pp. 202–204.
4. Rogge, op. cit., p. 158.
5. John Colville, op. cit., p. 223.
6. Churchill's Underground Fortress

   The Cabinet War Rooms were located in the basement of the Treasury building next to the Foreign Office, on the other side from Downing Street. This building, which overlooked St James's Park and Parliament Square, was the only building with a steel framework and the most fortified in Whitehall, London's government offices district. Work to convert its cellar into the Cabinet War Rooms began in 1938 and it was more or less complete when war broke out. The first War Cabinet meeting, presided over by Neville Chamberlain, took place there 21 October 1939.

At that time, the air raids were yet to begin, and the British government was struggling to find a countermeasure to the new type of mine the Germans were laying around British harbours, causing much damage to shipping. Churchill was then the First Lord of the Admiralty; it was in May 1940 that he took over from Chamberlain as Prime Minister. The Cabinet War Rooms were subsequently reinforced three times, so that they could even withstand large-scale bombs, and were further expanded and improved. Bedrooms were created for Churchill and his wife, his aides and secretaries. There was of course electricity, plumbing and air conditioning, and every measure was taken for the safety and welfare of the many staff who worked there.

A key piece of equipment was Churchill's private telephone, which he frequently used to talk to Roosevelt across the Atlantic. The machine was developed by the American Bell Telephone Company's research facility. It enabled the electromagnetic waves to be scrambled before being transmitted, so that confidential conversations were completely secure against phone tapping, and it was installed in July 1943. It was thirty-seven-feet tall and weighed eighty tonnes; it was so complex and large that it could not be housed on site, so it was placed in the basement of the Selfridges department store some distance away on Oxford Street. Churchill's words were first encoded to a basic level then sent to this machine, where they were thoroughly scrambled before being transmitted to Washington. Of course the Americans had the same machine, and the British and American leaders could safely exchange opinions on world-wide strategies or the command of the War. Londoners had absolutely no idea that such an important facility was beneath their feet as they shopped in Selfridges.

The Cabinet War Rooms seem to form an enormous underground fortress on their own, but in fact they were also linked to a number of similar facilities constructed deep under central London. They were interconnected mainly by the London Underground tunnels, and there was a lift descending from the Cabinet War Rooms to one such passage. One of the underground installations, used by the RAF Command Headquarters and dubbed 'Fort Horseferry', was designated the reserve Cabinet War Rooms for use in an emergency, and by the spring of 1943 its conversion work was complete. The room where Churchill presided over his last Cabinet meeting on 14 August 1945 is still preserved exactly as it was and is open to the public. (Source: *The Cabinet War Rooms*, IWM, 2001.)

7. Hideo Kojima, *Memoirs of Naval Attaché in Germany*, Recollections on Japanese Navy, compiled by Suikō-Kai, Tokyo: Hara Shobō, 1985, p. 157.
8. Eiji Seki, *Hangarī no Yoake : 1989nen no Minshu Kakumei (The Dawn In Hungary: The Democratic Revolution of 1989)*, Tokyo: Kindai Bungeisha, 1995, p. 60.

Chapter Three 'Play For Time In Asia'

1. *The Situation In The Far East In The Event of Japanese Intervention Against Us*, Chiefs of Staff Committee, C.O.S. (40) 592, 31 July 1940, *CAB* 66/10, The National Archives: Public Record Office (TNA:PRO).
2. *WAR CABINET 222 (40)*, Conclusions of a Meeting of the War Cabinet held at 10 Downing Street, SW1, on Thursday, 8 August 1940, at 11:30 A.M., CAB 65/8, TNA:PRO.
3. *Assistance to the Dutch in event of Japanese aggression in Netherlands East Indies*, Report by the Chiefs of Staff Committee, 7 August 1940, C.O.S. (40) 605, CAB 66/10, TNA:PRO.
4. Selected quotations from ANNEX 1 of the report *The Situation in the Far East in the Event of Japanese Intervention Against Us*, op. cit., *Strategy in the Far East*, CAB 66/10, TNA:PRO.
5. Compiled from British government documents including: *COVERING MEMORANDUM TO FAR EAST APPRECIATION*, Chief of Staff Committee, 31 July 1940, C.O.S. (40) 592, TNA:PRO, '*The Situation in the Far East in the Event of Japanese Intervention Against Us*', opt. cit, '*Assistance to the Dutch in the Event of Japanese Aggression in Netherlands East Indies*', opt. cit. and the *WAR CABINET 222(40)*, op. cit.
6. Quoted from WAR CABINET 222 (40), op. cit.
7. Quoted from WAR CABINET 222 (40), op. cit.
8. *Prime Minister to Prime Ministers of Australia and New Zealand*, CAB 65/14, TNA:PRO.
9. Rogge, op. cit., pp. 100–101.
10. *Nichi-Ei Gaikō Zassan (Anglo-Japanese Diplomatic Relations, Misc.) A134-1*, the Diplomatic Record Office (DRO), Ministry of Foreign Affairs (MOFA), 4 April 1941.

11. Prime Minister's Letter to Foreign Minister Matsuoka (*Foreign Office to Moscow*, No. 276, 2 April, 1941, FO 371/27889, TNA:PRO.)

I take advantage of the facilities with which we have provided your Ambassador to send you a friendly message of sincerity and goodwill.

I venture to suggest a few questions, which it seems to me deserve the attention of the Imperial Japanese Government and people:

1. Will Germany, without the command of the sea or the command of the British daylight air, be able to invade and conquer Great Britain in the spring, summer or autumn of 1941? Will Germany try to do so? Would it not be in the interests of Japan to wait until these questions have answered themselves?
2. Will the German attack on British shipping be strong enough to prevent American aid from reaching British shores with Great Britain and the United States transforming their whole industry to war purposes?
3. Did Japan's accession to the Triple Pact make it more likely or less likely that the United States would come into the present war?
4. If the United States entered the war at the side of Great Britain, and Japan ranged herself with the Axis Powers, would not the naval superiority of the two English-speaking nations enable them to deal with Japan while disposing of the Axis Powers in Europe?
5. Is Italy a strength or a burden to Germany? Is the Italian Fleet as good at sea as on paper? Is it as good on paper as it used to be?
6. Will the British Air Force be stronger than the German Air Force before the end of 1941 and far stronger before the end of 1942?
7. Will the many countries which are being held down by the German Army and Gestapo, learn to like the Germans more or will they like them less as the years pass by?
8. Is it true that the production of steel in the United States during 1941 will be 75 million tonnes, and in Great Britain about 12.5, making a total of nearly 90 million tonnes? If Germany should happen to be defeated, as she was last

time, would not the seven million tonnes steel production of Japan be inadequate for a single-handed war?

From the answers to these questions may spring the avoidance by Japan of a serious catastrophe, and a marked improvement in the relations between Japan and the two great sea Powers of the West.

12. Sir S. Cripps to Foreign Office, No.350–1, 13 April 1941, FO 371/27927, TNA:PRO.
13. Sir R. Craigie to Foreign Office, No.619, 16 April 1941, FO 371/27890, TNA:PRO.
14. Captain Kumao Toyoda, Adviser, the Ministry of Justice, *Hearings of Former Captain Katsuo Shiba*, in three parts, 1960–61. Southwest Malaya/Java 11, Military Archives, the National Institute for Defence Studies (MA/NIDS), Tokyo.
15. Minister of Navy to Foreign Minister, *Churchill's Letter of Thanks*, Nichi Doku Sensho (Japan-Germany War Record), T3-5, 462, MA/NIDS.
16. Kijuro Shidehara, 'Gaikō 50nen' (The Fifty Years Diplomacy), *The Yomiuri Newspaper*, 1951, pp. 202–204.
17. *Nihon Gaikōshi Jiten* (*Dictionary of Japanese Diplomatic History*), DRO:MOFA, 1979, p. 888. Professor Masao Maruyama described Matsuoka as a borderline case of mental disturb-ance, *Gendai Seijino Shisō to Kodō (Idea and Conduct of Modern Politics)*, Miraisha, 1964, p. 94. Also Shunichi Matsumoto, *Gaikō Fuzaino Jidai (The Age of Absence of Diplomacy)*, *Ekonomisuto* magazine, Mainichi Newspaper, 14 December 1971, p. 92.
18. John S. Mill, *On Liberty*, Penguin Classics, Penguin Books, 1985, p. 187.

Chapter Four   Atlantis, Predator of the Seas

1. The *Schlageter* (1,869 tonnes), a sailing ship built in 1937 at the Blohm & Voss shipyard in Hamburg which was used for German naval training. Today, almost seventy years after she was built, she is still in good condition and serves as a training vessel for the Portuguese navy under the name *Sagres II*. She has a capacity for 153 crew and ninety trainees. From time to time her beautiful triple-masted form presents itself at her port of origin, Hamburg.
2. K. Dunn to Gabe Thomas, 'Automedon and Rogge', mail, 30 August 2003. Also Mohr & Sellwood, *Atlantis: The Story of a*

German Surface Raider, Werner Laurie, 1955, p. 13. and Joseph P. Slavick, *The Cruise of the German Raider Atlantis*, Annapolis, Maryland: Naval Institute Press, 2003, p. 2.
3. Rogge, op. cit., pp. 3–9.
4. The *Kashiimaru* was built at Aioi Shipyard (near Kobe) by Harima Zōsensho (Shipbuilding Company) in 1936. It was one of the most modern vessels in those days with a 8,595 h.p. diesel engine, being capable of doing twenty knots. During the war, its owner the Kokusai Kisen Kaisha (Steamship Company) was amalgamated with the Osaka Shōsen Kaisha (Shipping Company).

Chapter Five The Trunks and the Cabinet Papers

1. Statement by Philip Walter Savery, Master of SS *Helenus, SS Helenus and SS Automedon*, 16B, IWM, Reading Room.
2. Rogge, op. cit., p. 102.
3. Statistics of the Nihon Junshoku Senin Kenshō Kai (Association To Honour Seafarers Who Died On Duty), 2003, Tokyo. Junior seamen under twenty years old bore the brunt of sacrifice accounting for 30%. In addition to the merchant ships, more than 4,000 vessels including fishing boats and motor/sail ships were sunk by hostile actions resulting in the loss of another 30,000 men according to the estimates of the same organization.
4. E. Seki, *Nichiei Dōmei: Nihon Gaikōno Eikō to Zasetsu (The Anglo-Japanese Alliance: Glory and Decline of Japanese Diplomacy)*, Tokyo: Gakushū Kenkyū-sha, 2003, pp. 172–5. Also, Rear Admiral Sōkichi Takagi, *Takagi Shiryō (Takagi Papers)*, MA/NIDS, Tokyo.
5. Mohr & Sellwood, op. cit., pp. 126–7.
6. Harper, op. cit.
7. Harper, ibid.
8. Harper, ibid.
9. Madge Christmas, Interview with Author, 10 October 2003 and Letters. Also Ann Nelis, Letter, 10 November 2003.

Chapter Six A Gift From Hitler

1. H.N. Smyth, 'Straits Steamship Co. Ltd. Singapore', personal memos, August 2003.

2. A formal agreement for military cooperation between the Tripartite Pact countries had not been concluded until 18 January 1942. Under the agreement the participating nations divided the Indian Ocean at longitude 70 degrees east for their respective theatres of operations.
3. *Australian Navy office signal dated 14/11/1940*, The National Archives of Australia.
4. From Singapore to Admiralty, *Secret Message*, 30 December 1940, FO 371/28814, TNA:PRO.
5. *Senshi Sōsho, Daihonei Kaigunbu/Rengōkantai (The Imperial General Headquarters: The Naval Division/The Combined Fleet)*, vol. 91, MA/NIDS, Asagumo Shinbunsha, 1975, pp. 426–7.
6. Lamotrek Atoll (7°30'N 146°20'E) is a triangular reef surrounded by three islets at each corner covered with coconut and breadfruit trees. The water inside the atoll is about fifteen metres deep except for a few patches of shallow sand. The passageway south of the Pugue Island at the northern end is the widest providing the best entry. There is an anchorage towards the west end where ships can shelter against the strength of the easterly wind.
7. Edited and translated by John Chapman, 1982, *The Price of Admiralty, The War Diary of The German Naval Attaché in Japan, 1939–1943*, Saltire Press, vol. II & III, 23 August 1940 to 9 September 1941, pp. 77–8.
8. S.W. Roskill, R.N., *The War At Sea, vol. 1, The Defensive*, London: Her Majesty's Stationary Office, 1954.
9. Craigie to Foreign Office, 29 January 1941, FO 371/28814, TNA:PRO.
10. Naokuni Nomura, *Report of Naval Mission to Germany*, June 1941, 1 Zenpan 242, MA/NIDS.
11. The report of the Secret Police, 1939, *Activities of Foreign Missions*, The National Diet Library (NDL), p. 137.
12. Ibid. 1940, p. 70.
13. 'Report on the leakage of information from H.M. Embassy', *The Times Weekly Edition*, 29 July 1942, p. 6, Column 3 (Interview with American repatriates at Lourenço Marques), FO 850/75A, TNA:PRO.
14. An espionage network operated by Richard Sorge, German communist journalist and his Japanese journalist friend Hotsumi Ozaki penetrated the Japanese leadership and the German Embassy. The German ambassador Ott so trusted

Sorge that he gave the master spy a room in the German chancery building! The group supplied extremely valuable information to the intelligence organization of the Soviet Red Army in the 1930s to 1940s. The spectacular example was that the top secret Japanese policy of southward advance decided in the Supreme Council in the presence of the Emperor in September 1941 soon became known to the Sorge group and was transmitted by short-wave radio to Moscow enabling the Soviet Army to redeploy its forces in Siberia to the front against Germany. The spy ring was discovered by the secret police and Sorge and Ozaki were arrested in October 1941 with their accomplices. They were put on trial and the two men were executed on 7 November 1944.

15. Erwin Wickert, *Senjika no Doitsu Taishikan: Aru Chūnichi Gaikō kan no Shōgen (German Embassy in the War: Testimony of a German Diplomat in Japan)*, Japanese translation of *Mut und Übermut – Geschichten aus meinem Leben*, Tokyo: Chūō Kō ronsha, 1998, pp. 18–19.
16. Chapman, op. cit. What is described in this chapter about the transactions of Admiral Paul Wenneker and his staff as well as their working relationship with the Japanese Navy is mainly based on J. Chapman's op. cit., *The Price of Admiralty.*
17. German Ships That Sought 'Emergency Shelter' at Kōbe and Yokohama

Name	Type	Tonnage	Arrival Date	Crew	Port
Scharnhorst	Passenger Ship	18,184	1 September	292	Kōbe
Kulmerland	Passenger-freighter	7,362	2 September	58	Kōbe
Burgenland	Passenger-freighter	7,320	3 September	76	Kōbe
Munsterland	Passenger-freighter	6,408	7 September	56	Kōbe
Rickmers	Freighter	5,198	7 September	40	Kōbe
Elsa Essberger	Freighter	6,103	3 November	38	Kōbe
Annelise Essberger	Freighter	5,172	3 November	38	Kōbe
Regensburg	Freighter	8,067	3 September	185	Yokohama
Elbe	Freighter	9,179	3 September	60	Yokohama
Odenwald	Freighter	5,097	15 September	33	Yokohama
Spreewald	Freighter	5,083	20 September	38	Yokohama

18. *Consul Sokobin to the Department of State, 17 December 1940*, Decimal file 1940–44, 740.0011 EW 1939/7208., Microfilm m982, Roll No.39, The National Archives and Records Administration (NARA), Washington, DC.
19. Chapman, op. cit., p. 338.
20. The Military Archives of the National Institute for Defence Studies, Tokyo, holds a photocopy of the original edition of the pamphlet *Read This and We Will Win* owned by Masanobu Tsuji in 1960. Today the booklet can also be read in English translation at the National Archives at Kew: FO371/31817.
21. FO371/6701,TNA:PRO.
22. According to *The Imperial General Headquarters: The Naval Division/The Combined Fleet)*, vol. 91 (p. 427) quoted above, Captain Katsuo Shiba, who was in the First Division of the Military Affairs Bureau of the Naval Ministry, describes in his post-war memoirs that the actual extent of the Japanese Navy's assistance to the German Navy is covered by a thick veil of secrecy for the reason that the officers dealing with the matter were limited in number. Therefore it is now difficult to obtain accurate historical records.
23. Kiyoshi Ikeda, 'Aru Jōhōsen', (An Intelligence War), *Bunka Kaigi magazine*, February 1986, Tokyo, pp. 17–18.
24. The Japanese Naval Mission Report (MA/NIDS, 1 Zenpan 90).

    The Japanese Navy's mission in Germany led by Rear Admiral Katsuo Abe left Berlin on 6 February 1941 and visited German air bases, fortifications and other military installations on the English Channel over a period of two weeks. In the mission's report dated 28 February it is indicated that, even when escorted by fighters, the Luftwaffe's large formations of bombers carrying out daylight raids on Britain had suffered extensive losses from British fighters. Partly owing to this, the report notes, and partly due to sustained poor weather conditions, the Germans were now carrying out surprise attacks by solitary bombers or attacks by squadrons of Messerschmitt 109 and Messerschmitt 110 bombers which had a capacity for 500kg and 1-tonnes bombs, respectively. The report also states that the RAF's attacks on German airbases were severe and that the Luftwaffe was attempting to limit the damage by dispersing its aircraft. Further, the following observations are listed as lessons learnt on Britain's capabilities through the aerial battles:

1. The Spitfires display considerable strength and flexibility, and a sophisticated steering capability.
2. Fighters are positioned in layers between the altitudes of 2,000 metres and 10,000 metres. The aircraft with the most steering capability take up the highest positions.
3. The fire power of the Spitfire, which is mounted with ten guns, is extremely strong and any opponent must exercise particular caution.
4. The Wellington and the Blenheim bombers have recently been escorted by fighters. The four guns mounted at the tail end of the Wellington are highly accurate.
5. The British shipping convoys' evasion tactics against bombing raids are highly ingenious and an attack is made very difficult.

25. Ikeda, op. cit., pp. 18–19.
26. Toyoda, op. cit.

Chapter Seven The Days of Captivity

For Chapter 7 the author owes a great deal to the written recollections, interviews and other valuable material made available by the late Mr Samuel Harper, Mr Frank Walker, Mrs Madge Christmas and Mrs Ann Nelis and their families as well as to Mr Gabe Thomas for his book *MILAG: Captives of the Kriegsmarine.*

1. NACAP, op. cit., pp. 12–14.
2. 'Tea Table Topics', *The Herts Advertiser and St Albans Times*, Friday, 12 March 1943.
3. Ms. Andrea Biberger, Interviews, 7 October 2003, Stiftung Liebenau, Ravensburg, Germany
4. *Ilag Liebenau-Ravensburg*, 10 March 1942, *Ilag Liebenau*, visited 28 November 1941 and *Letter from Kathleen Lambert*, 28 October 1940, FO 916/253, TNA:PRO. *Inspection of Civilian Internment Camp at Liebenau bei Ravensburg,* Vice Consul Robert P. Chalker, the United States Emabassy, Berlin, 23 January 1941, FO 916/35, TNA:PRO.

Chapter Eight The Atlantis *Meets Her End in the South Atlantic*

1. Rogge, op. cit., pp. 112–13, 116 and 118. Also Bernhard Rogge and Wolfgang Frank, *The German raider 'Atlantis'*,

translated by R.O.B. Long, Toronto and London: Bantam, 1979, p. 135.

2. Hisashi Noma, *Shōsenga Kataru Taiheiyō Sensō (Japanese Merchant Ships: The Story of Mitsui and O.S.K. Liners lost during the Pacific War)*, 2002, pp. 60–2. Also, N.Y.K., *Nihon Yūsen Senji Senshi (Wartime History of N.Y.K. Ships) Vol II*, 1971, pp. 586–8.
3. Rogge, op. cit., pp. 134–44.
4. Story by Charles J.V. Murphy; Pictures by David E. Scherman, 'The Sinking Of The "Zamzam"', *Life* magazine, 23 June 1941, New York, pp. 21–79.
5. *Report of the Destruction of Enemy Raider No. 16 by H.M.S. Devonshire*, 12 July 1948, ADM 1/20024 and *The Log of H.M.S. Devonshire, 22 November 1941*, ADM 53/114104, TNA:PRO.
6. The *Thor* Destroyed at Yokohama

   With the outbreak of the Pacific War, the Japanese Navy threw off its former hesitation and openly began to collaborate with Germany. A large number of German ships began to enter Japanese ports and utilize her waters to receive supplies and to rest their crews. On 30 November 1942 the *Thor* was lying in the port of Yokohama. She had been serviced and was due to depart the following day. She was broadside to the tanker *Uckermark* (12,000 tonnes), which had arrived from Germany just a few days earlier, and her crew were loading ammunition onto the *Uckermark*. There was an enormous explosion on the *Uckermark* and the *Thor* too caught fire. She burnt for a number of days before sinking. Seventy-five people died, and severe damage was caused to a British ship, the *Nanking*, which had been captured by the *Thor*, and other vessels in the vicinity as well as to the port facilities. The cause of this incident was never determined, but Wenneker believed it to have been an act of sabotage.

Chapter Nine Conclusion

1. G. Thomas, op. cit., pp. 202–203.
2. WO 208/3501, TNA:PRO.
3. *Gds Armd Div Int [sic] Summary No 291, Up to 2300 hrs 27 Apr 45*, War Diary, WO 171/4104, p. 2, TNA:PRO.
4. *Gds Armd Div Int Summary No 292*, Up to 2300 hrs 28 Apr 45, War Diary, WO 171/4104, p.1, TNA:PRO.

5. *War Report of the Liberation Army by an Officer of the British Field Intelligence*, manuscript, p. i, IWM, Reading Room.
6. Ibid., pp. ii–iv.
7. Dunn, op. cit.
8. Harper, op. cit.
9. Walker, op. cit.
10. Ibid.
11. Ibid.
12. The St Albans Central Library, The Maltings, St Albans, Hertfordshire.
13. The Straits Steamship Company and Singapore

    The Straits Steamship Company was founded in January 1890 under the auspices of British traders and shipping agents with Chinese Singaporean businessmen as its stakeholders. Initially the company owned no more than five 400-tonnes-class motorized steamships. It was subsequently managed by Mansfields of Liverpool and received investment from the Blue Funnel Line, and developed into a cornerstone organization for the maritime transport of produce in South East Asia revolving around Singapore. The company flourished through relaying the goods of global trade. Its ships transported Malaya's principal exports to Europe and the United States, tin and rubber, to Singapore for refinement; they then travelled up mangrove-lined rivers all over South East Asia to deliver machinery, chemicals and consumer goods brought to Singapore by the Blue Funnel Line and other British and American shipping companies.

    Singapore grew as the heart of the British colonial territory along the Straits after Raffles of the British East India Company built a trading post there in 1819. One hundred years later its population had surpassed 300,000 through the influx of Chinese immigrants and it was a thriving entrepôt, handling six million tonnes and one billion dollars' worth of imports and exports a year. By 1922 the Straits Steamship Company owned twenty-four vessels totalling 25,446 tonnes. Its second Ocean Building, shared with Mansfields, was proud and imposing.

    Not surprisingly many British, following their dreams or yearning for adventure, left their homeland for the economically thriving Singapore in the exotic tropics. According to the census of 1937, the number of Europeans resident in

Singapore had reached 8,478, but this only represented 1.6% of the population. The majority of these Europeans were of course British.

Japan, which had opened her doors to the West much later than Singapore, had grown in political and military strength, and her interest turned to the natural resources of the southern regions, such as rubber and oil. By the 1930s, Singapore was conscious of Japan as a threat. Around the time the Fergusons first emigrated to Singapore, Anglo-Japanese relations were progressively becoming strained over the Japanese military presence in mainland China and the armed conflict between Japan and China. By May 1940, when the Fergusons visited Britain on their first holiday since their marriage, Japan's expansionist ambitions had increasingly become clear in tandem with the developments of the European war that had started the previous September, and Singapore felt more threatened than ever. Added to this was the menace of the German commerce raiders, which was already a reality. At that time Singapore was nicknamed the 'Dollar Arsenal' of the Commonwealth and fulfilled an extremely important role: the dollars earned from the export of Malayan rubber and tin via Singapore paid for the arms that Britain acquired from the United States. Malaya produced 38% of the world's rubber and 58% of its tin. As it would have hit the British extremely hard to lose one billion dollars' worth of trade, unsurprisingly they searched for means of appeasing Japan, so long as America did not go to war against her, to preserve the stability of the region while they were fully occupied with the European war. Japan's attack on Pearl Harbor at a stroke resolved the situation for Churchill in a most unexpected manner.

On 15 February 1942, the Japanese occupation of Singapore began and the British nationals who had not left were interned in Changi prison and other camps. Soon the technical staff of the electricity, gas and water systems were required to return to work and help with their maintenance or rebuilding. Their selfless efforts, not for the occupying forces but for the 700,000 residents of Singapore, did not fail to make a strong impression on the Japanese. However, the Japanese occupation of Singapore was tainted by two detestable policies which heightened anti-Japanese sentiment among the Chinese population all the more: the mass-execution of civilian Chinese males and the extortion of large sums of money from Chinese businesses. Any chance of a successful occupation evaporated in the early stages. Chinese volunteer forces courageously resisted the Japanese in defending the Johore Channel and Bukit Timah Hill, and this resulted in many Japanese casualties. The Japanese Army responded ferociously, exacting revenge by capturing and then executing approximately 6,000 Chinese males following the defeat of the Commonwealth forces. The people of Singapore suffered under Japanese oppression for three-and-a-half years during which they reached a state of near-starvation and their economy collapsed.

The Straits Steamship Company lost thirty-one of its fifty-one ships in the Pacific War. Many fleeing civilians and merchant seamen died when their ships were mercilessly bombarded by Japanese aircraft. A large number of the Straits Steamship Company's crewmembers, technicians and administrative staff were taken prisoner. Under such abnormal circumstances the Straits Steamship Company's vessels responded to the British government's call for service, and risked danger to assist in war transport and minesweeping. For example, the Company's prized flagship the *Kedah* (2,499 tonnes) dodged and evaded Japanese warships and aircraft and safely transported General Sir Archibald Wavell, Commander-in-Chief for India and Supreme Allied Commander for Malaya and the Dutch East Indies, and his staff as well as 400 refugees, to Colombo. When the British fleet, led by Admiral Mountbatten, arrived off the shore of Singapore on 5 September 1945 to accept Japan's surrender, the *Kedah* carried the advance guard of the British command staff into the port of Singapore and gained the honour of becoming the first ship to dock there since the war. The *Kedah* was a high-specification vessel built in 1927 by Vickers in Barrow-in-Furness in northern England. With its speed of twenty knots, it was regularly seen overtaking Blue Funnel Line ships in the Straits of Malacca.

It is worth pointing out that shortly after the fall of Singapore the Straits Steamship Company's management in London, which included Sir John Hobhouse and director Charles Wurzburg, had already begun to plan for the re-establishment of the business. By around 1944 they had even discussed a programme of building and overhauling ships and had already commissioned three new vessels. Many of their employees were captured by the Japanese and were subjected to unspeakable suffering in prison camps in Singapore and elsewhere in Asia. A considerable number did not survive and died before their time. Even under such extreme circumstances there was a draftsman who drew ship designs, dreaming of a brighter future. It was precisely this sort of passion that enabled the Company to overcome all manner of difficulties and rise again after the war.

The Straits Steamship Company's staff went on to transport, with hardly a hitch, not only the usual cargo but also essential commodities such as food and drink, mail, newspapers and medical supplies from Singapore to far-flung destinations for many years after the war. They helped to improve standards of living in different parts of the world and through their interactions with local societies contributed to their economic development in all kinds of ways. (Source: K.G. Tregonning, *Home Port Singapore: A History of Straits Steamship Company Limited 1890–1965*, Oxford University Press for Straits Steamship Company Limited, Singapore, 1967; Eric Jennings, *Mansfields Transport and Distribution in South-East Asia,* Singapore: Meridian Communications (SEA) PTE Limited, 1973; *Shōnan Tokubetsushi Shi* (History of Special City of Shō nan), Japan-Singapore Association, 1986, Tokyo Metropolitan Central Library.

14. H.N. Smyth, 'Straits Steamship Co. Ltd. Singapore', Personal Memos, August 2003.
15. Ibid.
16. Nelis, op. cit.
17. Smyth, op. cit.
18. Christmas, op. cit.
19. Tregonning, op. cit., p. 227.
20. Elphic, op. cit., p. 267.
21. Rogge, op. cit., pp. v–vi.

Bibliography

Records

(Japan)

Ministry of Foreign Affairs (MOFA), Gaikō Shiryōkan (Diplomatic Record Office),

Nich Ei Gaikō Kankei Zassan (Miscellaneous Records of Anglo-Japanese Diplomatic Relations) A134–1.

Bōei Kenkyūsho Toshokan (Military Archives, National Institute for Defense Studies),

Senshi Sōsho (War History Series), Daihonei Kaigunbu/Rengōkantai (The Imperial General Headquarters: The Naval Division/The Combined Fleet), vol. 91; Daihonei Kaigunbu: Daitōa Sensō Kaisen Keii (The Events Leading to the Outbreak of the Great East Asian War), vol. 100, The Imperial General Headquarters Navy Division; Daihonei Rikugunbu: Daitōa Sensō Kaisen Keii (The Events Leading to the Outbreak of the Great East-Asian War), vol.1–4, The Imperial General Headquarters Army Division; The Reports of Naval Mission to Germany 1 Zenpan 90 and 242; Nichi Doku Sensho (Japan-Germany War Records), T3–5, 462.

The National Diet Library (NDL)

Gaiji Keisatsu Gaikyō (Secret Police General Survey), 1938–40, edited by Naimushō Keihokyoku (Interior Ministry, Police Bureau), AZ-357-37, Vol. 4–6, Ryūkei Shosha, 1980.

Tokko Keisatsu Kankei Shiryō Shūsei (Collection of Secret Police Records), Vol. 15, 17, 23, 1939–1941, AZ-357-E6, Fujio Ogino, Fuji Shuppansha, 1993.

Kaijō Hoanchō Suirobu (Coast Guard, Maritime Traffic Department),

Maritime Traffic Records for the South-western Islands of the North Pacific 1994 and *Maritime Traffic Records for the Alaska Coast* Vol.2 1932.

(UK)

National Archives: Public Record Office,

CAB65/8, 65/14, 66/10.

FO371/6701, 371/20288, 371/12525, 371/18186, 371/25162, 371/26904, 371/26949B, 371/27889, 371/27890, 371/27927, 371/27962, 371/28814, 371/3187, 369/2828, 850/75A, 916/35, 916/227, 916/228, 916/229, 916/253, 916/501, 916/521, 916/845.

WO171/4104, 208/149, 208/151, 208/163, 208/886, 208/892, 208/3270, 208/3501, 392/9, 392/19, 224/101.

ADM53/114104, 1/17353, 199/2435, 177/31, 199/2231, 1/20024, 199/2216, 199/2233, 53/121219, 199/1014, 1/18222, 1/10294.

AIR 14/1240,40/262, 41/14, 41/15.

HS1/189, 1/185, 1/186.

Imperial War Museum, Reading Room,

Letter of Captain D. Stewart to Captain S.W. Roskill, R.N. of 23rd October 1961, The Statement of Samuel E. Harper, 27th June 1941 and S.S. 'Helenus' and S.S. 'Automedon' and Statement by Philip Walter Savery, Master of S.S. 'Helenus'.

National Museums & Galleries on Merseyside,

The Plan of S.S. Automedon.

(USA)

US National Archives and Records Administration,

Secret Reports of Naval Attachés,1940 to 1946, May 3rd 1941 (entry 98B, Record Group38), Pre-Pearl Harbor Naval Despatches (Entry 9002 Box120), State Department Records (Movements of German Merchant Vessels, Release of crews of the Teddy and Ole Jacob, December 9, 1940), Consul Sokobin to the Department of State, 17 December 1940 (Decimal file 1940–44,740.0011 EW 1939/7208., Microfilm m982, Roll No. 39), Japan – Miscellaneous Information from German Sources (Naval Intelligence Report 2447-S-45, 6 June,1945), War Operations-Raiders (Naval Intelligence Reports Roll 20).

(Germany)
Wissenschaftliches Institut für Schiffahrs-und Marinegeschichite GmbH, *Das Kriegstagebuch Atlantis, Atlantis papers, etc.*
Der Stiftung Liebenau,
Liebenau – ein Internierungslager für Ausländerinnen.

(Switzerland)
Comité International de la Croix-Rouge,
Official Record on Mrs. Violet Clair Ferguson.

Unpublished Manuscripts, Papers and others

Andrea Biberger, Stiftung Liebenau, Interviews.
Madge Christmas, Private Written Recollections, letters, interviews, photographs.
Samuel E. Harper, Private Written Recollections, letters, interviews, photographs.
Ann Nelis, Private Written Recollections, letters.
H.N. Smyth, 'Straits Steamship Co. Ltd. Singapore', Personal Memos, August 2003.
Dr. K.G. Tregonning, Private letters.
Frank Walker, Private Written Recollections, letters, interviews, photographs.

Publications

The Battle of Britain, August–October 1940, The Stationery Office Ltd.
'The Sugiyama Memo from the Minutes of the Imperial General Headquarters Government Liaison Meetings', Hara Shobō, 1967.
Military History Society of Japan, *The Secret War Diary of the Imperial General Headquarters Army Section War Command Unit*, Kinseisha, 1998.
The History of Anglo-Japanese Relations 1600–2000, The Political-Diplomatic Dimension, Vol. 1, 1600–2000 (edited by Ian Nish and Yoichi Kibata), Vol. 2, 1931 – 2000 (edited by Ian Nish and Yōichi Kibata), Vol. 3: The Military Dimension (edited by Ian Gow and Yōichi Hirama).

The Society for the Study of Modern Japanese History, *The Systems, Organisations and Personnel of the Japanese Army and Navy*, Tokyo University Press, 1979.

Die Stiftung Liebenau unter Direktor Josef Wilhelm 1910–1953, Stiftung Liebenau 1995.

SIA: Take-off to Success, Singapore Airlines Limited, 1990.

Conway's All The World's Fighting Ships 1922–1946, Conway Maritime Press.

The Cabinet War Rooms, IWM, 2001.

Aldrich, Richard J., *Intelligence and The War Against Japan*, Cambridge University Press, 2000.

Best, Antony, *Britain, Japan and Pearl Harbour: Avoiding war in East Asia, 1936–1941*, Routledge.

Peter Calvocoressi, Guy Wint and John Pritchard, *The Penguin History of The Second World War*, Penguin Books Ltd, 1999.

Chapman, John W.M., *The Price of Admiralty:* The War Diary of the German Naval Attaché in Japan, 1939–43, Vol. II & III, Saltire House, 1984.

Churchill, Winston, *The Second World War*, Pimlico, 2002.

Colville, John, *The Fringes of Power: Downing Street Diaries 1939–55*, Hodder and Stoughton, 1985

Denniston, Robin, *Churchill's Secret War*, Sutton Publishing Ltd., 1997.

Doenitz, Karl, *Ten Years and Twenty Days*, Weidenfeld & Nicolson, 1959.

Dörr, Manfred, *Die Ritterkreuzträger der Überwasserstreitkräfte der kriegsmarine*, Biblio Verlag, Osnabrück 1996.

Elphick, Peter, *Far Eastern File: The Intelligence War In The Far East 1930–1945*, Coronet Books, 1998.

Elphick, Peter, *Life Line: The Merchant Navy At War 1939–45*, Chatham Publishing, 1999.

Foot, M.R.D., *SOE The Special Operations Executive 1940–1946*, British Broadcasting Corporation, 1984.

Gröner, Erich, *Die deutschen Kriegsschiffe 1815–1945*, Bernard & Graefe Verlag, 1985.

Haws, Duncan, *Merchant Fleets 6*: The Blue Funnel Line, TCL Publications, 1984.

Hildebrand, Hans H. and Ernest Henriot, *Deutschen Admirale 1849–1945*, Biblio Verlag, 1996.

Hough Richard and Denis Richards, *The Battle of Britain*, Penguin Books, 2001.

Jennings, Eric, *Mansfields Transport and Distribution in South-East Asia, Meridian Communications (SEA) PTE Limited, Singapore, 1973.*

Keegan, John, *The Second World War*, Pimlico, 1989.

Kiyoshi Ikeda, 'Aru Jōhōsen' (An Intelligence War), *Bunka Kaigi* magazine, February 1986.

Kojima, Hideo, *Memoirs of Naval Attaché in Germany*, Recollections on Japanese Navy, compiled by Suikō-Kai, Hara Shobō, Tokyo, 1985.

Lewin, Ronald, *Ultra Goes To War*, Penguin Books, 2001.

Masao Maruyama, *Gendai Seijino Shisō to Kodō (Idea and Conduct of Modern Politics)*, Miraisha, 1964.

Mill, John S., *On Liberty*, Penguin Classics, Penguin Books, 1985.

Mohr, Ulrich and A.V. Sellwood, *Atlantis: The Story of a German Surface Raider*, Werner Laurie, 1955.

Murphy, Charles J.V. and David E. Scherman, 'The Sinking Of The "Zamzam"', *Life* magazine, 23 June 1941.

Nihon Gaikōshi Jiten (Dictionary of Japanese Diplomatic History), DRO:Gaimushō, 1979.

Noma, Hisashi, *Shōsenga Kataru Taiheiyō Sensō* (*Japanese Merchant Ships: The Story of Mitsui and O.S.K. Liners lost during the Pacific War*), 2002.

NYK Maritime Museum, *NihonYūsen Senji Senshi (Wartime History of NYK Fleets) Vol II*, 1971.

Ōkubo, Toshitaka, *Kaisō: ōshū no Ikkaku yori mita Dainiji Sekaitaisen to Nihon Gaikō (Memoirs: The Second World War and Japanese Diplomacy as Seen From One Corner of Europe)*, Kajima Institute, 1976.

Okumiya, Masatake, *Taiheiyō Sensō; Itsutsuno Gosan (The Five Miscalculations in the Pacific War)*, Asahi Sonorama, 1994.

Rogge, Bernhard, *Under Ten Flags as told by Admiral Rogge*, Weidenfeld & Nicolson, 1957.

Roskill, Captain, S. W., R.N., *The War At Sea 1939–1945 Vol I. The Defensive*, Her Majesty's Stationery Office, 1954.

Roskill, Captain, S.W., R.N., *A Merchant Fleet In War*, Alfred & Holt Co. 1939–1945, Collins.

Rusbridger, James, *The Sinking of the 'Automedon' and the Capture of the 'Nanking'*, Encounter Magazine, May 1985, London University Library.

Saitō, Ryōei, *Azamukareta Rekishi: Matsuoka to Sangoku Dōmei no*

Rimen (Decieved History: the Truth behind Matsuoka and the Tripartite Alliance), Yomiuri Shinbunsha, 1955.

Schmalenback, F/kapitän a. D., D. Paul, *Profile Warship series 6, Prinz Eugen/Heavy Cruiser 1938–1947*.

Sebag-Montefiore, Hugh, *Enigma: The Battle for the Code*, Phoenix, 2002.

Seki, Eiji, *Asakamaru wo Bakuha seyo (Destroy The Asakamaru)*, Rekishi Kaidō (Historical Vista), PHP Institute monthly magazine, March-April 2000.

Seki, Eiji, *Hangarī no Yoake : 1989nen no Minshu Kakumei (The Dawn In Hungary: The Democratic Revolution of 1989)*, Kindai Bungeisha, 1995.

Seki, Eiji, *Nichiei Dōmei: Nihon Gaikō no Eikō to Zasetsu (The Anglo-Japanese Alliance: Glory and Decline of Japanese Diplomacy)*, Gakushū Kenkyū-sha, 2003.

Shidehara, Kijuro, *Gaikō 50 Nen (50 Years in Diplomacy)*, the *Yomiuri Newspaper*, 1951.

Shigemitsu, Mamoru, Gaikō Kaisōroku (*Diplomatic Memoirs)*, Mainichi Shinbunsha, 1978.

Slavick, Joseph, P. *The Cruise of the German Raider Atlantis*, Naval Institute Press, Annapolis, 2003.

Stafford, David, *Churchill And Secret Service*, Abacus, 2000.

Hinsley, F.H. and Alan Stripp, *Code Breakers, The Inside Story Of Bletchley* Park, Oxford University Press, 2001.

Suketaka Tanemura, *Daihonei Kimitsu Nisshi (The Secret Diary of the Imperial General Headquarters)*, Fuyo Shobō, 1979.

'Tea Table Topics', *The Herts Advertiser and St. Albans Times*, Friday, 12 March 1943.

Thomas, Gabe, *MILAG: Captives of the Kriegsmarine, Merchant Navy Prisoners of War,* the Milag Prisoner of War Association,.

Tregonning, K.G., *Home Port Singapore*, A History of Straits Steamship Company Ltd 1890–1965, Oxford University Press, 1967.

van Der Vat, Dan, *The Pacific Campaign*, Birlinn Ltd., 2001.

Von der Porten, Edward P., *The German Navy in World War II* , Arthur Barker Ltd., 1970.

Wickert, Erwin, *Senjika no Doitsu Taishikan: Aru Chūnichi Gaikō kan no Shōgen (German Embassy in the War: Testimony of a German Diplomat in Japan)*, Japanese translation of *Mut und Übermut – Geschichten asu menem Leben*, Chūōkōronsha, 1998.

Shōnan Tokubetsushi Shi (History of Special City of Shōnan), Nihon-Shingaōpōru Kyōkai (Japan-Singapore Association), 1986.

Website

S.S. Automedon-The Ship That Doomed A Colony, http://www.forcez-survivors.org.uk/automedon.html.

Appendices

Appendix 1

Ships Sunk or Captured by the *Atlantis* (See map)

No.	Date	Name	Status	No.	Date	Name	Status
1	3/5/40	Scientist	sunk	12	10/11/40	Ole Jacob	captured
2	10/6/40	Tirranna	captured	13	11/11/40	Automedon	sunk
3	11/7/40	City of Baghdad	sunk	14	24/1/41	Mandasor	sunk
4	13/7/40	Kemmendine	sunk	15	31/1/41	Speybank	captured
5	2/8/40	Talleyrand	sunk	16	2/2/41	Ketty Brøvig	captured
6	24/8/40	King City	sunk	17	17/4/41	Zamzam	sunk
7	9/9/40	Athelking	sunk	18	14/5/41	Rabaul	sunk
8	10/9/40	Benarty	sunk	19	24/5/41	Trafalgar	sunk
9	20/9/40	Comissaire Ramel	sunk	20	17/6/41	Tottenham	sunk
10	22/10/40	Durmitor	captured	21	22/6/41	Balzac	sunk
11	9/11/40	Teddy	sunk	22	10/9/41	Silvaplana	captured

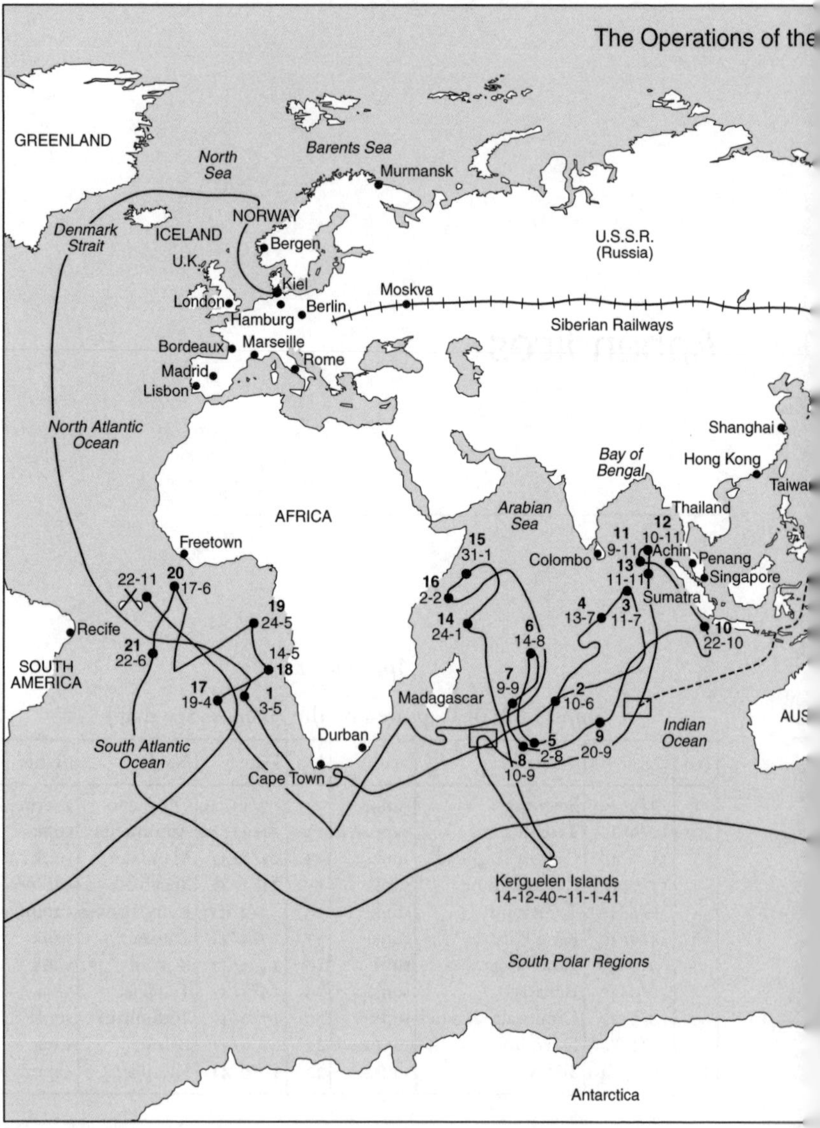

NOTE: Bold numbers correspond to Appendix 1's listing of ships sunk or captured by the *Atlantis*

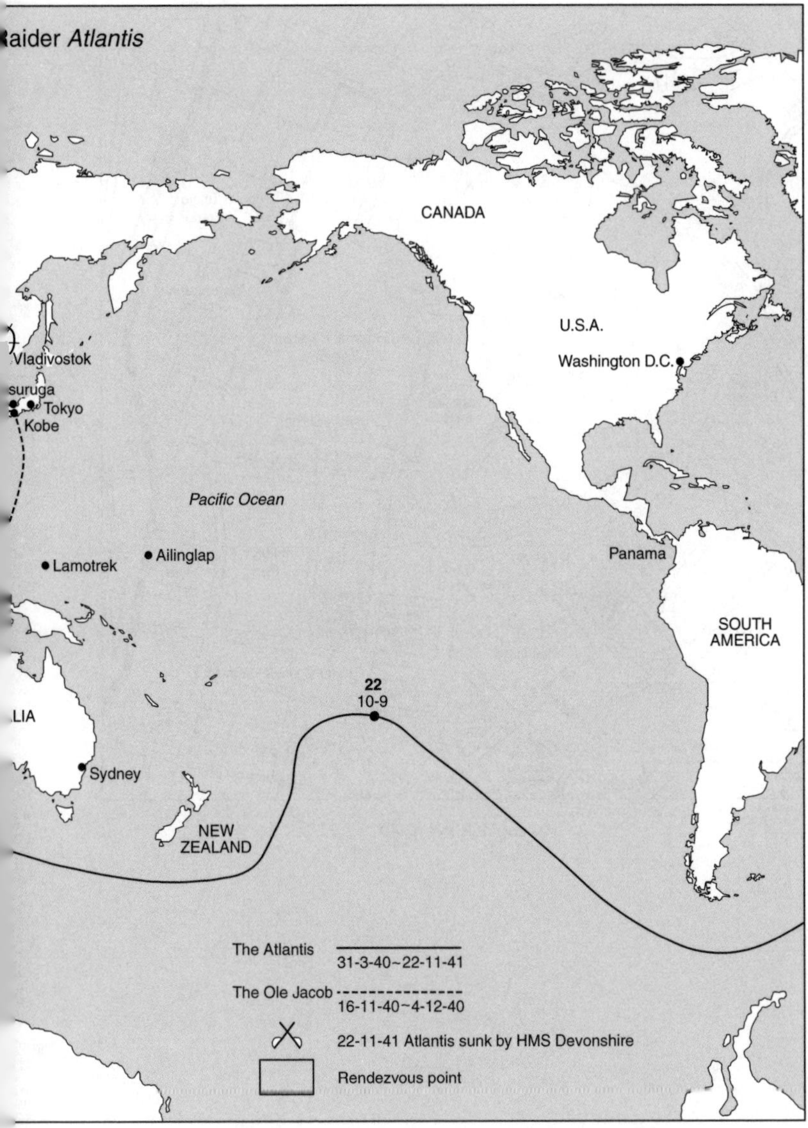

aider Atlantis
CANADA
U.S.A.
Washington D.C.
Vladivostok
suruga
Tokyo
Kobe
Pacific Ocean
Lamotrek
Ailinglap
Panama
SOUTH AMERICA
22
10-9
LIA
Sydney
NEW ZEALAND
The Atlantis
31-3-40~22-11-41
The Ole Jacob
16-11-40~4-12-40
22-11-41 Atlantis sunk by HMS Devonshire
Rendezvous point

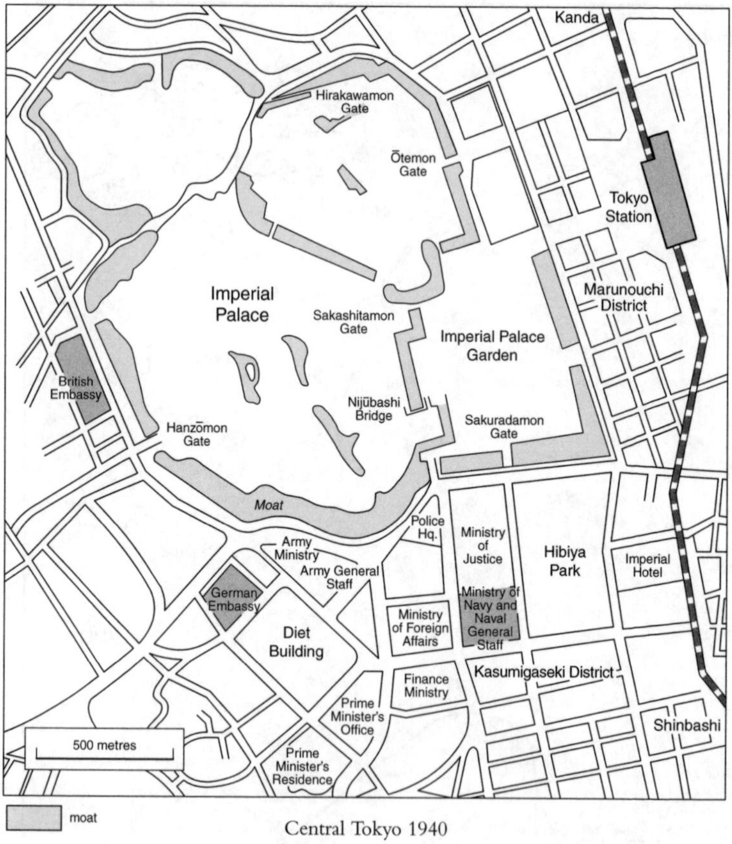

Central Tokyo 1940

30th March 2006

Dear Mr Seki,

Donald Stewart was born in Liverpool on 20 November 1906. He was educated at Cauldy Grammar School and then was a student on HMS Conway, a merchant navy training school. His father was Charles Ruthven Stewart, also a captain in the Merchant Navy. His mother was Mabel Stewart nee Caruthers. Donald married Winifred Cockburn and they had one son, Donald Ruthven Stewart (my father who died 6 years ago). Until his retirement he lived in Upton on the Wirral.

His wife had several miscarriages before becoming pregnant with Donald Jnr. My grandfather was captured in the November 1940 and my father was born in the March. My grandmother did not know for a long time what had happened to my grandfather, but eventually, with the help of the Red Cross contact was made and she was able to let him know that he had a healthy son and was allowed to send photos to him. My father was 4½ years old before he met his father.

Once back from the POW camp my grandfather appears to have simply put it all behind him and got on with his life. He rarely mentioned the incident on the Automedon or made any comment on life in the camp. He retired from the Merchant Navy on November 20th 1966 and within the week had moved to a bungalow in Conway, North Wales. He lived there with my grandmother until her death in 1974 and then on his own until about 1985 when he went into a nursing home in Colwyn Bay, North Wales because he was finding it difficult living alone.

He did not have many hobbies but liked walking in the countryside, enjoyed the company of several dogs over the years and was a keen observer and record-keeper of the weather. I recall that he was a man who liked everything to be organized and efficient. He was always smartly turned out and he was proud of being known as The Captain or Captain Stewart by his friends and neighbours. We – my younger sister Dawn and myself – used to like visiting him because he had a veritable treasure trove of goodies from around the world . . . in those days all very unusual and exotic to our eyes. Wooden statues, ivory trinkets, rolls of beautiful silks, jade ornaments, huge travelling chests that smelt of cedar, chop sticks, embroidered pictures, Turkish slippers, a stool shaped like a camel and he would entertain us by showing us his cine films taken on his travels. These included film taken in eastern waters from a junk, film taken on the back of a rickshaw and other things from far off lands. He would spend hours teaching us how to pick things up with chopsticks or how to tie various knots.

As I mentioned, he rarely spoke of his time on the ship or in the camp. I would remember, however, that he used to make my sister and me laugh by telling us about a man trying to get out of the camp by pretending he was injured. (Please bear in mind we were very, very young at the time and didn't realize the significance of this in the slightest.) He would act out the parts of the camp doctor looking at a man who was limping very badly indeed. Then he would limp up and down the room making us giggle and he said the man in question had put a very sharp stone in his shoe to make himself limp but the doctor hadn't realized. The doctor eventually agreed he could leave. The man was so relieved to be going that when he left the room, without thinking he took the stone out of his shoe and walked normally . . . and the doctor saw him not limping and ordered that he should remain in camp. Not a great story to recount but I remember it because we used to make him act it out every time we saw him because we thought it amusing.

Regards, Heather Stewart

Index